Designing Disability

Designing Disability

Symbols, Space, and Society

Elizabeth Guffey

Bloomsbury Academic
An imprint of Bloomsbury Publishing Plc

B L O O M S B U R Y
LONDON · OXFORD · NEW YORK · NEW DELHI · SYDNEY

Bloomsbury Academic

An imprint of Bloomsbury Publishing Plc

50 Bedford Square	1385 Broadway
London	New York
WC1B 3DP	NY 10018
UK	USA

www.bloomsbury.com

BLOOMSBURY and the Diana logo are trademarks of Bloomsbury Publishing Plc

First published 2018

© Elizabeth Guffey, 2018

Elizabeth Guffey has asserted her right under the Copyright, Designs and Patents Act, 1988, to be identified as Author of this work.

British Library Cataloguing-in-Publication Data

A catalogue record for this book is available from the British Library.

ISBN:	HB:	978-1-3500-0428-3
	PB:	978-1-3500-0427-6
	ePDF:	978-1-3500-0425-2
	ePub:	978-1-3500-0426-9

Library of Congress Cataloging-in-Publication Data

A catalogue record for this book is available from the Library of Congress

Cover design by Louise Dugdale

Cover image © Liam Bailey/Getty Images

Typeset by Integra Software Services Pvt. Ltd.

Printed and bound in India

To Matt and Ellen

CONTENTS

LIST OF ILLUSTRATIONS

ACKNOWLEDGMENTS

For all their advice, comments, and research leads, I want to thank David Serlin, Aimi Hamraie, Bess Williamson, Rosemary Garland Thomson, and Sara Hendren. I also want to say special thanks to Maggie Taft, Claire Constable, and Rebecca Barden.

I also want to thank, for all their patience, Tucker Beachak, Emma Bobb, Daniella Chiaramonte, Brian Cranston, Lauren Douglas, Spjamal Drummond, Brandi Eby, Jerielys Estevez, Mary Fennell, Raissa Fomerand, Julie Godefroid, Adam Hamdy, Steven Hummel, Lamease Jamal, Ashley Johnson, Dane Kranjac, Gail Martin, Briana McKenzie, Daniel Nassimos, Julianne Olori, Caroline Perthuis, David Peterman, Octavia Poenix, Alan Publielli, Tyreck Rand, Emely-Ann Rodriguez, Nathaniel Rojas, Ashly Sajous-Turner, Tristen Stafford, Kristin Stella, Allyson Taylor, Kim Toffali, John Tognino, Nicolas Umpierrez, Boris Yanez, and James Yarusso.

Introduction

Disability by Design?

FIGURE I.1 Rehabilitation International, International Symbol of Access. 1969.

At its heart, this book aims to show how the International Symbol of Access (ISA) came into being, not just as a design, but also a manner of thinking (Figure I.1). When I began writing this book, I was under the illusion that this would be a short article on a design that had shaped my life for many years. As a disabled person, I've long been aware that this seemingly simple symbol has profoundly shaped my day-to-day movements in a way that able-bodied persons scarcely realize. But I'd never understood that it also shapes the world at large in a way that able-bodied persons barely know.

Then, in 2012, I began to consider it more carefully after I saw the Accessible Icon Project (AIP). The older symbol I'd known for years—little more than a schematic wheelchair with a head placed on it—was increasingly criticized as cold and mechanical. The newer symbol echoes the rise of a disruptive, participatory disability culture. The AIP thrusts its wheelchair user into a more active and dynamic role. With the grace of a wheelchair athlete, its figure pushing itself headfirst, leaning dynamically to propel itself forward. At first, I was amused by the AIP, then irritated by the debate that began to surround it, engulfing the small figure with questions of passivity and assertions of personal agency. Finally, I was roused enough to jot down my own, highly personal feelings about the symbol already in use. I began to keep files of scattered references and wrote occasional articles related to the subject. In one, I told the story of the ISA's conception by a Scandinavian student. In another, I described the newer symbol's inclusion in art collections, even as the museums themselves can overlook real-world questions of access. I eagerly exchanged ideas with colleagues whenever circumstances brought me into contact with people who shared my growing obsession with the subject. But each time I dipped into the history and meaning of the access symbol, looking for books or other writing on the subject, I was startled to see how little research had been done and how infrequently the topic had been considered from scholarly point of view; to put together any kind of history of the symbol—or even the idea of environmental access—meant maneuvering through a web of primary sources. Slowly, it dawned on me that there was an untold history here, and it is larger than simply the story of one symbol's design and implementation.

Even after I came to this realization, however, I labored under the illusion that I could write a simple history of a symbol—the story of a designer, a design, and how it was used. Chapters were plotted, researched, and written—only to be ultimately discarded. In my more despairing moments, I wondered why a focused design history of a single symbol ended up looking more like a history of the ideas and technologies of access. Why was my study of a graphic symbol becoming a history of mobility devices? Why was I studying post-Civil War hospital design? Gradually, I realized that this wasn't just the history of a symbol. It was a multilayered story of ideas—about people, accommodations, barriers, architecture, and human rights. And, as I found it necessary to look beyond the creation of a simple graphic symbol, I was immersed in debates on segregation, definitions of disability, the role of humanism in medicine, and changing global perceptions of disability. While this remains a historical case study, it is also an exploration of public policy, public relations, and the profound power of visual rhetoric.

Disability and access remain issues of real and pressing concern. Because of this, *Designing Disability* does not foreground theory; it aims to be as user-friendly in style and format as possible, shifting between ideas of access to the incidents and individuals who have lived and known those issues. At the same time, this remains an account of the development of the iconic wheelchair symbol. Of course, that symbol has been used many ways, and to represent accommodations for many types of disability. But, as originally understood, it was developed with mobility-impaired persons in mind. Necessarily, in *Designing Disability*, this type of impairment looms large. Simply put, this is an account of how one device—the wheelchair—and one type of disability came to stand in for many others.

Design's misfit

The problem of access is a new idea, but its connection to design is even newer. Attending Brooklyn College in the early 1950s, student Frieda Zames quickly discovered how Boylan Hall and Ingersoll Hall, two "mirror images facing each other across a central quadrangle" at the center of campus, impeded her ability to get to class. Each building required Zames "to go up two steps. On rainy days I was terrified of falling because my crutch tips would slip. Snowy or icy days were worse. Never once at Brooklyn College did I think that those two steps in any way could be changed. I had to make do as best I could. I thought that it was my responsibility to fit in" (Fleischer and Zames, 2011: xiii). Today, Zames' problem is understood as a question of access. But in the 1950s, when Zames arrived at Brooklyn College, she, like most people, interpreted issues like this as a kind of personal challenge. It was her responsibility to "fit in."

The question of fit—and misfit—haunts this book. But "access" is the better-known term and is used more often. To the casual observer, access and disability come together visibly, in the ISA. In this context, the idea of access flags a host of very real accommodations, including Braille signs, ramps, and elevators. But for disabled people, such access does not exist in a void. As scholar Tanya Titchkosky relates, the word can be tied "to a complex form of perception that organizes socio-political relations between people in social space" (Titchkosky, 2011: 4). And yet linguistically the word "access" remains a rather formal or legalistic term. The Americans with Disabilities Act (ADA) ensures access to the built environment, while the UK's Equality Act considers equal opportunity to access.

At the same time, "fit" and "misfit" more closely capture the problem of disability today, particularly in terms of design. Certainly, ideas of being fit, fitting in, and fitness suffuse our culture today. They are a part of our daily lives. They also have the advantage of being tangible. Fit can denote the state of one's own body as well as others' perceptions of it. Fitting in, on the other hand, suggests vast subtleties in social interaction. But it also aligns more closely with the topic at hand—namely, disability as a design problem. Just how do disabled bodies fit into cars, buildings, and other objects, or landscapes and spaces? Recognizing designs that aim to make a good fit highlights our efforts to shape a world usable for all types of bodies. In the end, a growing recognition of disability's profound engagement with design and the challenge of the misfit is what brought the access symbol into being.

Of course, ideas of disabled "fit" or access simply didn't exist when Frieda Zames enrolled in Brooklyn College. The groundbreaking work of scholars like Tom Shakespeare (2006) and Susan Wendell (1996) remains foundational in the field, but is also relatively new. I turn here to Rosemarie Garland-Thomson's work suggesting that disability is not a physical state but a social condition; here she introduces the provocative idea of disability's "misfit." Traceable to what she calls a feminist materialist disability concept or theory (Garland-Thomson, 2011a), Garland-Thomson builds on the useful distinction made between sex and gender. Gayle Rubin and others argue that bodily states or conditions must be separated from social processes (Rubin, 1975). In feminist theory, sex is a physiological state; gender, on the other hand, is a social construct. A parallel divide can distinguish between the widely used term "impairment," and disability itself. The former is about medical processes and bodily function; the latter, Garland-Thompson argues, is less a bodily state than a "social process of disablement that gives meaning and consequences to those impairments in the world" (Garland-Thompson, 2011b: 591). As an idea, misfit allows us to produce a humanist, rather than medical, view of how designers have imagined, practiced, contested, and revised our notions of disability.

Here, then, "misfit" is a physical state and a social attitude; the two are inextricably linked. Bodies exist in a wide variety of shapes, sizes, and abilities. The clash between this degree of variety and a society unwilling or unable to plan for bodily difference can cause many kinds of misfit. Through graphic communications, urban planning, and architecture, design weaves social attitudes into the very shape and texture of our built environment. Garland-Thomson notes how the "space through which we navigate our lives tends to offer fits to majority bodies and functioning and create misfits with minority forms of embodiment" (Garland-Thompson, 2011b: 594). Tall or short, wide or narrow, anybody outside the norm has—at one time or another—experienced what it is to misfit. This is especially the case for people with disabilities.

If physicality and sociality are closely linked, design has a clear role in negotiating the two. That is, designers have it in their power to invent better fits. They can, for example, avoid planning for staircases and include ramps for access to buildings. But they can also create misfits. Revolving doors, for example, continue to be widely used, but are a barrier to wheelchair users and visually impaired people alike. And yet, it's a sign of how little these issues are discussed that architects and designers almost reflexively continue to work with a limited vocabulary of construction and design forms. Some proponents of revolving doors, for example, still argue that they are more energy efficient than swing doors. Creating separate entrances that feature conventional swing doors, they argue, can accommodate disabled people. But do we really need to create two sets of entrances? New ideas often meet with skepticism or are ignored. Unchallenged, many designs repeat forms that are assumed to be useful, or important, or universal. And on occasion, they really are all of these things. But how often might a staircase be replaced by a sloped ramp? Or a set of double doors simply replace those that revolve? More accessible—and sustainable—alternatives to revolving doors do exist. Automatic double doors, for example, allow everyone to use the same entrance. And they create a vestibule or "air curtain" that helps control interior temperatures while being both energy efficient and accessible. One set of conventions—in this case the air curtain—can create an easy "fit" between disabled bodies and constructed spaces, while another— the revolving door—can transform an impaired person into a "misfit." This book argues that design both produces different notions of disability, and responds to them.

Designing Disability aims to do more than highlight a simple binary of fit and misfit in the world around us; by applying this binary historically, this book links ideas of disability to design. Implicitly, it also deals with wayfinding, that is, the systems used to guide people through physical space, and the signage that publicly communicates messages of direction. But it also touches on some of the best-known landmarks in design and architectural history. These gain unexpected significance when seen from the perspective of access. Familiar landmarks, like the elegant parterres of Versailles and the open halls of the Crystal Palace in London, acquire new meaning when viewed in terms of workaday accessibility. So too does the disability-friendly environment of late eighteenth-century Bath. Of course, applying current ideas of disability and accommodations to historical spaces is anachronistic. These sites were not always designed with disabled people in mind. But, in the end, understanding the history of access, design, and disability is still useful. It helps us better understand these issues in our contemporary world.

Defining disability

In 1975, Victor Finkelstein, a South African anti-apartheid activist and early leader in the disability rights movement, asked: What if we designed an "upside-down world created for wheelchair-users?" (Finkelstein, 1975). Finkelstein imagined a very different world with a village shaped entirely around wheelchair-users' needs. As opposed to the real world, here, he proudly announced, all residents were wheelchair users. Here, he proclaimed, they could finally "control all aspects of their lives." In this small utopia "they make the goods that they sell in their shops with special aids, they work the machines that clean the street, run their own educational colleges, banks, post offices, and transport system." Of course, in this village a resident using a wheelchair was not just normal, but also "like everyone else in their world of people that she or he meets in daily life." Naturally enough, this village would be constructed with different building codes. The very vocabulary of architectural and design forms might change. For one thing, in a world of wheelchair users, everything could be lowered. Wheelchair-using architects, he speculated, would realize that all ceilings and doors could be dropped in height. Now, Finkelstein posited, "There is no need to have the ceilings 9ft 6 in. or the door heights at 7ft 2 in. Soon it becomes standard practice in this village for doors to be designed to a height of 5ft, and ceilings of rooms to be 7ft. 4in. Now everyone is happy in this village, all the physical difficulties in the environment have been overcome." But so far, Finkelstein's story was really only a thought experiment. The real provocation comes when he asked, what would happen to able-bodied people who might choose to live there too?

Of course, Finkelstein's tale was presented as an extended experiment appearing in a larger article that explored the social nature of disability. But in this situation, he argued, able-bodied people would become the misfits. When non-wheelchair users initially arrived in this imaginary village, Finkelstein continued, "one of the first things they noticed was the height of the doors and ceilings. They noticed this directly, by constantly knocking their heads on the door lintels." Seeing how the able-bodied members of the village went about with dark bruises on their foreheads, the village doctors, themselves wheelchair users, fretted that able-bodied people could suffer from a "loss or reduction of functional ability." Thus handicapped, special aids like helmets and braces were developed for non-wheelchair users. But still, Finkelstein added, they stood out and "when they sought jobs no one would employ them." In time, voluntary "societies were created to collect charity and many shops and pubs had an upturned helmet placed on the counters for customers to leave their small change." The situation was strained. Only when the able-bodied got together did they realize that their "disability" had a social solution—the wheelchair users needed to change door and ceiling heights. In the end, Finkelstein speculates, "The able-bodied disabled" began to hope for something better: "Perhaps, just perhaps, their disabilities could be overcome (and disappear!) with changes in society" (Finkelstein, 1975).

Throughout his career, Finkelstein challenged society's role in creating outsiders. Whether in this fictional world, or in the real one in which we live, Finkelstein argued, we must take a deeper look "at what is meant by disability" (Finkelstein, 1975). And yet, there is not now—nor has there ever been—a comprehensive and static definition of "disability." As Finkelstein's parable suggests, the meaning of "disability" can shift depending on the context. Moreover, some societies are more willing to accommodate impairment—in both material and social terms—than others. But also, symptoms and states of disability can be made more visible or hidden. In the industrialized West, institutionalization of disabled people in the nineteenth and early twentieth centuries meant that many lived their lives out of public view. Deinstitutionalization, normalization, and ever-extending lifespans in the twenty-first century make impairment, old age, and infirmity evermore present in our society today.

Bearing such changes in mind, it is important to situate the term "disability" historically. The American Civil War brought the term "disability" into common parlance. The term was commonly used to define who could or could not fight in the war or those who would later seek support or compensation for wartime injuries. The debilitating conditions claimed by veterans included amputation, deafness, blindness, as well as conditions like lung disease and incapacitating rheumatism. Some devastating physical and mental states passed under still familiar terms like "combat fatigue"; others, like the cryptic "soldier's heart," defy modern categorization. But in all of this, it is easy to recognize the sober list of core or iconic impairments that still dominate our understanding of disability today. With social, technological, and medical change, however, our twenty-first-century definitions have expanded to encompass neurodiversity and conditions like chronic fatigue syndrome that were not previously recognized.

In 1990, when the ADA was passed, disability was defined anew. This time it referred to any mental or physical impairment that substantially limits one of more major life activity. It encompasses those with physical impairments, including mobility, hearing, and visual impairment, as well as cosmetic disfigurement or anatomic loss impacting some key kind of bodily or mental function. On the other hand, it also recognizes mental impairment or psychological disorders as forms of disabilities.

Keeping the evolving definition of disability in mind, *Designing Disability* is a limited tale. It examines how designed fits and misfits have reconfigured our understanding of disability in the years between the Civil War and the passing of the ADA. But its focus on the ISA means that its scope is restricted. Although the wheelchair symbol claims an international audience, questions around its worldwide impact remain unanswered here. Just how global is this symbol? And does it carry the same meaning everywhere? Outside the industrialized West, other cultures have entirely different ways of conceiving disability. In much of Asia, for instance, it is considered appropriate for individuals with impairments to live entirely within a family framework; this situation, as Cherie S. Lewis observes "ensures that disabled individuals will not live in isolation, [but] it often mandates against independence for disabled persons" (Lewis, 1994: 190). If living with familial caretakers, many such disabled people don't access public spaces in the same way as in the West. Vision- or mobility-impaired persons accompanied by family members may not need accommodations like Braille lettering or automatically opening doors. For that matter, signage can also be of secondary importance (Figure I.2).

휠체어, 유모차 길

way of wheelchair and stroller

FIGURE I.2 Example of a text-based access sign in Korea, c. 2008. Creative Commons License.

Even when access is provided, it does not always follow the signage standards established in the West. In fact, the access symbol may in some ways be read as a marker of Western attitudes, not only toward disabled persons, but also of who shapes and uses public space. The wheelchair symbol may be found in airports from Dubai to Fairbanks, but how common is it in rural or undeveloped parts of Africa or Asia? And is it even necessary there? In China, the very idea of access is relatively recent. Just before the 2008 Beijing Olympics and Paralympics, the city sprouted ISA symbols where tourists and athletes might visit, even adding seventy wheelchair accessible taxis to the city's fleet. Here, as well as on the Olympic grounds, the ISA was used. But outside Beijing, the symbol is much less known. And when access has been introduced, textual—rather than pictorial—signs have sometimes replaced the ISA. But in the West as well, the access symbol is relatively new.

Defining a symbol

Designing Disability is broken into three discrete parts: before the access symbol, the symbol's creation, and, finally, its reception and uses. No history of the access symbol can be told without acknowledging the deep connection between mobility and the designed environment. In the end, this book aims to be a multilayered history, opening with an examination of the age-old issue of misfit between impaired bodies and the built world.

Chapter 1, "Origins of a Misfit Design," explores the notion of environmental misfit by looking at the ways in which mobility impairment has been dealt with in the West historically. I argue that the origins of the access symbol must be linked to the advent of a particular design: the modern wheelchair. Before its development, many mobility-impaired persons were irresolvably homebound. Gradually, with the professionalization of medicine in the nineteenth century, wheelchairs became more and more common; but still, they were largely connected with hospitals, sanitaria, and other institutions associated with serious illness. This tradition was still dominant when the modern, folding wheelchair was first introduced in the 1930s. It was no coincidence that, with the advent of the modern wheelchair, large numbers of seriously disabled people could leave the confines of home and hospitals. And yet, with this change the question of misfit became exaggerated; only then was it evident how poorly public space and the built environment fit the mobility impaired.

Chapter 2, "Fitting In," explores the gradual dissemination of the modern wheelchair and the growing awareness of impairment as not only a medical problem, but also a reflection of the question of fit. In the years after the Second World War, the proliferation of this modern wheelchair might suggest a sudden change in the lives of many disabled people. But many gradually realized that wheelchairs could not "fit" into the built environment until widespread changes were made. For the first time ever, the minutiae of building design, for example, staircases, sidewalks, even doors, had to be reevaluated. Only when such reassessments were made did planners, builders, and government officials begin to realize how profoundly the built environment could disable people. Understanding this shifted concern away from disabled bodies and toward an examination of how design contributes to socially designed misfit, thus paving the way for access signage.

I focus on several sites where, in the years after the Second World War, this radical rethinking began to take shape. In Southern California, where the modern wheelchair was first invented, personal mobility was already equated with wheels. Perhaps unsurprisingly, the pavement that accommodated the region's many cars also offered an infrastructure that unintentionally enabled disabled mobility. A second model developed more purposefully in the 1950s, at the University of Illinois. Here, an entire school and, later, the college town around it were refitted as a vast experiment in wheelchair access. But, by the early 1960s the simple modification of a single American college campus was clearly not enough. Infuriated by the architectural and design conventions that prevented their integration into society, a diverse group of disabled people joined forces with the President's Committee on Employment of the Physically Handicapped to demand a nationwide "attack" on design barriers that prohibited physical mobility. Their various demands on design came to a head in 1961 when, after almost five years of research, the group nudged the American Standards Association to endorse the first ever set of building standards written with disabled access in mind. Here is when the book's central theme—the intertwined problem of fit and misfit—began to capture the imagination of a larger audience.

The second part of this book addresses the development of the wheelchair symbol and its role in broader debates around access, rights, and space. Chapter 3, "The "Personal Politics of Signs (1961–1965)," deals with the question of signage, and its intersection with ideas of disability. The barrier-free architecture movement succeeded in drawing public attention to design's role in creating disablement. But how to confront the problem remained unclear. While pragmatists argued that the existing environment could—wherever possible—be altered and adapted for disabled people, signage advocates asked how persons with disabilities would be able to find these accommodations. They argued for consistent and easily understood labels that would publicly announce these adaptations to disabled and non-disabled people alike.

This way of thinking developed more rapidly in the UK and Europe than in the United States. In both places, access was linked to politics. In Europe's new welfare states, the bond between government planners, architects and designers, and society's weakest members was foundational. Because public accommodations made for disabled people were viewed as an assertion of that bond, experts argued that special access and retrofitting should be publicly announced with signs. Meanwhile, in North America, a political system that favored independence held with accommodations that helped mobility-impaired people "fit in" as seamlessly as possible. Ultimately, by the mid-1960s, advocates for disabled people on both sides of the Atlantic began to introduce access signage. Anyone could see that humanity came in a vast variety of abilities. The aim, though, was not to abolish all barriers, but to piece together accommodations whenever possible, until the broad outlines of a more equitable environment might be composed.

By the mid-1960s, Chapter 4, "Signs of Discrimination (1965–1968)," proposes, several very different approaches to access symbols had developed. In the United States, people tended to view access as an emerging Civil Right. Accessible pathways were constructed, but the legacy of racial segregation complicated the project. The idea of separating or distinguishing disabled citizens from all others made many people uncomfortable. As the government systematically dismantled discriminatory signage that had segregated the nation into black and white, it also implemented a series of "secret" symbols newly developed to direct disabled people toward designated accommodations. In the UK, on the other hand, supporters not only framed access within the context of the welfare state but some even lauded it as a form of "positive discrimination." Without any need for secrecy, signage proudly advertised accommodations with clear, bold symbols based on the human form.

Chapter 5, "A Design for the Real World? (1968–1974)," tells the story of the development of the ISA, the globally implemented symbol that remains in use today. This symbol reveals both an awakening awareness of the need for visibility and the difficulty of expressing disabled people's humanity within a systematic program of design; it registers two very different approaches to disability, signage, and citizenship. Part of a radical design workshop, a Danish student designed the original icon as a schematic wheelchair. When the conservative international organization Rehabilitation International adopted it, they slapped a circle on top of the wheelchair form, transforming the chair into a body.

This may be seen as one of those wonderfully telling moments in the history of design, where a significant decision is made with unexpected consequences. I argue that in working to find an acceptable compromise, Rehabilitation International created a profoundly misfit symbol, that, through efficient marketing, nevertheless became the universal symbol of access.

The final two chapters of this book examine the ISA's reception, and its recent evolution. When first introduced in the late 1960s, the ISA represented a vast social promise, a kind of commitment and assurance that the built environment would be accessible wherever the sign appears. But by the early 1970s, other connotations also began to emerge. As Chapter 6, "Signs of Protest (1974–1990)," describes, the access symbol made disability itself more visible. Using the Civil Rights movement as a model, some disabled people began advocating for full access to the rights, protections, and duties of citizenship. As this disability rights movement took shape, demonstrators began agitating through sit-ins and protests, and by acting out in civil defiance. As meetings and demonstrations began to coalesce around disabled access to housing, transportation, education, and other rights, the ISA jumped from urban planners' signage to flags, cardboard signs, and the other paraphernalia of this protest movement. In the United States especially, many disabled people appropriated the symbol as a powerful expression of political will that culminated in 1990 with the signing of the ADA.

Finally, Chapter 7, "A Critical Design? (1990–Today)," explains how and why the once radical access symbol is increasingly seen as limited and out of date. Practically, it may seem an international success, functioning world over by identifying mundane or everyday accommodations like automated doors, restrooms, and parking spots for people with disabilities. But the internal compromises and tensions evident in the image itself remain unresolved. Even more telling, the symbol that once added cohesion to the disability rights movement stands accused of being strikingly out of step with changing ideas of disability in the twenty-first century. This chapter explores two recent revisions to the ISA: the 1993 remake introduced by Brendan Murphy under the auspices of the Society of Environmental Graphic Design, and the 2010 Accessible Icon Project. I use these two case studies to ask just how extensive change can really be.

From the very start, or perhaps because of its very start, the access symbol was and remains a misfit design. It still does not fit easily in professionally designed communications systems. But it's also a sign for misfits—those whose bodies don't fit the ways in which the built environment is so often designed and constructed. Ideas of environmental, social, and philosophical fit crisscross this simple symbol. Finally, this is more than a study of a single design; it is a story of the particularly modern juncture between design, bodies, and power.

PART ONE

History of an Idea: Access (–1961)

1

Origins of a Misfit Design

The Advent of the Modern Wheelchair (–1945)

After she'd grown up, Ruth Bie couldn't remember meeting Franklin Delano Roosevelt (FDR) or patting the dog on his lap (Fischer, 2008) (Figure 1.1). And perhaps FDR would have preferred this. In the last twenty years we have become increasingly accustomed to depictions of Roosevelt in his wheelchair. But during his lifetime, images like this were rigorously repressed. This candid snapshot of FDR, the three-year-old granddaughter of his caretaker, and his terrier shows the president in a wheelchair on the porch of his Hyde Park, New York, retreat Top Cottage. But even out of camera range Roosevelt tried to avoid being seen using his chair. A polio survivor, the president had been paralyzed from the waist down since 1921. In many ways, we could argue that Roosevelt suffered from a double misfit. On the one hand, his body did not "fit" the environment around it. On the other, Roosevelt worried that if others saw the extent of his disability they might judge him as incapable, weak, and unfit to lead. He worried for his political career and feared becoming a social "misfit."

The issue received its first public airing when Hugh Gallagher published *FDR's Splendid Deception: The Moving Story of Roosevelt's Massive Disability* in 1985. The photograph of Roosevelt with Ruth Bie graced the book's cover. Gallagher's argument is clear-cut: while Roosevelt was alive, wheelchairs were, at best, an oddity. At worst, they carried a kind of stigma. The president worked furiously to hide just how dependent he was on one. But Gallagher built Roosevelt's fears into a larger intellectual edifice. Wheelchairs were stigmatizing at that time, Gallagher argued, and Roosevelt strategically concealed his use of one; his wheelchair use was suppressed because the American electorate would never choose a "crippled President to lead it back to prosperity" (Gallagher, 1985: 97). The development of today's

FIGURE 1.1 Margaret Suckley, Franklin D. Roosevelt in his wheelchair on the porch at Top Cottage, Hyde Park, NY, 1941.

access symbol must be understood within the larger context of disability and culture. It can, in fact, be tied to a much longer history. The wheelchair, a key component of this symbol, is itself a modern invention; for many years, it was something to cover up and conceal rather than represent on signage.

How did the wheelchair transform from a device that people like Roosevelt tried to hide to one of the most widely known—and accepted— graphic symbols of the late twentieth century? This book traces not only the development of a symbol, but also the processes, the social and environmental pressures, and the designs that together answer this question. In less than a generation after FDR's death, the wheelchair came to represent an entirely new way of thinking about disability. At the heart of this radical upheaval lies an extraordinary, yet easily, stated idea: disability is created not by impairment but by a mismatch between bodies and the environments in which they exist (Garland-Thomson, 2011).

What could be simpler? In fact, there is nothing easy or simple about disability and design. During Roosevelt's lifetime, disability was something to be overcome. A contemporary example might be the 1937 film *Heidi*. The public embraced Shirley Temple's portrayal of the Swiss farm girl who relentlessly urges the spoiled Clara to abandon her wheelchair and instead breathe and walk in the clean mountain air of the Alps. Roosevelt never climbed in mountain meadows, but he did present himself publicly as the man who "beat" polio. To fit in, he stage-managed this persona, masterfully building a political reputation on a brand of persuasive, if relentless, optimism that would have made Heidi proud (Tobin, 2013: 204–212). In photographs, FDR appears worldly, avuncular, and supremely self-confident: FDR working industriously at his desk or a table; FDR casually sitting in a car, smoking a filtered cigarette and pince-nez in place; FDR gripping a lectern while leaning forward with the full force of his weight. Photographers helped perpetuate this persona simply by not taking pictures of the president in his wheelchair. Of course, if they ignored polite requests, the Secret Service would routinely seize their cameras. For all his contagious, cheerful bonhomie, Roosevelt seems to have viewed his wheelchair as a painful symbol that, to a degree that he found shameful, marked his own disablement.

FIGURE 1.2 Boy using wheelchair outdoors, c. 1910. Courtesy Wellcome Library, London.

To explore Roosevelt as a case study, however, risks missing a larger and even more compelling picture. The International Access Symbol and the wheelchair depicted on it represent a break with tradition. For most of human history, people with mobility impairments negotiated their way through life with an ad hoc assortment of assistive devices. Most made do with a wide variety of canes and crutches. More seriously impaired persons could be carted around in litters or even wheelbarrows. The earliest wheelchairs were an improvement for some, though for a host of social and practical reasons they were more often avoided. As late as 1910, users—and their attendants—who ventured to take these chairs outside did so at their own risk. Any turn off the beaten path might mean a tumble, getting mired in mud, or worse. This anonymous early twentieth-century photo palpitates with thwarted desire (Figure 1.2). Open fields beckon, while boy and attendant stare fixedly at the camera, his wheeled chair stranded on a rocky dirt berm. The boy's predicament explains a great deal about the relative powerlessness of wheelchair users. For much of its short history, the wheelchair embodied an entire frame of mind; its very form signaled "resignation, decline, and defeat" (Bartolucci 1992: 29). No history of the access symbol can be told without acknowledging this pre-history.

Examining the vast pre-history of crutches, canes, and early proto-wheelchairs makes it easier to recognize the revolutionary introduction of another design, what I call the modern wheelchair. Of course, better medicine, a refinement of surgical techniques, and other innovations all helped extend the life spans of both disabled and able-bodied persons alike in the early twentieth century. But no single invention more clearly shifted attitudes about disability—as well as ability—than the advent of the modern wheelchair. Just before Roosevelt died, the White House ordered several of these chairs. Had he lived longer, Roosevelt's highly personal sense of fit and misfit might itself have changed. But for most of his adult life, Roosevelt understood one profound truth: the nature of disability is not defined so much by impairment as by the ways in which society—and the designed environment—bolsters and shapes our definition of ability.

An environmental misfit

Although the sheer fact of bodily impairment has remained constant through human history, few mobility aids were available before the mid-twentieth century and most have obscure origins.[1] Indeed, even at the dawn of the Industrial Revolution, when the French artist Théodore Géricault visited London in 1819, he left a keenly observed depiction of a device used for transporting disabled people living among the urban poor (Figure 1.3). His *Paralytic Woman*, a lithograph depicting an impaired woman being carted in a shabby, if slightly modified, wheelbarrow, demonstrates how

FIGURE 1.3 Théodore Géricault, A paralytic woman being transported along the street in a Wheelchair, 1821. Courtesy Wellcome Library, London.

long this medieval device continued to lumber through urban streets and country lanes alike. It also highlights a series of misfits. A subtler social drama plays out behind him. A young woman passes the wheelbarrow, casting a sidelong, fearful stare while an accompanying child hides her face, as if the invalid's infirmity were catching. The pair of interlopers signals a second, social misfit, in which disabled persons were often marginalized by society. Around 1800, the side-long, piercing glances cast at the paralytic woman were both normal and ordinary. Like many disabled persons at this time, she is viewed through a veil of pity and fear. But her predicament was environmental as well. Rolled through the rough and turbulent streets of London's East End, the woman's wheelbarrow does not fit the hardscrabble environment in which she is placed; vaguely in the distance we see the hurly burly of other wheeled vehicles passing through the urban hubbub; the stout man touting her cart pauses for breath, but also appears to be taking it all in, as if assessing how to safely enter the melee of the busy London street in front of him.

Studying the predecessors of the wheelchair—and especially their interface with the built environment—raises more questions than it answers. For example, at what point is a wheelchair a wheelchair and not a wheeled chair? The question may seem pointlessly obscure, but wheelchairs are constructed for human mobility; chairs with wheels, on the other hand, can fill multiple functions. Whisked across a smooth floor, for example, wheels may be installed on pieces of furniture so they can be easily arranged and rearranged; they protect delicate floor finishes from scuffing. The wheelchair's obscure origins force us to ask, too, how often must mobility devices be limited to chairs? Both ancient Greek and Chinese art contain images of beds with wheels (Kamenetz, 1969: 8). We know that disabled people have long had to make do in a world that was not configured for their bodies, but how widely were such conveyances really used? In the Middle Ages, those disabled persons fortunate enough to own a wheelbarrow (that is, a box placed on wheels) might be moved around like so many barrels of wine or bundles of wood (Kamenetz, 1969: 10, 11). Such transport was a common enough sight for centuries to come.

Certainly, until the mid-twentieth century, mobility-impaired persons resorted to a variety of devices for transport, but in this history a second truth quickly emerges—canes, crutches, and walking sticks dominated through much of human existence. The orthopedist and amateur historian Sigmund Epstein even argued that the crutch was a kind of marker of civilization, especially when "woven" into "a story of how the genus homo rose above the handicap of disease, trauma and deformity" (Epstein, 1937: 304). Canes, crutches, and walking sticks date at least to ancient Egypt and their value—for non-disabled, temporarily disabled, and permanently disabled persons alike—is well established (Loebl and Nunn, 1997). Of course, they are easy to construct; a single tree limb easily makes a rudimentary walking stick. But also, crutches were often the best "fit" available within the built—and unbuilt—environment. In a world where most people's lives were shaped by farm work, physical labor, and a rough and ready terrain, the crutch, cane, and walking stick all have an advantage. They aren't only better suited for uneven terrain but can help all bodies—able and otherwise—navigate the uneven patches of ground. By contrast, wheeled devices of all sorts need smooth, flat, and preferably paved surfaces. These were a constellation of characteristics difficult to find anywhere before the twentieth century. To this day, even the most developed cities present a host of problems for wheelchair users. Ruts, holes, uneven paving, and open gutters can make street travel difficult. In the past, carts and carriages were specially built for uneven paving and cobblestone streets. And, unlike the modern wheelchair, these were built to carry their passengers high off the ground and insulate them from the muck and clamor of pre-modern towns and cities.

However one reckons it, crutches offered a better environmental "fit" for the semi-ambulatory. Outside of cities, crutches could negotiate uneven or boggy ground. But they had an advantage in urban spaces. Here, crutches helped disabled people with a built environment that included curbs and staircases, too. In William Kidd's early nineteenth-century painting *The Army,*

FIGURE 1.4 William Kidd, The army or two Chelsea pensioners descending stairs arm-in-arm, c. 1840. Courtesy Wellcome Library, London.

the Scottish-genre painter presents us with two elderly and disabled British pensioners, veterans of the Napoleonic wars who still wear their striking scarlet coats (Figure 1.4). Behind them we glimpse an open door and through it a long hall within the Royal Hospital, which doubled as an old soldiers' home for retired troops injured in service. Exiting through the majestic entry of the eighteenth-century Royal Hospital, the modest pair proceeds down a set of stairs. Arm in arm, the two advance down the steps, with the one-legged veteran leaning on his mate's left arm while using a crutch to support his other side. No wheelchair could negotiate those steps or staircases.

From an architectural point of view, the link between environment and disability has often been obscured. In fact, in the late eighteenth and early nineteenth centuries, far from meeting the needs of disabled persons, architects designing hospitals saw the inclusion of large staircases as a hopeful sign of modernity. Strategically placed around buildings, large staircases would, reformers reasoned, provide a "reservoir for fresh air" in otherwise insalubrious spaces (Oppert, 1867: 16). Focusing on adequate ventilation, these buildings were often acknowledged to be inconvenient for sick and invalid patients, especially when they had to be carried from one floor to another.[2] In hindsight, an architecture built around stairwells helps explain why so many patients were all but bedridden, and the heavy use of small palanquins or litters to transport the mobility impaired within such buildings. Yet it also suggests a cultural blind spot, in which planners were scarcely aware of disablement, let alone how their ideas might heighten—not lessen—forms of impairment. If nothing else, crutches, canes, and walking sticks helped disabled persons like Kidd's pair of war veterans navigate a world that was not designed with people like them in mind. Up and down steps and across cobblestones, unpaved roads, and other obstacles, the crutch, cane and walking stick were simply more adaptive and operational in a pre-modern environment.

Even so, Kidd's casual glimpse of disabled life in the early nineteenth century hardly expresses the lived experience of those using crutches. Certainly, crutches were heavily used—in the nineteenth century, the British medical journal *The Lancet* reported that demand at Charing Cross Hospital was so great that the facility struggled to keep them in stock (Jones, 1836: 837). But many of the people who relied on them found crutches to be heavy and uncomfortable. Moreover, most people used ill-fitted crutches. And, worse still, the most commonly used designs could cause their own injuries, ranging from joint pain to thrombosis, if used for sustained periods of time.

Such difficulty and discomfort led the rich and powerful to resist using crutches. As a result, the well-to-do were the first to agitate for wheelchairs. The late sixteenth century marked the first appearance of "mechanical" chairs placed on wheels. Developments like the "chayre des goutes" or gout chair, first spotted at the court of King Philip II of Spain, were developed first and foremost as a mobility aid (Figure 1.5). The overstuffed chair was placed on wheels and designed to ease Philip's gouty arthritis by including a footrest, hinged arms, and a backrest upholstered with horsehair. But it was also fixed with an ingenious system of adjustable ratchets that could be shifted for maximum relief (Kamenetz, 1969: 14). The seat was considered so curious that Philip's valet, Jehan Lhermite from Antwerp, recorded the chair in side and back view, as well as from below, with special attention

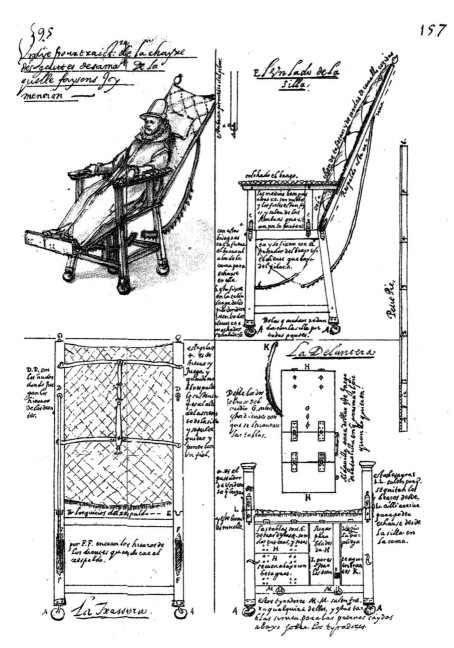

FIGURE 1.5 Jehan Lhermite, The "chayre des goutes" or gout chair, first spotted at the court of King Phillip II of Spain, c. 1578 (in *Le Passetemps de J. Lhermite*, J. E. Buschmann, 1896). Courtesy Wellcome Library, London.

given to the mechanics of its lounging mechanism. In this depiction the king of Spain, normally depicted in a manner that demonstrated his noble and honorable status, appears strangely doll like, his image clearly less interesting to the artist than the mechanics of the chair itself (Kamenetz, 1969: 14). But court etiquette determined the style of this rolling chair; it had to impress with elegance and avoid vulgarity. Philip had a large entourage capable of pushing and pulling the chair along. In the end, the same chair was transported from one palace to another, as Philip followed courtly protocol and proceeded to his different properties (Parker, 2014: xii). The chair was not designed for travel, and Philip used it only inside of his palaces. It is important to remember that this was not necessarily by choice, but because they were the only places to provide flat and polished floors ample enough to enable allow dragging the behemoth through rooms and down drafty halls.

A century later, at the court of Louis XIV, the sheer logistics of how and especially where such a machine might work may be found in the example of the French king's "roulette," or rolling chair (Figure 1.6). The king was first reported using a rolling chair in 1686, when recovering from surgery for an anal fistula. Though today there is little that sounds as antithetical to restful recovery as a trip around the palace's formal gardens surrounded by

FIGURE 1.6 Pierre-Denis Martin, King Louis XIV in his wheelchair in front of the Swiss Lake at Versailles (detail) 1713. Photo by FA/Roger Viollet/Getty Images.

a phalanx of retainers, Louis took delight in his roulette. Its bulky wheels, larger than those on Philip's chair, were able to negotiate the manicured paths of Louis' palace grounds. When, in 1713, Pierre-Denis Martin depicted the king on a promenade through the gardens of Versailles, the illustrated landscape that stretches out behind the king reveals Versailles' elegant and carefully laid out parterre; with its flat walkways, ramps, and broad lanes, the king's palace provides a rare glimpse of a space that, before the twentieth century, was well suited to a wheelchair. The French king turned to the chair to avoid walking distances and always insisted that one be at hand in case of sudden bouts of pain or fatigue (Perez, 2007: 109, 110). Of course, just because these chairs were wheeled does not mean that they functioned like later wheelchairs. For Philip and Louis, these proto-wheelchairs were more like mobile thrones. They may have accommodated physical frailty and infirmity, but they were also declarations of wealth, comfort, and power.

Stately and regal, Louis' roulette and Philip II's gout chair looked fitting enough for a king and each, in its own way, was widely imitated in the years to come. A less grand version of Philip's device, the Merlin chair, was introduced into London society in the mid-eighteenth century. In spite of its whimsical-sounding name, taken not from Arthurian legend but from its eccentric Belgian inventor John Joseph Merlin, this chair was not designed for a prince surrounded by courtiers. Though the Merlin chair seized on the gout chair's inventive mobility, placing the seat on two front wheels, with a third balancing wheel positioned at its back, this chair, unlike its predecessors, was self-propelled. The chairs favored by Philip and Louis relied on fleets of servants to push them. The Merlin chair, however, used a clever system of winding handles, hand-cranks, and gears, all of which linked to rotating levers that controlled the chair's wheels. Merlin's wheelchair gave the sitter a new degree of agency.

Merlin took advantage of every opportunity to promote his innovation. In the 1780s he used the chair at balls, masquerades, and other assemblies of fashionable London. Sometimes Merlin even dressed as a quack doctor promoting his version of a "gouty chair" (Jacob, 1985: 26). His aggressive plugs paid off, earning him considerable fame in the eighteenth and nineteenth centuries. For the next 100 years the term "Merlin chair" was applied to virtually any chair on wheels that allowed the sitter to propel him or herself around a room. Even when a somewhat simpler self-wheeled chair was introduced in the early nineteenth century (this one had a second rim placed on each wheel, so its user could use his or her hands to roll the chair forward), this too was often called a Merlin chair.

But, the Merlin chair was almost impossible to maneuver outside. Urban and rural landscapes were ill adapted to them. Where Louis' and Philip's throne-like conveyances could be used in palaces and princely grounds, both versions of the Merlin or "invalid" chair revealed a deeper truth—they made a poor environmental fit even for those wealthy enough

FIGURE 1.7 Merlin's mechanical chair for the elderly or infirm, 1811 (in R. Ackermann, R. *The Repository of Arts, Literature, Commerce, Manufactures, Fashions, and Politics*, 1st series, vol. 6). Courtesy Wellcome Library, London.

to afford them. Merlin's ingenious mechanism was complex and delicately formed, but its promise of access was, by today's standards, limited. Carved from expensive wood and covered with padded upholstery, its delicate design would suggest that these chairs were meant for indoor use. An illustration of a Merlin chair that appeared in an 1811 issue of

Rudolf Ackerman's *Repository of Arts*, a popular periodical at the time, suggests as much (Figure 1.7) (Ackermann, 1811: 225). Riderless, this Merlin chair is encircled by a well-tended lawn, every bit as rarefied as the manicured estate of Louis XIV's palace gardens. Unlike the rugged wheelbarrows and pushcarts that roamed London's eighteenth-century streets, the Merlin chair's dainty wheels, low-hung stretcher bars and elaborate footrest leave it open to the smallest of impediments; a small pebble, for instance, might stop its wheels, while a puddle would soil its delicate finish. In 1836, the Scottish inventor and historian Sir David Brewster offered a realistic assessment of its use. Noting the Merlin chair's fragility, Brewster reminds us that most are "fitted only to move on the smooth surface of a floor, and not to overcome the inequalities of a common road" (Brewster, 1831: 6). Certainly, its inventor never promoted the chair as an all-terrain vehicle and the wealthy gout and palsy sufferers who bought it scarcely expected to go outside at all. The chair very much reflected social expectation that impaired or disabled people wanted to stay at home and not partake in society. It was a delicate chair designed for delicate people.

It was not that doctors at the time urged their patients to stay home. Those wealthy enough were urged to travel and take treatments at spas. In Britain, the city of Bath was a common destination. There, disabled people were encouraged out of doors, if only for their treatment at the city's many spas. Bit by bit, Bath was remade into a city reconfigured for disabled people, and no design better expressed these accommodations than the hulking and robust Bath chair. Lower to the ground than the Merlin chair, it was also sturdier (Figure 1.10). Though today the Bath chair seems utterly antique, its appearance and purpose hint at a connection between disability, access, and the environment in a way that today seems utterly modern. The Bath chair is a symbol of an emerging idea about disability as much as it is a unique design to serve impairment. Reordering the priorities of Merlin's invention, the Bath chair was designed specifically for outdoor use.

The origins of the Bath Chair were humble enough. It took the shape of a sedan chair or litter, a mode of transport fashionable across Europe in the early years of the eighteenth century (Peach, 1893: 129). By the late eighteenth century, however, politics and a scarcity of labor made the uncompanionable and undeniably elitist sedan chair less popular. In much of Europe, they were replaced by horse-drawn carriages. But in small, walkable cities like Bath, the sedan chair was a practical feature of spa life, gently carrying invalids short distances about town for their treatments. Here a somewhat more egalitarian version of the sedan chair emerged, its cab placed on three wheels, with a single person pushing it from behind. The Bath-based inventor John Dawson is generally credited with introducing the Bath chair to British society by 1780 (Peach, 1893: 148). But after his death in 1824, James Heath, another Bath-based manufacturer, began to promote his version of the chair; James Heath advertised extensively in local newspapers and was so successful that he was often cited as the chair's inventor by the late nineteenth century (Gloag, 1964: 245).

The Bath chair's roots are evident enough but less obvious is how much of the city of Bath was shifted and altered to accommodate it, and disabled people as well. Treatment at Bath, of course, was prescribed for a variety of ailments, ranging from recovery from febrile diseases to diabetes. But many of the maladies that touched on mobility disabilities led visitors to Bath. Visitors suffering from lumbago and sciatica sought its healing waters, as did those afflicted with gout, rheumatism, and paraplegia. When the ancient Roman spa town in southern England began to make its principal income from wealthy and infirm visitors, easy access became an issue of concern. By the mid-eighteenth century, the local government started to invest in its built infrastructure. Problems of access and public planning abounded. The spa was hilly in places and the approach from London fraught. Hoping to make arrival and access "safe and easy," the town fathers lobbied to begin "repairing, amending, and enlarging the principal roads leading to Bath," as well as "cleansing, paving and enlightening" its actual streets (Warner, 1801: 338). The elegant Georgian buildings of the Circus, and particularly its paved streets, are more than a testament to town planning. As a system of transportation in which the infirm or elderly could make their way around, the city's manicured streets allowed easy movement.

While the city's famous waters and cosmopolitan atmosphere attracted visitors and attention, Bath became known because of its accommodations. As an 1821 guidebook proudly announced, "besides the rich boon of its waters, its high social privileges, and many other attractions," the city possesses "every variety of surface and aspect which can benefit the aged, the consumptive, and the constitutional invalid, or the convalescent from recent disease" (Anon, 1825: 15). Many who came hoping to be cured by its healing waters stayed for its disability-friendly atmosphere, and its population of elderly, frail, and unwell visitors swelled. In 1860, the doctor and amateur historian James Tunstall noted, "The houses on the Parades and streets adjacent were erected exclusively for the accommodation of the invalid. The pavement is on a level with the street doors, so that, by means of the wheel chairs—which take their name from this city—even the cripple may enjoy the fresh air without fatigue, and partake, in some degree, in the amusements, so necessary to his forlorn condition" (Tunstall, 1860: 19). Not only was the town well planned, but also it was gradually improved with certain kinds of bodies and devices in mind. In nineteenth-century Bath, impairments might not disappear, but disability was lessened. It provided a good fit.

Though the Bath chair had emerged as a fixture on the local scene by the turn of the nineteenth century, the design—and the access it provided—only burst into the popular imagination at the 1851 Great Exhibition. The city of Bath sent to the Exhibition a display of three-wheeled chairs intended to showcase local industry. But Heath also persuaded the Exhibition's

THE GREAT INDUSTRIAL EXHIBITION OF 1851.

FIGURE 1.8 Anonymous, The Great, Exhibition of 1851, 1851. Courtesy Library of Congress.

organizers to allow him to rent his chairs to visitors. As the newspaper *The Guardian* would later note, because of Heath, "many an infirm or invalid lady, and others deprived of the power of locomotion" were able "to go through and inspect at their ease the countless art treasures in the Exhibition" (Anon, 1857: 3). The space was so accessible that exhibition organizers opened the hall an hour early specifically for elderly and infirm visitors. For visitors like the elderly writer Amelia Opie, the Exhibition became a rare chance to venture out in public. Opie, an octogenarian by this point, took full advantage of the Exhibition's early opening hours and went often in her Bath chair. Encountering other invalid friends she hadn't seen in years, she joked that they should hold races down the Exhibition's vast interior side aisles (Brightwell, 1854: 389). As it happened, Opie waited for the general public to be let in, watched the arrivals, and was delighted that people, pleased to see her in public, frequently came over to greet her (Brightwell, 1854: 389).

But, just as in Bath, the environment played a unique role in allowing this proto-wheelchair to work (Figure 1.8). Joseph Paxton's innovative Crystal Palace proved remarkably well suited to the Bath chair's needs, especially as it provided a space for its wheels to easily glide or be pushed across its surfaces. The vast iron and glass building was over 1,800 feet long with a total floor area of almost a million square feet. Built to enhance visual spectacle, including a stuffed elephant covered with the richly ornamented trappings of an Indian prince and a machine that made cigarettes in front of visitors, the structure's massive barrel vault allowed open spaces around individual features. It also left the vast interior of the building entirely open. Recalling the palatial homes of Philip II and Louis XIV, Paxton's Palace was the first large-scale, barrier-free environment open to the public. (Many years later, after the Crystal Palace was dissembled and reconstructed in Sydenham Park, Paxton himself, now elderly and infirm, returned to the building in a Bath chair.)

But unlike the city of Bath, the building was accessible by accident, and the fit between bodies, spaces, and building was never entirely seamless. No one, for example, thought to provide disabled access ways into the building, which was raised on a plinth and approached only by stairs. And visitors confronted even more stairs leading up to the second-floor galleries and down to the subterranean basement. Access was the product of accident rather than ambition.

The Great Exhibition set a precedent of access that was carried forward at subsequent World's Fairs. In the United States, at both the 1855 World's Fair in New York and the 1876 Centennial in Philadelphia, the main exhibition halls imitated Paxton's innovative architecture. And at both events, disabled and able-bodied visitors were invited to rent wheelchairs. Organizers at the 1893 Columbian Exhibition provided an entire landscape of flat, accessible routes around the massive fair grounds. They also contracted with the Columbian Roller-Chair Company to provide rentals (and attendants) that were available at some twenty booths throughout the fair. By the end of the fair, the company reported that they had rented approximately 794,100 chairs to visitors (and reportedly made over $400,000) (Johnson, 1897: 385). There is no record of how many of these visitors were disabled, but it is clear that this Exposition and subsequent ones uniquely accommodated impaired visitors. Indeed, the parameters of wheelchair use were beginning to shift.

A symbol of defeat?

Matthew Brady's 1863 picture of a ward in Carver General Hospital in Washington DC presents a cheerful space carefully decorated with ivy bunting and American flags, patients siting at attention in dress uniform, and the unit's nurses arranging themselves on seats, mindful of staying out of the photographer's main gaze (Figure 1.9). Down the center of the photograph, a flat and accessible path leads to a young man, his right leg amputated just below the knee. He stares at us from a wheelchair. This photograph signals a shift in the conception and use of wheelchairs in the mid-nineteenth century, when wheelchairs came to be used as medical tools.

FIGURE 1.9 Matthew Brady. Ward in the Carver General Hospital in Washington DC, 1863. Courtesy National Archives and Records Administration.

The medicalization of wheelchairs is traceable, in part, to advances in surgery and sanitation. As battlefield medicine and attention to cleanliness improved in the mid-nineteenth century, more and more amputees survived. This was especially true of the American Civil War, the first war in which the injured survived long enough to be taken off the battlefield and into the hospital. Such a large casualty rate meant that administrators were pressed for space and put a premium on patient mobility. Moving large numbers of patients into, around, and out of hospital wards caused doctors and mechanics alike to reevaluate the wheeled chair.

Of course, outside hospital contexts, wheelchairs were flimsily made and even dangerous. Throughout the century it was widely acknowledged that these chairs provided a ride so bumpy that many users complained "of pain, not only when jolted over a rough road by an unsteady hand, but even when they passed over a pebble in a garden-walk" (Tilt and Etter, 1881: 48). Nineteenth-century novels like J Haggard Rider's 1895 *Joan Haste* give casual mention that, when used indoors, they were ill-proportioned, and rammed into furniture and doorjambs with alarming frequency (Rider, 1895: 225).[3]

But, for several decades, doctors had been examining non-wheeled invalid or "therapeutic" chairs arguing for more support for the spine, ideally in chairs with high backs and reclining features. As early as 1863, the enterprising Charles Bander had devised a supportive chair, specially designed to move the injured or sick around for transport. His patent for an "ambulance" or "traveling" invalid chair placed particular emphasis on an adjustable spring mechanism in its back (Charles L. Bander, November 10, 1863, patent No 40,547). The profile of Bander's chair signaled a broader shift from the chubby and relatively low-lying chairs associated with the Merlin to seats with higher backs, like the one captured in Brady's 1863 photograph. The styling and production of these chairs was not complex; most drew from ladder-back and other chair construction typically made by skilled craftsmen of the period. Since they were meant for transport around hospitals, these chairs were constructed of cheap, light, and practical materials like lightweight Indian reed and inexpensive wooden frames. What they lost in luxury, they gained in a new seriousness of purpose.

For the first time, wheelchairs were truly on the threshold of something new. They were being used not merely for wealthy persons—sick and healthy—but for large numbers of people in serious medical need. Invalid and Merlin chairs had been advertised in surgical and medical instrument catalogs in the late eighteenth century (Woods and Watson, 2004: 407). But it was in the mid-nineteenth century, with the development of modern healthcare and especially with the Civil War, that, as scholars Woods and Watson point out, wheelchairs "became primarily medical devices" (Woods and Watson, 2004: 407). Private individuals may have continued to own wheeled chairs, but by the end of the Civil War, the professionalization of medicine brought wheeled chairs increasingly within the realm of well-defined medical practices.

Hospital-issued wheelchairs were also labor-saving devices. Made with special "push" rims, they allowed patients to push themselves along. Furthermore, emphasis was put on practicality and especially safety. In the decades following the Civil War, innovation focused primarily on technical changes, particularly in the development of chair wheels. Under the influence of innovations in bike manufacture, chairs began to incorporate wire bicycle wheels and braking systems as well. In 1874, the French-Canadian inventor Peter Gendron patented a wheel originally developed for bicycles, wagons, and baby carriages, but adapted for wheelchairs (Peter Gendron, April 21, 1874, patent No 150022 A). Soon, even smoother riding hollow rubber wheels were developed and sold.

The medicalization of wheelchairs, however, also fixed their place in the center of professional medicine—the hospital. As hospital architecture shifted away from the pavilion model with its ventilated staircases, interiors were increasingly flat and accessible. No longer were the frail, impaired, or sick expected to limp down hallways on canes or be arduously carried on special litters as they mounted staircases. Wheelchairs helped to facilitate the functionality and smooth running procedures favored by builders and doctors alike. Training manuals and hospital advice books urged medical facilities to keep at least one "invalid chair" or "wheel chair" on hand, if only "for the conveyance of patients" (Swete, 1870: 137). Most inventories or annual reports of healthcare institutions in the late nineteenth century mention at least one or two on site.[4] However, as they became increasingly common in hospitals, wheelchairs also became increasingly suspect outside of them.

How to behave in a Bath-chair

The medicalization of the wheelchair made its private use and ownership more complex. Nobody knew this better than the poet and novelist Joseph Ashby-Sterry. Self-identifying as a "heretic," when the fifty-year-old writer temporarily injured his knee in 1883, he took to a Bath chair. Humorously chronicling his experience in his regular *Punch* magazine column, "Lays of a Lazy Minstrel," Ashby-Sterry confronted the very serious question of how a chair user is expected to act in public. Smiling as he greeted onlookers, Ashby-Sterry began to:

> Fancy my bearing is too jovial. Rather too much of the Bath-brick! I temper it by putting on a sentimental expression and end by appearing like a faint fool. A disgusting red man who has just passed shakes his head, says something to his friend, looks at me, and taps his forehead. (Sterry, 1883: 253)

Tired of parsing "how to behave in a bath-chair," he suggested that someone write "Rules for Behaviour in a Bath-chair" (Sterry, 1883: 253). Had anyone bothered to write an etiquette manual for wheeled chair users, they might have consulted Frank R. Stockton's *Pomona's Travels*. Here, Stockton's humorous advice is voiced by the practical Pomona, a naïve servant, who fecklessly explains appropriate behavior. The key, she recounts, is for a man to sit "in the bath-chair, with the buggy-top down, and his pipe lighted, and his hat cocked on one side a little, so as to look as if he was doing the whole thing for a lark" (Stockton, 1900: 182, 183).

When the Empress Eugenie climbed onto a Bath chair in order to see the Great Exhibition in 1851, she was exerting the prerogative of some wealthy but able-bodied persons. Indeed, by the late nineteenth century, the Bath chair in particular was increasingly associated with pampered wealth. This type of Bath or invalid chair user haunts the margins of Victorian literature. Charles Dickens provided a short and sharp verbal portrait of the elderly Cleopatra Skewton in *Dombey and Son*. Here he describes "her attitude in the wheeled chair (which she never varied)" was like that of her namesake. She was like a "Princess as she reclined on board her galley." Mrs. Skewton's beauty, Dickens assures us, had long ago "passed away, but she still preserved the attitude, and for this reason expressly, maintained the chair … there being nothing whatever, except the attitude, to prevent her from walking" (Dickens,

1848: 204). Just as wheelchairs became more and more common in hospitals, in many luxurious resorts, the Bath chair was increasingly marginalized. Visiting the seaside around the turn of the century, Beatrix Buchanan described how her mother's crippling arthritis made a Bath chair necessary. At the same time, the daughter claimed "a fierce, ferocious, smoldering hatred" for the chair, which made a spectacle of them both. The daughter's "martyrdom" was made complete as she accompanied her mother—in the chair. Quickly, she noted onlookers' disapproval. Above all, she hated "how passers-by would glance at mama's large, red face, make unfeeling remarks, and snigger brutally to themselves" (Buchanan, 1903: 155). Though some die-hards continued to use "the 'bath chair' of Brighton and Bournemouth, in which fat dowagers go forth," it was, as one observer noted in 1915, "a poor old-fashioned thing" (Rhodes, 1915: 12) (Figure 1.10).

In fact, the growing disdain for Bath chairs can at least be traced earlier. In 1859, a furniture maker was listed in a New York City directory as specializing in chairs "for the comfort and convenience of sick, lame, and lazy people" (Anon, 1859: 140). While truly ill persons were increasingly sent to hospitals, observers like the essayist James Hain Friswell inveighed against "The hypochondriac who... lounges about in an invalid chair." In his "character formation manual," Friswell went so far as to claim that chair users were among "the most self-indulgent and lazy people" he knew (Friswell, 1864: 144). These attitudes were widely held and filtered into memorable characters like Clara, the spoilt child and wheelchair user in Swiss author Johanna Spyri's 1880 book *Heidi*. Born into a wealthy and indulgent family, Clara thinks she cannot walk and uses a wheelchair until she visits Heidi in the Alps. Removed from the comfort of her urban home and embracing the simple lifestyle of the mountaineers, Clara blossoms; in fact, she learns that she can thrive without a wheelchair.

At the same time that wheeled and Bath chairs were considered increasingly suspect in public spaces, workaday crutches were almost ordinary. From beggars in the streets of Rome and New York to the disabled veterans who crowded cheap Parisian cafes, crutches could be found everywhere in the eighteenth and nineteenth centuries. In sheer day-to-day visibility, wheelchairs were uncommon. Indeed, while the wheelchair was increasingly associated with luxury and laziness, the crutch, which requires labor and strength to use, was perceived differently. Unlike the wheelchair, the crutch could adapt to a number of different environments and required few, if any, special accommodations. Little wonder the device became a quick signal or stand-in for active disability in the public's imagination. Crutches were visible everywhere. In this respect, nineteenth-century literature is filled with iconic invalids like Dickens' charming waif, Tiny Tim, and Thomas Hardy's "fallen" woman, Fanny, in *Far From the Madding Crowd*. Furthermore, Robert Louis Stevenson drew one of the most vivid pictures of disabled dexterity yet when depicting the pirate captain Long John Silver in *Treasure Island*; in the ship's tight quarters, Silver fixed "his crutch by a lanyard round

FIGURE 1.10 H. K. Browne, Cleopatra Skewton in Charles Dickens' Dombey and Son, 1848 (in Charles Dickens, *Dombey and Son*, London: 1848).

his neck" (Stevenson, 1884: 79) but could also use it to stabilize himself while cooking and on dry land he might emphasize a point by crushing the crutch in the ground while speaking.

Would Stevenson's wily and unprincipled pirate have been the same character had he used a wheelchair instead of a crutch? Could he have even managed on the schooners and rocky jungle islands portrayed in Stevenson's novel? Such literary reflections explain, at least in part, the role of the crutch in the public's consciousness by the early twentieth century. For all their liabilities, crutches were the most practical solution to many forms of mobility impairment. No nineteenth-century wheelchair would fit on a cramped pirate schooner or scoot across the untamed jungles of the Caribbean. Crutches met with fewer barriers in the environment. They were so ubiquitous, too, that no one saw the need for a crutch etiquette manual— that is, an equivalent of Sterry's suggestion "how to behave in a Bath chair."

Thus it was the crutch, and not the wheelchair, that served as the first modern symbol of active disablement. As recently as 1938, the crutch was used as the symbol for the National Foundation for Infantile Paralysis, a group formed by Franklin Roosevelt. Now better known as the March of Dimes, the organization's aggressive fundraising techniques are still memorable for their ingenuity. Volunteers organized parades and square dances, telethons, and tag sales. But one of their best fundraisers was "blue crutch days," referring to a plastic blue-crutch lapel pin sold to the public as a fundraiser (Rose, 2003: 56). Following a moneymaking initiative begun by a California Lions Club, state legislatures across the United States began to declare official "blue crutch days," while boy and girl scouts, civic or veterans' groups sold miniature representations of the crutch that could be worn as lapel pins (Rose, 2003: 56). Little more than a simple, single bright blue plastic crutch, at the top of this small pin were three silver circles resembling the US coins. On each "coin" was printed the words "MARCH" "OF" "DIMES." The little lapel pin ratified a symbol that expressed solidarity with polio survivors.

When FDR helped found the March of Dimes in 1938, he still avoided using assistive devices in public, except when absolutely necessary. Bearing in mind the wheelchair's increasing association with institutional care, it is unsurprising to find that Roosevelt, himself much preferred using a cane or crutch when seen before audiences, and usually employed these while leaning on the arm of a son or assistant. In later years, the president's attitude toward his various mobility aids shifted. Late in his presidency, FDR began using a new type of folding wheelchair, and although he refused to be photographed in it, he did speak openly to others about his use of this new chair. When, for example, in 1945 he was returning from the Yalta conference, Roosevelt spent the better part of a day entertaining Abdulaziz Ibn Saud, the king of Saudi Arabia, on a navy cruiser moored off Egypt. Saud was also disabled with acute arthritis, walked with pain, and often used a wheelchair himself. On first meeting Roosevelt, the Saudi king immediately proclaimed that they were like "twin" brothers because of "their close ages, their responsibilities for their nations' well-being, their interests in farming, and the grave physical infirmities" that each faced (Yergin, 1991: 386). Ever the diplomat, Roosevelt replied to the king, "You are luckier than I because you can still walk on your legs and I have to be wheeled wherever I go." But Ibn Saud would have none of this, responding, "No, my friend, you are more fortunate. Your chair will take you wherever you want to go and you know you will get there" (Yergin, 1991). Clearly touched by this response, Roosevelt gifted the king his backup wheelchair, calling it a "twin" of the one he was using (Eddy, 1954: 31).

The Saudi ruler went on to request a custom-made wheelchair that had silk and antique brocade and was equipped with a fringe cover. The king's specially commissioned chair recalls the elaborate devices used by Philip II and Louis XIV, centuries earlier. Its California-based maker went so far as to describe the chair as "a throne on wheels" (Anderson, 1977). By the mid-twentieth century, of course, there was little interest in chairs like this. But the basic design was identical to the less ostentatious version originally given by Roosevelt. Lightweight and collapsible, Roosevelt's new chair demonstrated a significant rethinking of the wheelchair, and the environments in which it could be used.

The chair that changed the world

His rigid wicker chair wouldn't fit on the back of the family Buick, or so Herbert Everest would always explain to reporters, investors, and anyone else who would listen. Everest was a mining engineer who became disabled in 1918 when a wall fell and fractured his spine while he was fighting a fire in an Arkansas mine. As a paraplegic, he struggled with the wheelchair problem for the next fifteen years. Everest's largest frustration was how to strap his delicate but also rather bulky wicker chair onto a vehicle. He strove to make a living as an independent consultant in electronics, but "found my greatest difficulty was the lack of a usable, folding wheelchair. It just was not practical to tie the hospital chair on the back bumper to go on business errands" (Anon, 1955b: 4). Out of this misfit the modern wheelchair was born.

As Everest would later recall, one day his wife "found a self-propelled, wooden, folding chair which could be put in the car." Although "the chair was a wonderful help," it was made for use up and down hospital corridors, was held together with lightweight and flimsy wicker caning, was easily frayed and crushed in the back of his car, and "had to be rebuilt after nearly every long trip" (Anon, 1955b). Trained as an engineer, Everest approached another engineer, his neighbor Harry Jennings. Working with industrial materials and using the folding chair as a model, they created a sturdy wheelchair with tubular steel and welded joints. Moreover, it could be folded and used in careful coordination with cars. The result, patented in 1937 (H. A. Everest et al., October 12, 1937, patent No 2095411 A), was, in the words of the writer Freda Bruce Lockhardt, a "comparatively peaceful revolution, which has made wheelchairs familiar features of modern life" (Lockhart, 1971: 5). This was the chair that FDR used in his final years. This was the chair that would be pictured on the International Symbol of Access. Because of its revolutionary design, construction, and uses, I call this the first modern wheelchair (Figure 1.11).

To be clear, Everest and Jennings' first chairs invoke the best-known mechanisms of modernity. Certainly, for Everest himself, the wheelchair was not a medical device. It was a social tool, essential to being in and of the world around him. And it made little sense for his wheelchair to be constructed like the chairs used to transport patients through the wards of hospitals. It was wrong, too, for his chair to be fashioned from the same materials as cheaply crafted furniture. Unlike the hand-crafted cane and wood chairs then in use, these chairs were made in factories, and they were constructed from the materials of the machine age—steel, chrome, and vinyl. But they didn't just look more modern. They were also designed specifically with the automobile in mind. This new wheelchair was anchored to the interconnected, sped-up world of modern mobility. Everest and Jennings conceived their first prototype wheelchair as belonging in the world of machines.

It is especially difficult today to appreciate the impact of this first, modern wheelchair design. Although it took time for the chair to be widely introduced, it gradually made the wood and wicker chairs used in hospitals look obsolete. Its introduction was an act of empowerment that fundamentally changed ideas around mobility, access, and disability itself. Herbert Everest "became a rolling advertisement" for the chair he developed and put into production (Cooper et al, 2003: 281). Everest would later explain to the readers of the Paralyzed Veterans Association newsletter *Paraplegia News* that as late as 1935 "anyone wishing to buy a chair had a choice of a restricted few." Chair users usually "took what the dealer had, or went without" (Anon, 1955b: 4).

Eschewing the padded upholstery, wood and rattan or rush seating of prior chairs, Everest & Jennings' (E&J) chair was a strikingly "dramatic departure" from those that came before (Bartolucci, 1992: 32); it had more in common with the stripped down, functionalist furniture design coming out of the Bauhaus in Germany than the Victorian-era spas of Brighton and Bath. Instead of padding, it employed a plain and sturdy fabric that could collapse like a hammock on its seat and back. And its spare, chrome-plated structure recalls the tubular steel chairs of Marcel Breuer and the cantilevered steel-bar chairs of Mies van der Rohe.

The first E&J wheelchairs were sturdy but also lightweight, and made for *both* indoor and outdoor use. Not only were they collapsible, but also the company continued to innovate its design. Unlike the Merlin chair, and most of the chairs used in hospitals after the Civil War, the company quickly

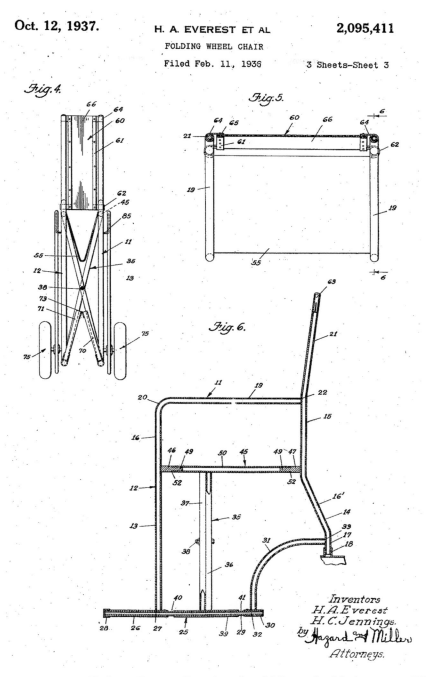

Oct. 12, 1937.   H. A. EVEREST ET AL   2,095,411

FOLDING WHEEL CHAIR

Filed Feb. 11, 1936   3 Sheets—Sheet 3

Fig.4.

Fig.5.

Fig.6.

Inventors
H.A. Everest
H.C. Jennings.
by Hazard and Miller
Attorneys.

FIGURE 1.11 Herbert Everest. Drawing for folding wheelchair patent (US 2095411 A), 1937.

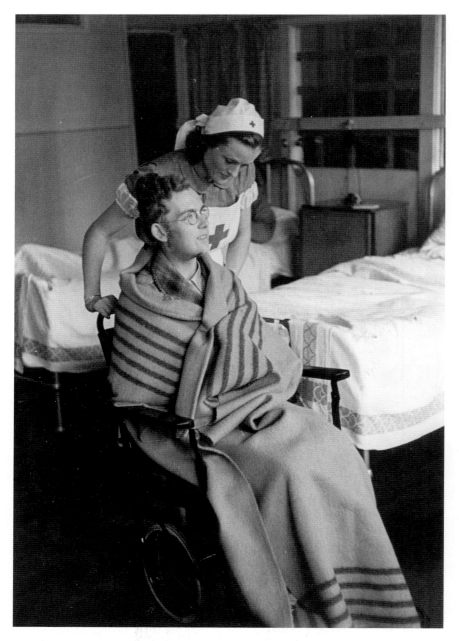

FIGURE 1.12 Kurt Hutton, Nurse tends an injured soldier, 1941. Picture Post/Getty Images.

enlarged the rear—propelling—wheels of E&J chairs. While almost all chairs produced by this time were fitted with small wheel rims that allowed users to propel their chairs forward, because the E&J chair led with smaller, lighter, and more responsive casters, it was easier to guide and steer. Thus the newer design combined hand rims with a relatively lightweight frame, meaning that it was easier for the user to move him- or herself. Indoors, this wheelchair could be maneuvered well in small spaces, fitting through doorways without first having to carefully line the chair up with the doorjamb. But also, unlike the Bath chair that was designed for outdoor use, the E&J chair was more compact and its user could manoeuver it up single steps and around curves. And, of course, addressing Everest's original need, it could also be easily folded and placed in a car. This feature would, as we shall soon see, help shape a new attitude toward chairs—and their fit into the larger environment. In the final analysis, E&J chair was more than a convenient new chair design; it also reflected changing attitudes about personal mobility.

The new wheelchair's promise of light, compact mobility led the White House to acquire several E&J chairs in early 1944. To be sure, the foldable wheelchair was not invisible. But to Roosevelt, who had struggled for years to find a practical and inconspicuous way of getting around, it must have been a welcome alternative to earlier wheelchairs. The president began using a standard issue E&J design, and several more were quickly acquired. When the Secret Service oversaw a redesign of Roosevelt's airplane, E&J was asked to build a more compact version, without arms, so he could fit in an unusual elevator. The president did not want to enter the plane in public, carried up steps, or be seen wheeling across the tarmac and up a ramp. Instead, he chose to board the plane privately, by way of a special elevator that opened on the aircraft's door (Gallagher, 1985: 176). Roosevelt's wealth and power allowed him to find or make special accommodations necessary to use a wheelchair. His wheelchair did not change the world; the turning point in attitudes toward the disabled came only after his death. But, as more and more people started to use the E&J wheelchair, it gradually becomes clearer: the modern wheelchair required an environment built with it in mind.

Even in FDR's day-to-day life, Hugh Gallagher observes, "the President moved in a ramped world" (Gallagher, 1985: 142). As early as 1933, on the bright and sunny porch where Roosevelt relaxed with the three-year-old Ruth Bie and Fala, the setting was clearly accessible to his chair, as was the rest of the residence at Hill Top cottage. The modest Dutch Colonial Revival home was designed by architect Henry Toombs, but with considerable input from FDR, who fitted it to his needs.[5] The first floor had no stairs or steps at all. For instance, the small porch where Roosevelt sat was accessible to the grounds via an earthen ramp. Inside the cottage, windows were built lower, for maximum viewing from a wheelchair, and doorways lacked thresholds or other impediments to wheeled access. Roosevelt's assistants went to great lengths in order to accommodate his chairs, particularly in the nation's capital. Ramps were built in front of public buildings and railings placed to enable walking from backstage to podium. Sometimes, the Secret Service even constructed ramps "not just for the President, but for his car too" (Gallagher, 1985: 98). Traveling around the country, FDR liked to ride in his car all the way up to a speaking platform, waving his hat along the way, and even delivering speeches from the vehicle. Those early accommodations remind us how ill-fitted Roosevelt's surroundings were to his impairment, but also suggest that clever design allowed FDR to cultivate the appearance of normalcy.

Roosevelt died just as the war was ending and legions of veterans, many of them injured, were returning home. Companies like Everest & Jennings were uniquely poised to meet their wheelchair needs. But after the president died in April 1945, the accommodations around Washington were seen as having fulfilled their purpose. Without Roosevelt there, "the ramps constructed in the White House and other places across Washington for the use of the President's wheelchair were soon taken up" (Gallagher, 1985: 209). Even FDR's church, an institution that might pride itself on access, did not see a continuing need. At St. John's, the place of worship favored by presidents and just across Lafayette Square from the White House, "removed the small ramp from the two steps at the church's nave" (Gallagher, 1985: 209). Here, as elsewhere, access was available on a case-by-case basis, through individual accommodations. Most of the public continued to believe that seriously disabled persons should adapt themselves to the environment, or else stay in infirmaries, in hospitals, or at home.

Roosevelt's needs were not an aberration. In fact, E&J wheelchairs became standard issue for the waves of injured veterans returning home. But the invention of the modern wheelchair and its widespread dissemination was not enough. It still remained for society to recognize disability as a matter of environment as much as one of technology or medicine. The product of need, innovation, and technology, the modern wheelchair could not be put into widespread use until there was the social and political will to make it fit within the built environment. The invention of the modern wheelchair thus highlighted a heretofore unrecognized kind of misfit, suggesting it as a new way of thinking about disability and the role that design could play in mitigating its effects. And signage would be integral to this changed mind-set.

Notes

1   Of course, some physical impairments, diseases, and accidents have remained consistent through history. But the nature of others has, to some extent, changed over time. Two hundred years ago, incapacitation and death came early and was often from infectious diseases, malnutrition, and injuries. In the industrialized world today, people live longer and suffer from heart disease, strokes, and a variety of conditions often connected with old age.

2   Although high-profile reformers like Florence Nightingale worried that seriously ill patients "get no good by going through the air, and being jolted up and down

stairs" (Florence Nightingale, 1858: 84), most architects and administrators took for granted many features that would later prove to be barriers for access. The most up-to-date hospitals always featured a "fine and spacious entrance hall" graced with "tolerably wide" entry stairs; these functioned partly as airshafts and partly because "they must afford space for carrying up the patients" (Oppert, 1867: 16). Typically, patients were put in chairs and carried up and down these staircases, though, as one Victorian-era author admitted, "I have sometimes seen patients carried up who groaned from pain caused by the uncomfortable chairs which the porters use in some establishments" (Oppert, 1867: 16).

3 Most nineteenth-century wheelchairs lacked even the most simple safety mechanisms like brakes. Visiting Russia in the 1840s, Mary-Ann Smith observed a memorable moment in wheelchair safety when visiting the Tsar's wife, Alexandra Feodorovna, in her private quarters in St. Petersburg's Winter Palace. The invalid empress approached in a wheelchair that two of her younger sons began pushing across the palace floors, "propelling the Tzaritza at unwonted speed." Then their father entered the room, and with military discipline, the boys immediately moved to salute their father, letting go of the chair. The Tsarina continued to speed across the elegant anteroom outside Alexandra's private apartments, coming to a rough stop in front of a range of chairs set against a distant wall (Smith, 1859: 108, 109).

4 See, for example, Horace Swete's account of the tools and equipment necessary for a well-functioning clinic (1870).

5 Toombs had already designed a number of accommodations in Warm Springs, FDR's rehabilitation center in Georgia. The president had numerous ideas and special requests when Toombs designed his Hill Top residence; in fact, Toombs would later claim that FDR should be noted as architect, not he (see correspondence, Henry Toombs to M Le Hand, 1938, Franklin D. Roosevelt Library).

2

Fitting In (1945–1961)

In 1950 Marlon Brando hit the big screen. Standing at the cusp of a critical career in film, his best-known performance until then was his searing portrayal of Stanley Kowalski in Tennessee William's 1947 Broadway plays *A Streetcar Named Desire*. But Brando was persuaded to come to Hollywood and star in *The Men* (1950), the tale of a veteran embittered by paraplegia (Figure 2.1). Studio publicists held Brando in ambivalent admiration and struggled to sell such a dark film to the public. As he prepared for the role, Brando was shadowed by *LIFE* magazine, whose correspondent documented him eating, drinking, and living with paraplegic veterans in Los Angeles' Birmingham Veterans Hospital during the four weeks before

FIGURE 2.1   Marlon Brando practicing for his role as a paraplegic veteran in *The Men*, 1950. Ed Clark/Life Picture Collection/Getty Images.

production began (Cosgrove, 2014). A state-of the-art facility, the hospital was filled with Everest & Jennings' (E&J) new wheelchairs. Brando slowly learned to use one. The young and physically active Brando went to great lengths to pass as one of the guys. When *LIFE*'s photographer caught up with the patients on an outing, Brando suddenly pulled back from the studio's scripted press event, reverting to his mischievous, bad-boy image. In an impulsive rush, he comically took his chair over a specially ramped sidewalk curb only to take a pratfall in front of the magazine's camera. As Brando performed for the camera, a group of patients gathered around the actor and laughed appreciatively at his stunt. But to them, the mishap was all too familiar.

The Men focused on the psychological state of men with little chance of returning to their former lives, but it also revealed how simple daily actions like mounting steep sidewalk curbs dogged them day in, day out. Ultimately, critics praised *The Men* as "extraordinarily fine" (Crowther, 1950: xi), but the film was as earnest as the *LIFE* photo-op was light-hearted. *The Men* ends on an ambiguous note. Newly married, Brando's wheelchair-using veteran Ken ("Bud") Wilozek has misgivings on his wedding night. Leaving his bride, he returns to Birmingham Veterans Hospital. Buoyed by his comrades there, Bud finally sees the error in his way of thinking and drives all night to find his wife. She has moved away and returned home to her parents, who never approved of her marriage to a disabled veteran to begin with. In the final scene, Bud struggles to get his folding wheelchair out of the car and then transfers onto it. Proceeding up the path to his in-laws' home, Bud makes it as far as the front step. Wheel to step, rubber to brick, his progress stops short of the door. The wheelchair can't go any further up the short path; seeing him, his wife rushes out of the house. The film closes with the pair embracing on the path.

Like the pratfall Brando took for *LIFE*, this closing scene reveals a hidden truth—although it had been introduced some ten years earlier, the modern wheelchair still had to be fitted into a world that was not built for it. When *LIFE* published a photo spread promoting *The Men*, the magazine's editors breezily described Brando as learning the "technique of getting his chair up an incline, which looks deceptively easy" (Anon., 1950a: 132). No doubt, E&J folding wheelchair had the potential to change lives. But it was also a very demanding device. Even as the doctors at Birmingham treated veterans and the government provided them with lightweight, chrome-plated wheelchairs, these chairs were useful only if the spaces in which they moved were accommodating.

Like Brando, the veterans at Birmingham Hospital quickly learned that little problems—steps, curbs, uneven surfaces, narrow doors, and a host of impediments small and large—conspired against them. In fact, wheelchair mobility and access slowly brought to light a larger terrain in which physics, philosophy, and social convention intersect. Bluntly put, wheels function only under certain conditions. This chapter deals with the misfit between the modern wheelchair's promise of mobility and the modern environment's inhospitability to it. For the modern wheelchair to function as designed, curb cuts, ramps, and a variety of tweaks and adjustments had to be developed—to this day they form the basis for the barrier-free access movement. But even just recognizing the need to integrate these changes into the environment was difficult; it was harder still for able-bodied people to understand that the built environment was itself disabling. The modern wheelchair promised far more mobility than anything offered earlier generations of disabled people. But for it to be integrated into modern life, the modern environment had to be changed to accommodate it.

Without a doubt, the disabled access movement has its roots in the early postwar years, when the modern wheelchair first became normalized. Returning veterans to civilian life was a chief concern in the years immediately after the war. Part of this postwar adjustment included integrating those returning with disabilities. Hollywood documented this process in movies like *The Best Years of Our Lives* (1946), which chronicles the adjustments of ex-servicemen, including one who lost both hands during a shipboard accident, and *Bright Victory* (1952), the tale of a soldier's return after he was blinded by a German sniper's bullet. White canes, guide dogs, and hearing aids were all used in this process, but no device presented a more striking visual symbol of these efforts than the new and improved wheelchair. Veterans or not, it gave new promise to an entire class of severely disabled people. But, having embraced the wheelchair, the public—disabled and able-bodied alike—now had to be taught how it should be used.

Reading backward from today, it is easy to see the roots of this change in 1940s California, where thousands of veterans went to recuperate after the Second World War. There, they encountered a rudimentary wheeled culture of access organized around the car. Not coincidentally, this also was where E&J was based. But this retrospective view is dangerous as it might bury developments made in the middle of the country, at the University of Illinois, where researchers began a rehabilitation program for veterans that eventually transformed the entire campus into a kind of experimental test site for disabled access. Nevertheless, it was only in the 1950s, when the question of access was taken up in Washington, that the magnitude of the problem—as well as possible solutions—became clear.

Accessing a culture on four wheels

When *LIFE* photographer Ed Clark arrived at Birmingham Veterans Hospital for his publicity photo shoot with Marlon Brando, he caught the actor and friends hitching a ride around the hospital grounds (Figure 2.2). Rearview mirror, tail pipe, door handle, these wheelchair-using veterans were grasping any part of the car they could; as the car accelerated, they

FIGURE 2.2 Marlon Brando (far right) joking with wheelchair using veterans on the grounds of Birmingham Veterans Hospital, Los Angeles, 1949. Ed Clark/Life Picture Collection/Getty Images.

held on tight. This lighthearted gag caught Clark's eye and he captured it on film. While Brando's pratfall was met with rueful smiles suggesting that each wheelchair user recognized in Brando's accident the new challenges they would have to face, the actor's hitchhiking stunt was different. Its seemingly effortless bravado foregrounds a new form of liberation promised by both the modern, collapsible wheelchair and the automobiles it was designed to be used with. Nowhere was this pairing more apt than in Southern California. Los Angeles presented, as commentator David Brodsly would later observe, "a world that seems designed to run on four wheels" (Brodsly, 1981: 35). Though he was referring to cars, the patients at Birmingham Veterans Hospital were on four wheels, too. In California, rolling—that is, the autonomy of movement inextricably tied to the wheel—achieved iconic status, and its culture of independent mobility based on the wheel facilitated a kind of de facto access.

This was hardly happenstance. Los Angeles' culture of the wheel provided the critical impetus for the development of the collapsible wheelchair in the first place. When, in the early 1930s, Herbert Everest and Harry Jennings developed the folding wheelchair in Los Angeles, they had automobile access squarely in mind. When Everest, a paraplegic, moved to Los Angeles, he could drive himself all over the state, picking up jobs as an independent electronics consultant. He found the city's car culture amenable enough to his disability; however, he needed a wheelchair that could fit easily in the back of his car. Folding wheelchairs had already been developed, and some had even been patented. As early as 1894, Kansas native Sarah Potter developed a portable invalid chair (Sarah A. Potter, December 25, 1894, patent No 531,330). In London, J. and A. Carter, specialists in "invalid furniture," sold a wooden wheelchair for travelers who wanted to avoid the "inconvenience and annoyance of being carelessly moved about by Railway Porters" (Anon., 1902: 163). By 1914, the popular magazine *Scientific American* described at least one already in use in New York (Bond, 1914: 67). But Herbert Everest imagined a wheelchair for the American car culture typified by Los Angeles' smooth and relatively barrier-free asphalt and concrete landscape. With Jennings, Everest designed a chair that allowed him to drive his car to work, park, take out, and unfold the chair, then roll into work, moving seamlessly from car to parking lot, and then from lot into buildings. E&J built a wheelchair empire based upon the personal mobility that coalesced around the automobile.

Speaking broadly, car culture changed the American public's attitudes toward mobility in the early twentieth century. Fusing technology with mass production, the first inexpensive cars brought speed, distance, and independence to large numbers of people. At the same time as labor was becoming more regimented by 9 to 5 hours, punch cards, and train and tram schedules, the automobile offered a form of personal release. The car allowed drivers "their own way, their own view, and their own opportunities to interact with things. It meant freedom from railroad timetables, certainly, and perhaps from the stranglehold of corporate monopolies on time" (Gudis, 2004: 40). Propelling this novel sense of autonomy was a new reality—car drivers could travel across the city, state, or country, almost at will. Automobiles offered travelers a new form of freedom.

This new mobility was also egalitarian. White and non-white, rich and relatively poor, able-bodied and disabled all had access to the road, and all the freedoms it implied. Entire communities grasped this potential. For African Americans in the rural South, the advent of inexpensive automobiles helped spur the Great Migration. Disabled people, too, benefited from the advent of inexpensive automobiles. Amputees who could operate an automobile, for example, could take care of errands across town, or take a camping trip across the country. An Alliance, Ohio, man born with no legs and one arm became a racecar driver (Anon., 1919). A boy who lost both hands in a train accident went on to become a Dallas County judge, clocking 1,500 miles behind the wheel (Anon., 1920). In 1920, the *Literary Digest* reported "there are a dozen other cases I could mention of those cripples who are not cripples; of physically handicapped men whose handicaps vanish into thin air the moment they are seated in the driving seat of a motor-car" (Anon., 1920). Later, of course, FDR would take great pride in driving his own specially adapted cars, including a sporty four-door Plymouth PA Phaeton he kept at Warm Springs and that allowed him to travel around the Georgia back roads unencumbered. Less well-known disabled drivers experienced a similar sense of pride. On a lark, a recently discharged First World War veteran named Paul L. Bolin, who lost a leg fighting at Chateau-Thierry, drove a car across the continent to San Francisco (Anon., 1920). In each instance, the car did not solve the problem of impairment, but it did begin to give some disabled people a new sense of mobility and freedom.

When Herbert Everest moved to Los Angeles in the early 1920s, his situation was more marked than some, but to a greater or lesser extent everyone in far-flung, loosely populated Southern California experienced a problem with mobility. In the years shortly after the First World War, Los Angeles' strong attachment to the motorcar began to take shape. The population was scattered and, as cars were gaining in popularity, citizens eagerly advocated for an extensive infrastructure—unconstrained by the horses, pedestrians, and the trolleys that filled ordinary city streets— to support them. Carving divisions through the city, planners structured the region around automobile transport. With visionary fanfare, the first freeway opened in 1940. Where large cities like Chicago and New York were vertically oriented, Los Angeles was horizontal. Expanding on a grid of local streets, boulevards, and avenues, a spidery network of freeways connected far-flung corners of the city. By the 1930s, regional architecture was designed and built with wheels in mind. In this uniquely auto-friendly city, asphalt and concrete streets were routinely intercepted by the sloped aprons of driveways and driveways. These led, in turn, to large parking lots, which themselves connected to adjacent sidewalks. One-story buildings were constructed on flat, concrete pads that rested directly on the ground. The result was a built infrastructure that was— often enough—step free.

The Men depicted some of this terrain and the ways in which it accommodated and presented obstacles to wheelchair users. All the wheelchairs used in the film were made by E&J—this point was emphasized even before the film was released, when the film was featured in hospital journals (Anon., 1950b: 5). It highlighted the facilities at Birmingham Veterans Hospital, one of only a few places built to treat spinal cord injury. The sprawling hospital campus was constructed of one-story brick and stucco buildings like much the rest of the architecture around town. Although *The Men* was largely filmed at Birmingham Hospital itself, the film offers glimpses of the access available to Bud in Los Angeles. At key moments in the film, Brando's character tests the world outside the hospital. He goes out to a restaurant with his fiancée, and later accompanies other wheeled vets to a bar. Though his wheelchair makes him a source of constant—and often unpleasant—attention, it also allows him to roll through Los Angeles' flat environment with relative ease. It is only in the film's final scene, when he leaves Los Angeles to visit his in-laws in their neighborhood of multistoried houses and stepped brick paths, that he confronts a physical barrier.

Given that, in California, access to four wheels meant mobility to disabled and non-disabled people alike, driving was encouraged as part of veterans' recuperation. Largely at the behest of veterans' groups, the state was ahead of the nation when residents argued that automobiles were essential to morale and even aided faster convalescence. By 1944, California's American Legion Auxiliary launched an independent initiative to raise $10,000 to help disabled veterans purchase their own cars. This initiative quickly gathered national attention; by August 1946, backing came from Congress, which authorized the purchase of cars for disabled veterans nationwide.[1] Several major automakers concurred, with Ford and Oldsmobile providing adaptations to some of their most popular automobile makes. At Birmingham Hospital the program was so successful that the patient parking lot was informally dubbed "Oldsmobile Row" (Banks, 1997: 1). (Brando was meant to drive a specially equipped Oldsmobile in *The Men* and one appears in the *LIFE* magazine profile.) But no matter how many specially equipped Oldsmobiles were on the road and however many E&J wheelchairs were given to returning veterans to use with them, plenty of barriers remained, even in wheel-friendly Los Angeles.

Then in 1946, just down the highway from Birmingham Hospital and a stone's throw from E&J headquarters, the University of California at Los Angeles admitted four veterans, all wheelchair users, as students (Anon., 1948: 66). That year, the school took a calculated, pragmatic stance and admitted thousands of decommissioned soldiers on the 1944 GI Bill. But they also took a gamble, and included the quartet from Birmingham Hospital. To date, wheelchair users like Herbert Everest found Los Angeles' wheel-friendly environment accessible, though on an individual basis. But this was an attempt to integrate larger numbers of disabled people into institutional life beyond that of infirmaries. It was a leap into the unknown. And, although the city provided more access than many environments at the time, the university was different. No one, after all, had taken into account the campus' distinctive architecture, including its neo-Romanesque towers, grand staircases, and elevated cloisters. In contrast to a regional architecture that favored flatness, UCLA's monumental campus mimicked the majestic campus architecture of New England and European universities.

When the first group of chair users arrived, not everything went well. The campus proved so unaccommodating that a local group of veterans had to carry them into its most inaccessible classrooms (DeLoach, 1992: 37). But the plan continued. Over the next year, the university grew its Veterans Affairs Department and began strategizing better adjustments and modifications. Just as FDR relied on special accommodations, the school built special ramps and widened classroom doors to accommodate their wheelchair-using students

(Browning, 1947). By 1948, disabled students were permitted to park in a central lot reserved for faculty; UCLA had its own Oldsmobile row in the heart of its campus. But other accommodations came more slowly. When, for instance, administrators realized that the campus veterans' services office was up a flight of stairs, wheelchair-using vets had to be enrolled in the parking lot behind Murphy Hall (Figure 2.3) (Anon., 1948: 66).

In a certain sense, the increasing numbers of injured veterans elicited a genuine interest in change. Historian David Gerber reports that by 1945, about 671,000 soldiers had been wounded, and 300,000 seriously enough that they needed long-term care (Gerber, 2000: 73). Generally speaking, there was a governmental and social commitment to ensure that all veterans "lead useful, reasonably normal lives" (Gerber, 2000: 331). This charge extended to profoundly injured veterans who, benefitting from improved medicine and treatment, were increasingly able to survive their wounds. Now, too, civilians who were living longer with the aftermath of diseases like polio, as well as conditions like cerebral palsy and muscular dystrophy. Anyone could see that the nature of these impairments was hugely varied, and so too were the approaches toward integrating these veterans and civilians into society. For all these purposes, in 1945 President Harry Truman instituted a national Employ of the Physically Handicapped Week; the next year he inaugurated the President's Committee on Employment of the Handicapped. Together, both initiatives were continued under President Dwight D. Eisenhower, who actively supported vocational rehabilitation legislation. Yet presidential advocacy does not imply that American leaders or the public understood how profoundly access shapes disabled people's lives. Wheelchair users were uniquely able to do just that.

Although veterans, like those at Birmingham Hospital, used the same wheelchair as Franklin Roosevelt, their attitude toward it was fundamentally different. Rather than hide their chairs, they organized their lives around them. Special groups for disabled people, for example, the American Federation of the Physically Handicapped that was founded in 1940, already advocated strongly on labor issues. But the Second World War veterans also organized through informal channels like newsletters and physical therapy programs and met at the hospitals where they convalesced. They founded groups like the Paralyzed Veterans of America (PVA), whose informal motto was "empowering veterans lives."

However, even in wheelchair-friendly California, the notion of wholesale accommodation was new. These wheelchair users, historian Guy Tremblay insists, were "pioneers" of a new sort. This generation was unwilling to stay at home, using their wheelchairs to venture out into the world and forcing access to be an issue (Tremblay, 1996). What they discovered was that wheelchairs were not enough; the problem of access was pervasive, and it played out most visibly in institutions of education, where a serious commitment was made to accommodate returning GI veterans. A new approach toward environmental infrastructure was needed.

FIGURE 2.3 Paraplegic veterans registering for classes at the University of California, Los Angeles,1947. John Florea/Life Picture Collection/Getty Images.

The Nugent ethic

When most students applied to enter the University of Illinois's flagship campus at Champaign-Urbana, they mailed in an application. But in March 1949, when a group of fourteen wheelchair users sought admission, they

FIGURE 2.4 A semi-permanent wheelchair ramp constructed at Lincoln Hall, University of Illinois. Students staged a protest here in 1949, erecting an improvised ramp into the building. By 1956, the year this photograph was taken, a sturdier ramp was constructed, 1956. Courtesy University of Illinois.

went straight to campus and used 2 × 8 planks taken from a painter's scaffolding rig. The students were already enrolled at the university's Galesburg campus, where the Mayo Army Hospital had turned part of its wheelchair-friendly complex into a division of the University of Illinois (Brown, 2008). This trial program was brief. Opened in October 1948, it was forced to close almost immediately after it opened; the state government wanted to repurpose the campus as a research center for medical care of the elderly. Many of Galesburg's more able-bodied students transferred to Champaign-Urbana. But the paraplegic students were not included. Dubious university administrators suggested that the main campus could not provide the same medical facilities as the Mayo Army Hospital. They proposed other solutions, including the completion of two years of college work by correspondence or the establishment of an "isolated ward" for paraplegic students in the new medical center planned for the Galesburg site (Roberts and Criggger, 1949). Rejecting these suggestions, the disabled students and the chief administrator of their program, an educational psychologist named Timothy Nugent, joined forces. Together, they organized a rally at the main campus.

This protest quickly transformed into a demonstration of accessibility. Arriving at an imposing lecture hall in the center of campus (Figure 2.4), the students found some wooden planks and rapidly erected their own makeshift infrastructure; as Nugent would later recall, they laid these planks "up over some steps to show that these guys in wheelchairs could get into that building" (Nugent, 2004–2005: 63). With Nugent, the students proved how the campus could accommodate their chairs' needs. The Galesburg wheelchair users prevailed, and were allowed to attend school on a trial basis (Nugent, 2004–05: 63). But what began as a test, meant to integrate disabled students into existing classes, became instead an experiment in access. And it turned the campus—and later the small college town around it—into a space where disabled students could flourish. The planks that the Galesburg students used at Champaign-Urbana helped students "fit" into their environment or, to be more accurate, made the environment fit the needs of disabled students.

The program at Champaign-Urbana had few precedents. In the century prior, there had been little systematic knowledge about accommodating wheelchairs. At best, isolated individuals pushed as they could for small changes to help them function better. A feature in the 1883 issue of *Building News*, for example, noted that a Liverpool nursing home placed an "inclined plane" onto its terrace, "to allow of patients wheeling themselves about the grounds in their Merlin chairs. A second inclined plane was added to the patients' entrance on the west side of the building, to allow easy egress in and out of the building, too" (Anon., 1883). In a 1916 issue of *Popular Science Monthly*, a column for handymen demonstrated how a simple "inclined sidewalk" could be added to even modest homes and assist a wheeled invalid chair. For an even fuller environment of accommodation, one had only to look at FDR's Warm Springs hospital in Georgia, where a consciously designed environment of access included ramps and wider doors, but also electrically operated doors that swung open automatically when a beam of light detected movement (Watson and Woods, 2005b: 99). These cases, however, were still limited in their scope and ambition—especially when compared to the efforts that began to unfold at the University of Illinois.

This marks a profound shift in the very conception of access. The academics at Champaign-Urbana did more than simply bring a group of wheelchair-using students together. They also began remaking the built environment on campus. In the first year of the program, adjustments for wheeled access included the installation of ramps to seven buildings across campus (Nugent, 1950). And certainly, in the next several years, parking facilities were made available to disabled students, and classes moved from inaccessible spaces when necessary. But it was still more than that. In those first years, a series of narrow doors, smaller elevators, too high water fountains, and too small toilets all needed to be replaced. In at least one structure, a second-floor window was converted into a doorway; stretching up to it, a wheelchair ramp was joined to the new opening, allowing wheeled access to the building's upper floors. At first, the university committed to making changes incrementally. Campus-wide, for instance, when sidewalks became damaged and needed repairs, curb cuts might be added for wheelchair access. Some of this has assumed a mythology of its own. When the campus moved too slowly for Nugent's taste, recalled the activist and U of I alum Fred Fay, the "ingenious" Nugent and his physical therapist Chuck Elmer "got up in the middle of the night with a sledgehammer and destroyed curbs, and then the next day report them as needing ramps" (Fay, 2001). Like all the activity at Champaign-Urbana, such treacherous zeal was shaped by a broader set of assumptions: given good training in a friendly environment, even severely disabled students could attend university, receive an education, and lead successful lives.

Given such aspirations, Tim Nugent would insist, the University of Illinois program could not be limited to making buildings, sidewalks, and curbs accessible. The goal was to naturalize wheelchair use and disability itself. Nugent's own father was hearing and vision impaired, his sister would eventually be diagnosed as legally blind, and he himself had been diagnosed with a heart condition when young (Nugent, 2004–2005). As someone already familiar with disability, Nugent understood that wheelchair users' problems were not solved through new technologies, like the E&J wheelchair, alone. In many ways, the built environment—and by extension society as a whole—plays a profound role in determining who can access spaces, and who cannot.

For his part, even as he recognized this environmental misfit, Nugent also argued that disabled people should do everything possible to "fit" social expectations. The question of social fit and misfit had haunted disabled people at least since Joseph Ashby-Sterry proposed that someone write a "Rules for Behaviour in a Bath-chair." Yet the reality at the University of Illinois was much clearer. Nugent insisted that students in the school's rehabilitation programs fit into a certain attitude of mind and spirit. Nugent's program was thus a remarkably astute social mirror of the rest of campus, simply reimagining student life as carried out on wheels. Submitting to the task of assimilation, wheelchair-using students were taught how to spread picnic blankets so they could eat fried chicken dinners on the ground; they also organized their own dance parties (Brown, 2008). Wheelchair sports thrived at Illinois, the school becoming well known for its excellence in wheelchair football, basketball, baseball, and bowling. What is more, wheelchair cheerleaders promoted the men's teams at home and on the road (Figure 2.5).[2] With its sports, cheer squad, and dances, Illinois' incoming disabled students were urged to fit into this parallel campus

FIGURE 2.5 Male and female cheerleaders, affiliated with the University of Illinois's wheelchair basketball program, accompanied the team at home and on the road, 1955. Courtesy University of Illinois.

society as completely as possible, yielding to what would retrospectively be called "The Nugent ethic" (Goldsmith, 1983: 201). Nevertheless, it was a method that gained attention and the university's rehabilitation department saw its numbers swell as it enrolled not just military veterans but students with a variety of impairments ranging from polio to cerebral palsy and muscular dystrophy.

This approach was in some ways forced, and graduates of the program would look back on it with mixed feelings. Some imbibed its positivism, and took it deeply to heart. Graduate Fred Fay recalls how "Nugent brought this can-do philosophy and this spirit of competition to the campus that was really refreshing. … Having that kind of dominant role model really shaped the attitudes of a lot of students there" (Fay, 2001: 26). But others like former activist and U of I student Kitty Cone "had felt totally controlled and manipulated by the Rehabilitation Center. It was run by able-bodied people for people with disabilities" (Cone, 1996–1998: 81). Recalling her days as a wheelchair cheerleader at Illinois, Mary Lou Breslin remembered just how hard it was to be oppositional and resist the program's insistence that everyone participate in campus life. "I bought into the whole gestalt of U of I once I got there. I did not stand back and say, this is a terrible idea; let's reform the place. It was just the opposite: I thought, oh, yeah, I'm one of the insiders" (Breslin, 1996–1998: 47). It should be clear that this was, however, too simplistic a view.

For one thing, from its start the program did accommodate students with various impairments, but its main emphasis was on wheelchair users. The members may have had diverse attitudes, priorities, and expectations, but because the program itself was rooted in Mayo Hospital's spinal injury unit this early focus is not surprising. Nugent was energetically committed to the group, but he was originally hired as head of students' corrective physical education and therapy—essentially a rehabilitation program. Since the 1920s, the "rehabilitation" of disabled people meant that medical specialists identified various impairments, and then aimed to treat them through therapeutic interventions. As scholar Nora Groce notes, "blindness, deafness, mental retardation and mental illness were not usually included within the realm of 'rehabilitation' programs" (Groce, 2002: 4) as conceived after the Second World War. The latter were "often represented by people and organizations whose constituencies were concerned with specific disability groups—'the blind, 'the deaf' and so forth" (Groce, 2002: 4). When the University of Illinois started the Galesburg program in 1948, almost all the two dozen students were in wheelchairs (Nugent, 2004: 25). By the time Kitty Cone arrived at the Champaign-Urbana campus in 1962, that emphasis still predominated. As she later recalled, "they had, I think, between 100 and 200—I'm not sure—students in wheelchairs. That was really the focus" (Cone, 29). Though there had been several hearing and vision-impaired students enrolled in Nugent's program in the 1950s, it wasn't until the 1960s that the program began formally accepting and accommodating them.

Whatever the nature of their disability, Nugent expected all of his students to fit in. Writing in the 1955 issue of *Sigma Signs*, the newsletter of the U of I program's service fraternity, a student-reporter pointed to this neat assimilation, swearing that a "stranger to the campus can't help but be struck by the fact that even though these people are in wheelchairs or on crutches, they have the same bright, cheery, attitude, the same calm, but very obvious self-assurance visible in any student in the great university" (Anon., 1957b: 10, 11). Mary Lou Breslin, another program graduate, put it more bluntly. The goal was to create "people who can fit in" (Breslin, 1996–1998: 48).

Nugent's notion of a good fit was environmental as well as social. Buildings, Tim Nugent came to believe, were designed for healthy, non-disabled, young but still adult bodies. He gradually rejected this older habit of thinking, insisting it too simplistic. Instead of looking at a relatively narrow norm, Nugent reasoned, "it's a matter of considering all people ... It's a matter of conceptualization not just prescriptions or statistics or figures" (Nugent, 2004–2005: 157, 158). Society has given the real range of bodies and abilities very little thought. But, baldly put, any sizeable group of people is going to have a varied set of needs. On the other hand, he observed, able-bodied persons have long been given helpful accommodations. Imagine, he suggested, reaching a lecture hall on a second floor. How did you get there? Architects solved this problem millennia ago by providing steps or staircases. Nevertheless, Nugent recognized, most able-bodied users "don't realize that they're getting in on steps, but somebody had to design and build those steps" (Tim Nugent, 2004–2005; 138). Stairs, he explained, are an architectural convenience based on centuries of social convention, yet they are now so naturalized that we scarcely reflect on them long enough to realize that they are an accommodation. At the U of I, Nugent argued, "There's nothing special about what we're doing except that we're considering the whole population and not just a segment of it" (Tim Nugent, 2004–2005: 138).

Nugent spent little time speculating on how and why architects and designers had arrived at the standards in place; instead, his focus was on changing the world around him. And in the 1950s, that world was the University of Illinois campus. His administrative records in the early years of the 1950s reflect a flood of problems related to wheelchairs and access. A door in the basement of the Mathematics Building would not open fully enough to allow easy passage. An elevator in the same space was inaccessible from all parts of the building. Ramps were needed in another building. No doubt a great deal of the problems faced by the wheelchair-, brace-, and cane-using students were created through oversight, and were simply added reflexively. Most were also easily fixed. Nugent understood that if the built environment could be tweaked and adjusted, disabled students could function in it. But he gradually arrived at a larger truth; ultimately, he began to argue, lack of access could be hunted down and tied to the minutiae of design. These he began to call "barriers" (Nugent, 1960: 51). Staircases, too narrow doorways, and uneven surfaces on floors—it didn't matter. All obstacles were barriers not only to access, but also to his students leading normal lives.

Throughout the 1950s, by subtly widening doors, lowering drinking fountains, and generally altering the built environment to be accessible to wheelchairs users, Nugent staked out a new kind of "barrier-free" public space. His approach was not without critics; some doctors and parents consistently complained that Nugent's sink or swim approach was too cavalier or heavy-handed, particularly for the youngest paraplegic students who enrolled in his program.[3] Nevertheless, by the late 1950s Tim Nugent started to win attention—and money—for his work. Funds were donated through the national Polio Foundation, the Cancer Foundation, and the Paraplegia Foundation. Slowly, through these groups, Nugent secured an audience for his approach toward disability. But Nugent wanted more. He began to advocate for his broader goal—nothing less than a barrier-free world. But as support for and attention on Nugent's program grew, he was forced to confront a more fundamental problem: how could specifications for wheelchair access be codified? It took a 69-year-old insurance executive to answer this query, bringing the question of access to the attention of the political establishment in Washington DC.

An attack on barriers

In photographs taken when he met President Dwight D. Eisenhower and was named the 1956 Handicapped American of the Year, Hugo Deffner barely registers the ordeal he had just experienced. The award was given by the President's Committee on Employment of the Handicapped, a postwar organization formed in the fall of 1947 and whose very existence indicated changing attitudes toward disability. The committee was formed not only to help the many disabled veterans returning from war, but also to take advantage of the "new methods for rehabilitating and employing the handicapped (that) had been forming for several decades" (President's Committee on Employment of the Handicapped, 1972: 1). Created in 1951, the award brought attention to disabled people in the community, specifically those "who not only surmount their own handicaps but also facilitate the employment of other handicapped persons" (President's Committee on Employment of the Handicapped, 1972: 13). Deffner's efforts to advocate for ramps, elevators, and other accommodations in Oklahoma led him to be recognized by the Committee as "a one-man campaign for the elimination of steps in public buildings" (Banta, 1957: 10).

To accept the award, Deffner, a polio survivor and wheelchair user, had traveled from his native Oklahoma to Washington DC. But this was possible only after the president placed a call to the head of American Airlines, insisting that Deffner be allowed to fly with his wheelchair. A taxi driver at the airport then had to be bribed to help lift him into a cab (Nelson, 1986). Once Deffner arrived at the stately Willard Hotel in the capital, he couldn't climb the steps at its entrance and had to be carried into the hotel (Nelson, 1986). All of this was just a prelude to the difficulties that awaited Deffner when he arrived at the awards ceremony held at the Department of Labor.

While President Eisenhower waited on the stage, ready to make his presentation, Deffner waited outside on the sidewalk, unable to mount a staircase and enter the building. Eventually, two burly Marines, dispatched from the ceremonial Marine Corps band, went outside, picked up Deffner's wheelchair—with him in it—and carried the award recipient inside. Only then did they discover that there was no access to the stage, where Eisenhower was waiting. Deffner had to be carried there also, in front of the president and audience alike (Goldsmith, 1997: 12–13). Once he finally reached the stage, the ceremony proceeded. Deffner gave a short speech, describing his own experiences when, as a polio victim, he could not attend high school. "Safety begins at the front door," he said, "and nobody is going to be hired that can't get in the door" (President's Committee on Employment of the Handicapped, 1972: 30). Trying to minimize the embarrassment, Eisenhower alluded to the stairs when he told the assembled crowd that he congratulated Deffner on his drive to "make every building in the United

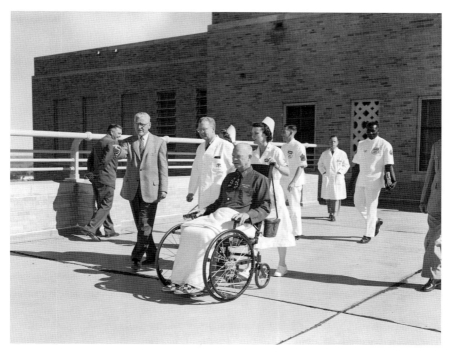

FIGURE 2.6 Himself no stranger to a wheelchair, two years before Dwight D. Eisenhower met disabled activist Hugo Deffner the president rolled into a press conference at Fitzsimmons Army Hospital after suffering a heart attack, 1955. Courtesy Bettmann/Getty Images.

States accessible to one who possibly cannot climb stairs. And I hope that he is having success in that effort, because sometimes they do seem steep even to me" (Eisenhower, 1960: 413). Indeed, Eisenhower was no stranger to wheelchairs. A little over a year earlier he'd been treated by a team of doctors based at Fitzsimmons Army Hospital (Figure 2.6). But with Deffner, things were different. The miserable awards ceremony shamed the President's Committee on Employment of the Physically Handicapped, the 1,000 or so delegates attending the group's annual meeting, and Eisenhower himself.

Astonishingly, all of this happened in a city that, only ten years earlier, had placed ramps in front of public buildings, making special access for FDR. These had since been taken down. Of course, Roosevelt was extremely sensitive about his disability. Yet the president and the Secret Service also went to great lengths to hide his need for special modifications. And so, by 1957 few federal buildings in Washington offered the open accommodations common at military hospitals in California and on the campus of the University of Illinois. Arguably enough, Roosevelt's secrecy also meant that few people were aware of the accommodations made to help him and how—if kept in place—they might help others. Even as ideas about a disabled person's ability were changing at institutions across the country, acknowledgment was slow in coming to Washington. This was precisely what Hugo Deffner wanted to change.

If any delegates at the 1956 meeting where Deffner was given his award were not already aware of the problem of "barriers," they were quickly educated. His ordeal helped him perform the problem in front of an audience. (Although it can be tempting to think that Deffner's fumbled presentation ceremony was stage-managed, there's no evidence to prove it.) Not only did the event point to an enormous environmental oversight, but also it highlighted how disability might be acknowledged and an individual celebrated, even as environmental barriers to his functioning were entirely overlooked. The committee changed its orientation after this. It began advocating for something like a national project, recognizing and researching what it would take to create a truly barrier-free society.

After Deffner's troubled appearance in Washington, the President's Committee on Employment of the Physically Handicapped held an executive board meeting and quickly opened discussions on how best to take national action (Goldsmith, 1993: 12). Of course, as its name indicates, the committee had been formed to deal with one form of barrier—namely getting jobs for disabled people. In this much, the committee was organized as little more than a "nucleus" that would coordinate the efforts of voluntary, state-led committees composed of figures from business, industry, labor, and the government; they meant to educate and promote the activities of vocational and rehabilitation agencies on a state-by-state basis (President's Committee on Employment of the Handicapped, 1972). To date, their efforts were diluted to an almost disheartening degree. But together, Deffner and Nugent shifted and expanded the discussion. Rather than helping specific people fit into the workplace on an individual basis, Deffner and Nugent asked how not just the workplace but the world might be fit to them.

With the verve and gusto of a military campaign, this committee and their advocates—many of whom were disabled veterans—began to advocate for change. They framed their strategy as a national "attack" on a world in which most forms of impairment were still characterized as "abnormal," and disability was long associated with dependency and weakness. Deffner's campaign caught the attention of the Paralysed Veterans of America (PVA). Citing Deffner's efforts in their newsletter, the PVA trumpeted his work. It declared him an "enemy of steps and stairs," and urged readers "to help Mr Deffner in his campaign to eliminate the step" (Editorial, 1955: 2). This militaristic phrasing both recast disability groups as powerful, and also offered a reminder as to how so many of these men had become disabled in the first place.

The operation was successful. The President's Committee on Employment of the Physically Handicapped formed a battle plan, allying themselves with a variety of civic and national organizations, including the PVA as well as specialized charities like the National Society for Crippled Children and Adults, as well as the Veterans' Administration itself. Going on the offensive, the committee began to outline the first building guidelines to recognize questions of access for disabled persons. What would become the American National Standards Institute 117.1 (ANSI 117.1) was introduced in 1960 as "A National Attack on Architectural Barriers" (Nugent, 1960: 51).

Developing building standards was a challenging endeavor. Existing information and empirical research was limited. Henry Toombs, the New York–based architect hired by Roosevelt to adapt Warm Springs Institute, had long been studying these issues; as early as 1931, in the Institute's in-house newsletter *The Polio Chronicle*, he published a short series of columns that he modestly titled "Architectural Suggestions" (Toombs, 1931a: 1). For the next thirty years, these low-key writings made him one of the country's principal experts on the subject. In the late 1950s, Tim Nugent was the other expert. By 1956, when authorities at the U of I decided to make all of the campus' more than 200 buildings wheelchair accessible, Nugent had begun producing reams of data regarding the necessary width of a door or grade of a ramp. It is thus no surprise that Deffner and Nugent consulted regularly by phone, and, following Deffner's 1957 trip to Washington DC, Nugent was invited to produce the first federal accessibility guidelines (Nugent 2004: 128).

From its compelling subtitle to its detailed guidelines, the American Standards Association's final report, called the "Attack on Barriers," is suffused with Nugent's ethos (Chatelain, 1961). Ingenuity, independence, and access itself—the ideas that shaped this program—gird ANSI 117.1. In his earlier reports, Nugent laid out his agenda. "Contrary to what most people think," Nugent contends, advancements like the wheelchair did not decrease the nation's sense of disability, but rather "tend to magnify the problem of increased numbers of the disabled" (Nugent, 1960: 51). Recent medical advances, he would argue, as well as new innovations like the wheelchair, allow disabled persons unprecedented opportunities. And yet, due to environmental barriers, a disabled person is prevented "from pursuing his aspirations, developing his talents, and exercising his skills" (Nugent, 1960: 51). Though the guidelines were meant to include the semi-ambulatory, the vision and hearing disabled, and others who didn't use chairs, Nugent's recommendations were once more focused on wheelchair accessibility. They would define conventional building standards, including sidewalk widths, building entrances and exits, doorway clearance, floor surfaces, toilet stall design, and most construction in the United States and elsewhere for the next quarter century.

Nugent had a vision of a barrier-free world and the recommendations Nugent drafted had the potential to benefit millions. But, for many reasons, these recommendations were difficult to enact. The federal government attempted to adopt them, with varying success. Some states and local governments also incorporated them into building codes, but only for new construction. Though never enforced as law, Nugent's building standards had a host of implications. Echoing other efforts in this period including the rise of anthropometrics and ergonomics, the building standards aimed to measure and quantify the human body.[4] Taking the E&J wheelchair as the standard, Nugent replaced the normalized body with the normalized wheelchair. Though ANSI 117.1 never mentioned signage, Nugent's research, with its emphasis on the E&J chair, nevertheless set the stage for the soon-to-come wheelchair emblem used in the International Symbol of Access (ISA).

Notes

1   Noting that "thousands of incapacitated men complained that they would miss driving a car more than anything else," California's director of the Department of Motor Vehicles began a program which trained disabled drivers and then granted them driving licenses (Anon., 1945: A1). The push for this came from veterans and their advocates; it was argued that returning veterans who were variously disabled were more easily assimilated if they could drive cars.

2   Initially, groups of veterans played in exhibition wheelchair basketball games. Quickly, however, wheelchair teams of students began to be developed at colleges and universities across the country. Timothy Nugent encouraged this development by helping found the National Wheelchair Basketball Association in 1949.

3   Nugent himself reported that doctors sometimes criticized him as too rough on some students, especially those with spinal cord injuries. He was also taken to task by some parents, who were especially upset by his desire to see even the most disabled students function without any kind of caretakers (Chamberlain, 2014).

4   See, for example, Flinchum (1997).

PART TWO

Redesigning Signs and Space (1961–1974)

3

The Personal Politics of Signs
(1961–1965)

In October 1961, Timothy Nugent, University of Illinois professor, coach, and herald of a new approach toward disablement stood before a symposium audience in Stockholm to introduce an international audience to the new American building guidelines for barrier-free access. Nugent received a warm welcome in Sweden, where he met with eager government officials and designers. He was even awarded the inaugural Patrik Haglund Lectureship from Sweden's Central Committee on Rehabilitation. Unlike in the United States, where easy access was spearheaded by disabled people and related organizations, in Europe, government welfare and health authorities were equally invested in bringing services to their disabled citizens. For instance, projects were under way in Sweden and Denmark, where sociologists and architects worked to perfect kitchens and bathrooms with particular focus on assisting the special needs of wheelchair users. But neither these programs nor others like them had conceptualized the vast scope of what Nugent was proposing: a barrier-free world. One observer reported that when Nugent described his work in Illinois during that first lecture in Stockholm, it was like a bomb went off in the room (Goldsmith, 1997: 17).

Nugent's conception of disability upended European assumptions. Nugent claimed disability as a condition that included the vision and hearing impaired, as well as those with mobility impairments. But he made his case especially forceful by asserting that "alarming as it may seem, approximately one out of every six people in the United States has a permanent disability" (Nugent, 1961: 51). For Selwyn Goldsmith, a British architect and recent polio survivor who would go on to become one of the principal theorists of designs for disability in the UK, Nugent's lecture was life changing. Aside from the limited experiment enrolling paraplegic veterans at UCLA, few programs had been instituted. But Nugent's work stretched much further. In addition to giving a transformative lecture, Goldsmith reported, Nugent also "came bearing with him the final draft of a document that was to change the world" (Goldsmith, 1997: 7). That text, of course, was the sum of Nugent's work at Illinois toward barrier-free access. For Goldsmith, the document and the meeting were revelatory: "I was unprepared for the explosive charge that Tim Nugent detonated" (Goldsmith, 1997: 17).

Now, as Nugent was speaking, the barrier-free architecture movement was just beginning to get widespread attention in the United States; but in Europe—as in the United States almost a decade earlier—the notion that the environment itself could be disabling was entirely new. It represented a significant reconceptualization of disability itself. Following Nugent's presentation in Stockholm, the argument quickly spread throughout Europe. And why not? In Europe, as in the United States, during the years after the Second World War, more and more disabled people lived longer, benefited from more sophisticated medical treatment, and began to use newer assistive devices like the modern wheelchair. For the first time, disabled people were increasingly present in public life. To be sure, some innovations—like the modern wheelchair—at first began to appear slowly (the Everest & Jennings (E&J) wheelchair, for example, was never used extensively in the UK, and it was only in the mid-1950s that a similar design was developed by the British Ministry of Health) (Woods and Watson, 2004a).

Gradually, in Europe as in the United States, between the 1940s and 1960s, the modern wheelchair would gain real force not only as medical hardware but also as an agent of social, cultural, and political change. Amid this cultural shift, the very notion of an environmental misfit—for chair and user—and the introduction of "barrier-free architecture" as its solution was as welcome as it was revolutionary. And there was no precedent for it. When Nugent developed this approach in Illinois during the 1950s, it was in relative isolation. And so, when he arrived in 1961 at the International Society for Rehabilitation of the Disabled in Stockholm, his work and point of view seemed strikingly new. But, rather than accept his ideas wholesale, some aspects of his thinking were transformed. Spurred by the logic of the social welfare state, there developed a somewhat different approach to disability and access itself.

As it happens, in the United States Nugent's findings were becoming increasingly entrenched. In October 1961, after the Society for Crippled Children and Adults in the United States published Nugent's findings from his work at Illinois, Nugent's ideas gained authority when they were adopted by the American National Standards Institute, a private group responsible for setting non-binding industry standards. The Society issued 50,000 copies of the guidelines, with 14,000 alone going to members of the American Institute of Architects. Now known as ANSI 117.1, Nugent's findings acquired the imprimatur of official acceptance, and were promoted by diverse organizations from labor unions like the AFL-CIO to assorted church councils. His specifications were seen as the impartial, scientific, and definitive solution to the question of disability and environmental change. They became a model for builders and architects. By 1967, the approach was so well established that the *Times* of London referred to Nugent's approach as a kind of "orthodoxy" (Anon, 1967c: 10). In the United States, the authority of Nugent's ideas was enshrined in 1968, when ANSI 117.1 became the core of the US Architectural Barriers Act.

And yet as Nugent's recommendations were becoming evermore entrenched, some of his supporters in Europe became less and less enamored of his ideas on access. Of course, Nugent's 1961 "Attack on Barriers" was strident in his support of access for all. There, he stressed that "the severely, permanently, physically disabled can be accommodated in all buildings and facilities used by the public ... independently and without distinction" (Nugent, 1961: 59). In the service of assimilation, Nugent implicitly argued, environmental changes were never announced publicly or marked explicitly. At the University of Illinois' huge campus, for instance, disabled students were expected to navigate the sprawling grounds without any form of signage marking accessible paths through buildings or between them. ANSI 117.1 detailed the width of doors and the grade of ramps, but nowhere in the entire document was there any provision for explanatory signs identifying facilities provided for disabled users.

Selwyn Goldsmith was one of Nugent's principal supporters in Europe. And yet, for his part, Goldsmith increasingly found Nugent's ideas on access deeply unsettling. As it was, by the mid-1960s Goldsmith became increasingly obsessed with the issue of signage, and its cultural significance. At first, Goldsmith interpreted the failure to take signage into account as simply an oversight on Nugent's part. But the more he studied Nugent's recommendations, the more he came to believe this oversight epitomized a more fundamental problem within the entire American approach to disability (Goldsmith, 1983). In contrast to what he called the almost secretive, "self-help" design culture of the United States, Goldsmith developed what has come to be called the "architectural model of disability," an approach stepped in the socially minded ideology of the welfare state (McIntyre, 2013). Applied to Europe and especially the UK, he went so far as to argue, these recommendations were, themselves, a cultural and political misfit.

What a good sign can do

Just how much should the built environment announce that it has been fitted to the needs of disabled people? A 1960 snapshot of the converted military barracks housing the University of Illinois's rehabilitation program—the hub of the disabled community on campus—demonstrates one approach to answering this question. In the photograph, a well-placed ramp leads to the program's headquarters; low-key administrative placards announce by name

FIGURE 3.1 Ramped entrance at the first Rehabilitation Center on the campus of the University of Illinois. In spite of its wheelchair-accessible entry, the building was marked by minimal signage, c. 1956. Courtesy University of Illinois.

the offices within (Figure 3.1). Nowhere are there access signs identifying the ramp, the best route to take inside, or any of the other accommodations available in these unassuming buildings. The same was true elsewhere on campus; curb cuts were ever-present and telephone booths and water fountains were uniformly lowered, but nowhere were these accommodations given signs. In Tim Nugent's scheme, the integration between disabled persons and the world around them should be seamless. There should be no demarcation of accommodations, nor should there be any kind of misfit between the students in his program and the general student body. But this led to a somewhat harsher reality. A small number of initiates—the students in Nugent's program—knew of the campus' special access. But, without signage, a casual observer might not. And, in its own way, Illinois's lack of access signs reveals a deeper truth. Signs make information public, and information is power.

In many ways this tactic was indicative of a broader approach to disability and design then taking shape in the United States. Even before the war, the United States embraced the notion of useful disablement (Rose, 2017). Above all, the ability to fit into the workforce was highly valued. Advocacy groups, for example the American Federation for Physically Handicapped Persons (AFPHP), were founded on this idea. AFPHP helped establish the national Employ the Handicapped Week in 1945 and campaigned under slogans like "Hire the Handicapped—It's Good Business." Herbert Everest's development of the folding wheelchair is emblematic of this attitude; Everest wanted to work, found mobility in his automobile, and made a wheelchair that could be used in tandem with his car while on the job. As the field of "rehabilitation medicine" gained force in the United States immediately after the Second World War (and large numbers of disabled veterans, polio survivors, and other impaired people were seeking treatment), its ambition was to help affected individuals fit back into "normal" society. Put simply, the goal was "to return affected persons to their own homes and back to their usual activities and to employment" (Verville, 2009, 3). Behind the orthotics, prostheses, speech pathology, and other aspects of rehabilitation, "vocational productivity through employment ... gave rehabilitation medicine its creditability" (Verville, 2009: 4). At Illinois, too, Nugent's program aimed to make "it possible for the talents and resources of millions of physically handicapped individuals to be put to use for the betterment of mankind" (Nugent, 1960: 53).

For Nugent and others in the United States, integrating those with disabilities to "normal life" meant finding them work and helping people with disabilities to blend in. Fundamentally, environmental access was touted not to draw attention to disability, but, rather, to make it less of a practical impediment in day-to-day life. In theory, the goal was to de-emphasize its impact. In effect, many of the accommodations on the University of Illinois campus were hidden in plain sight. The unmarked ramp and access route in front of the school's rehabilitation program were only the beginning. Students like alumna Mary Breslin were puzzled by the circuitous "routes to get to classes." Breslin recalled that "some of them were just amazing because you'd have to go in some back door where they figured out some way to get the ramp in, doing these very elaborate numbers with three elevators and a surface elevator and a freight elevator and a this and a that" (Breslin, 1996–1998: 56). Other concessions at Illinois were equally unobtrusive. In 1954, the school acquired two buses equipped with hydraulic lifts to help students move between dorms, distant classrooms, and the campus rehabilitation center. But the buses passed unmarked, had no publicly announced schedules, and generally traveled through the campus unobserved. Unpublicized accommodations or hidden routes of access were not only common on the University of Illinois campus. Across North America, they were the status quo.

Usually disabled people were responsible for finding forms of access on their own. Returning to Toronto at the end of the Second World War, the wheelchair-using veteran Ken Langford was encouraged to leave the hospital where he was recuperating and "experiment with going out into the community." In downtown Toronto, for example, he found that "there were usually level entrances somewhere. Certainly in hotels, theatres ..." But often these paths were private or unmarked, not to mention circuitous. For example, Langford recalled the difficulty of attending veterans' reunions at Toronto's Royal York Hotel; it "isn't the easiest place to get to because there are steps at every entrance. But the initial technique was that we would park at the back and go in through the service or garbage entrance, in through the kitchen and take the service elevator" (Tremblay, 1996: 161). The entrance for wheelchair users was so complex that no casual visitor could have guessed its existence.

Selwyn Goldsmith later discovered similar unpublicized accommodations while conducting an access study of the small English city of Norwich. Here, too, many older buildings were made inaccessible by steps or stairs. But at some, like the Norwich County Hall, the city library and the local Cathedral, intrepid wheelchair users willing to search out alterative entrances might find them down alleys, on side streets, or off to the side of the main doors (Goldsmith, 1969b: 42, 43). And yet, even if access were possible, a problem remained. These routes were hidden and went unmarked. With no apparent indication otherwise, the structure's main entrances made the buildings *seem* inaccessible. And so, Goldsmith argued, they simply went unused (Goldsmith, 1965: 974).

Of course, there was one fundamental difference between the roundabout accommodations at Illinois, and the quirky, unmarked routes wheelchair users discovered elsewhere. In most places, these simply provided unplanned—if de facto—access. But at Illinois, hidden access was premeditated. Ironically,

FIGURE 3.2 A two-storied wheelchair ramp leading to a second-floor window at the University of Illinois, 1956. Courtesy University of Illinois.

at the sprawling, yet well-ordered Illinois campus there was no lack of signage. Postings urged students to put trash in receptacles, directional arrows pointed them toward academic buildings, and ubiquitous placards showed the way to fallout shelters. Convenience and clarity ruled, except when it came to guiding disabled students to accommodations. Access signs for disabled students simply did not exist. Of course some structural changes were hard to miss. In one building, an otherwise inaccessible second-floor classroom was connected by an outdoor wheelchair ramp that led to a modified, second-story window (Figure 3.2). A point of personal pride, Nugent frequently guided visitors here. But while a sign identifies a trashcan next to the ramp, the ramp itself, spectacular as such things go, remained unmarked. Sheila Wolfe, a reporter from the Chicago *Daily Tribune*, visited campus around this time. Like a fine coat, she noted how unobtrusively the environment was "tailored" to the needs of the students (Wolfe, 1961: B17). But these changes were never trumpeted. Noting this approach, one British observer remarked that the object here was "camouflage rather than exposure" (Tomlinson and Stevens, 1972: 107). The ramps, curb cuts, and the rest were not hidden per se, but passed without recognition. At the University of Illinois, signage was everywhere. Ironically enough, the annual newsletter published by the Disabled Students Organization was titled *Sigma Signs* (Figure 3.3). But signage to announce accommodations for disabled persons was entirely absent there; even if special signs had been used, they would not "fit" the physical nor ideological landscape of the school.

As such, it's important to remember that Nugent had greater goals; for him, the Illinois campus was an example of what could be achieved anywhere, if only architectural barriers were abolished. Searching in a thousand ways, he aimed for an understanding of the world that could, on the one hand, speak to disabled students trying to comprehend their place in postwar society and, on the other hand, to colleagues struggling to integrate them into an often-inaccessible environment. By his lights, Nugent thought the problem lay in millennia of architectural conventions shaped around the needs of an idealized human body; designers provided a "fit" for able-bodied individuals, but in so doing also made others "misfit." If builders and architects simply stopped incorporating steps, too narrow doors, and other inaccessible features into their construction, he rationalized, people with disabilities could lead their lives much like anyone else.

Of course, much of Nugent's time was spent sorting and negotiating the needs of his disabled students, but he always refused to consider them "special." The problems they encountered were simply more evidence of a broader population that campus architects had, to date, ignored. At the same time, for Nugent, there was nothing extraordinary about the students themselves. In a 1961 television interview, the plainspoken Nugent put it more directly: "The word special bothers me" (Nugent, c. 1963). It troubled him so much, in fact, that over and over, Nugent would describe an incident

FIGURE 3.3 Cover of *Sigma Signs*, journal of Delta Sigma Omicron (the rehabilitation service fraternity at the University of Illinois), 1953. Courtesy University of Illinois.

that had occurred early in his career. At a conference in Cleveland, he recounted, when he had just finished giving a lecture on the accommodations at Illinois:

> there was a question- and-answer period, and one smart aleck got up and he said, "Yeah, Professor Nugent, you say all these things, but you've got special ramps, you've got special buses, you've got special this, you've got special that," and he thought I was going to argue with him. So I said, "Well, just a minute. How did you get in this building?" He said, "I walked in." I said, "Well, how did you get from the sidewalk to the door." He said, "I climbed up the steps." I said, "Oh, wouldn't you have looked like a jackass crawling up the face of that wall if someone hadn't thought of those steps first?" (Nugent, 2004–2005: 138)

At Illinois, he reminded other rehabilitation professionals, "The only thing 'special' about this whole scheme of things is that it is relatively new in its total format." Nevertheless, he proclaimed with characteristic optimism, "it will, in the relatively near future, be taken as much for granted as we take the wheel" (Nugent, 1963: 10).

Yet many things about Nugent's new "format" were, in fact, special. There were special ramps, special doors, special paths, special parking spots, special keys. And disabled students learned about how to find, recognize, and use them during their own special orientation. Called Functional Training Week, incoming disabled students were brought to campus a week before the school's official orientation. Meant partly to introduce students to the campus' special accommodations, it also was intended to wean students— many of whom had never lived unassisted—from their families. Many disabled students arriving for the first time were extremely dependent on assistance from family, and when they arrived at the University of Illinois, they were expected not only to clothe, bathe, and feed themselves with little to no assistance (students accustomed to help, for example, were taught how to transfer from a chair to toilet stool and back again or how to dress and undress themselves), but they also learned to navigate the campus on their own. Reflecting back on the program years later, Nugent would recall how staff "would take them about the campus and show them the entrances and the pathways from this place to that place and the bus stops and things like that" (Nugent, 2004–2005: 70).

In essence, Nugent's thinking began from the position that there was no real difference between students enrolled in the program and the rest of the student body. And, once accommodations were in place, a kind of parity could easily be established. Distinctive signs pointing to accessible facilities would imply that disabled students were different when, in fact, no real distinctions existed. Yet, with no signage of any kind directing them to accommodations, these instructions were essential to students. This meant, as Gloria Chin would later recall, getting "acquainted with the buildings in which our classes would be held, learning the secret formula of operating the elevators" (Chin, 1959: 7). In some ways, it could be argued, making students learn a "formula" that was often hidden to the casual observer left them heavily dependent on Nugent's program. To the new enrollees, independence on campus had to be learned. It also meant following closely the established parameters of the program put in place.

Reflecting back on Nugent's program, many graduates were laudatory. Like Marshall Wall, some even hailed the Illinois campus—and the access it provided—as a kind of "utopia" for disabled people (Wall, 2007: 106). And many individuals would agree with Fred Fay, who insisted that Nugent "shaped the attitudes of a lot of students there. ... [bringing] this can-do philosophy and this spirit of competition to the campus that was really refreshing" (Fay, 2001: 26). Some of the students even referred to Nugent as an almost mythic figure, calling him the "Great White Father" (Wall, 2007: 98). But there were also critics, even from within the program. Mary Lou Breslin, a graduate from the program at the same time, lamented its insistent idealism, and Nugent's emphasis on fitting in. As she recalled years later, "they should not have permitted this patriarch [Tim Nugent] this fanatical person to determine and direct so many people's lives" (Breslin, 1996–1998: 54). Kitty Cone put it more definitively: "All the disabled students went through the rehab program. They were like the personal property of the director, Tim Nugent. You had to do what Nugent said or you were out on your ass" (Cone, 1996–1998: 30). In a way this applied to access and functionality on campus too. If you were in the know and followed the rules, you could find your way around. Otherwise, there were no signs around to guide you. In effect, not making this information public also meant students followed a series of tightly configured attitudes and values.

The absence of signage kept accessibility hidden in plain sight for two potential audiences—first, those disabled students who relied on signage in order to identify accessible spaces, and second, for those able-bodied people who did not rely on it but would still have seen it anyway. The dearth of signage was, in some ways, a larger disservice. Except for those rare moments when the rehabilitation program was profiled in the press, it received scant attention on campus. For years, Illinois' rehabilitation services were self-funded and Nugent struggled for recognition from campus administrators (Nugent, 2004–2005: 113). Moreover, with total student enrollments exceeding 30,000 in the 1950s, it was easy enough for the hundred or so disabled students on campus each year to disappear in the crowd. With little fanfare and no environmental signage, the rest of the university's students were unaware that they were living on a vast testing ground. In his memoirs, the film critic Roger Ebert recalls growing up in Champaign-Urbana, where his father worked at the university's electrical plant. His family "would often go for dinner at a cafeteria on campus in a Quonset hut that had a wheelchair ramp. Here were budget-priced meals for faculty, staff, and war veterans in wheelchairs." When the young Ebert asked about the ramps here and elsewhere on campus, his father didn't mention the cutting-edge program, the years of attempts to make the entire campus accessible, or any other conscious efforts to accommodate wheelchairs. Instead, he rather laconically observed, Illinois' wheelchair users "like it here because they don't have to wheel those chairs up and down hills" (Ebert, 2011). To be sure, Walter Harry Ebert was right—the campus was as flat as the cornfields surrounding it. But the disabled students who flocked to the university came because of its rehabilitation program, not its terrain. On a more personal note, I should add that my own parents were enrolled at the University of Illinois in this period, and I was born and lived in Stadium Terrace, the ramshackle Parade Grounds where the university placed married students and also housed the rehabilitation program; to this day my parents recall nothing of Nugent or the hundreds of students he ushered through that campus, even though, apparently, they were our close neighbors there. And, to this day, I consider it an educational opportunity missed. While Nugent's efforts to promote access were profoundly influential, the question of visibility at Illinois was an unresolved problem. Since at least the nineteenth century, disabled people were largely segregated in society and remained invisible; the Illinois program hardly addressed the problem of visibility.

Down the "welfare path"

When Tim Nugent's "Attack on Barriers" was first published in 1961, it was circulated both in the United States and in Europe. Some of his European readers were incredulous. The Italian politician and union leader Raimondo Magnani recalled that he and countrymen were astonished to read American disability statistics revealing that one in every six persons could benefit by the elimination of architectural barriers (Nugent, 1960: 51). Several wry Italian observers suggested that disability might be a uniquely American problem. Puzzled, these critics speculated that perhaps this happens only "in America. Here, we do not see many of such disabled" (Associazione nazionale mutilate e invalidi del lavoro, 1965: 32). In some ways, the critics were right. Disability was not a uniquely American concern; there were plenty of disabled Italians, but they were out of sight and seemingly out of mind.

In the postwar years, Italy struggled to emerge from Mussolini's shadow. The fascist leader respected former soldiers like these disabled German veterans who saluted him from their Bath chairs when the Italian leader visited Berlin in 1937 (Figure 3.4). But, among the general populace, he had little use for "nonproductive citizens," a vast category of persons encompassing not only disabled persons, but also homosexuals, criminals, and dissidents (Knittel, 2015: 21). Magnani was silent on this legacy, but quick to address lingering assumptions. He alluded to these larger, problematic preconceptions when he stressed that "in Italy, we cannot see many handicapped in rolling chairs for many reasons. First: because

FIGURE 3.4 Mussolini giving a fascist salute to a group of disabled veterans on a visit to Berlin, 1937. Istituto Nazionale Luce/Alinari/Getty Images.

they hide themselves or else they are hidden. Second, because if they made any attempt to enter into others' lives, they would be rejected or carried away" (Associazione nazionale mutilate e invalidi del lavoro, 1965: 32). No doubt Magnani shared with American reformers like Tim Nugent and Hugo Deffner a pent-up frustration, but he was addressing a different set of concerns. In postwar Italy the government was weaving a vast social net meant to benefit all of its citizens from cradle to grave. It was one thing for a laissez-faire approach toward disability to develop in the United States. But in Europe and Canada, supporters argued, things should be different. Here, there should be no shut-ins or misfits.

The postwar settlement, what Selwyn Goldsmith would later call "the welfare path" adopted by many countries in Europe (Goldsmith, 1997: 19), meant not just designing the built environment but also reconceptualizing how society itself was structured. In the general reckoning and reorganization of postwar Europe, a variety of approaches to policy and governance began to emerge. But generally, there was a move—gradually in some places and rapidly in others—toward states taking responsibility for social ills (Briggs, 1962). Governments were expected to identify and serve people needing help. In the United States, people like Tim Nugent and Hugo Deffner emphasized personal empowerment. The goal was equal—not special— treatment. In much of Europe and especially the UK, Selwyn Goldsmith would later claim, different social goals began to emerge. By the mid-1960s,

FIGURE 3.5 A 1976 invalid car issued by Britain's National Health Service, 2000. Courtesy National Motor Museum/Heritage Images.

he insisted, European countries had developed an approach to disability that highlighted the "social welfare cultural values of compensation, special treatment and pragmatism" (Goldsmith, 1983: 200). To Goldsmith, this cozy culture of social welfare was more than rhetorical: it laid the groundwork for assertive, unapologetic signage that advertised special fittings, ramps, and other accommodations for disabled persons. While the specifics varied from country to country, Europe's "progressive" and "modern" states took a hopeful but also pragmatic attitude toward social change.

Northern Europe was especially proactive in its efforts to transform the resources available to those with disabilities. To be clear, the barrier-free access movement came to Europe with Timothy Nugent. But there were already a number of lively, government-sponsored initiatives to create housing and other services for disabled people. For example, in the Netherlands there already existed a robust "social insurance system," and there soon developed a network of residential centers and independent housing programs overseen by the nation's various entitlement programs (DeJong, 1984). In Sweden, housing was also of great interest and Fokus or cluster housing specially designed for disabled people was then just beginning to take shape (Brattgard, 2002, 1972).

In Goldsmith's native UK, the Ministry of Health was rapidly developing its own disability culture. That agency oversaw not only a sprawling new National Health Service (NHS), but was charged with providing surgical, medical, and other appliances free at the point of use. Almost inevitably, it also led to a number of design-led initiatives for disabled people. One of the most visible developments of this type—a fine example of the complex social and design work being done under the auspices of the postwar welfare state—was the new "invalid car," a design for the mobility impaired (Figure 3.5). Often known as the "invacar," "noddy car," or "trike," the diminutive three-wheeled vehicle was first distributed in the years immediately after the Second World War (and lasted some thirty years; the program was closed down amid a call for better safety regulations and production ended in 1977). It was not available commercially, but provided and maintained by the government, free of charge, to injured ex-servicemen as well as other disabled people. Originally introduced by Oscar "Bert" Greeves, a struggling motorcycle designer, the first model was designed for a disabled cousin. Greeves found that this makeshift endeavor had a ready market and, after the Second World War, quickly won a government contract for production (Sparrow, 2014: 10, 11). It was meant to hold a single person and their wheelchair, which could be carried behind the driver's seat. Vaguely resembling a motorized—and enclosed—Bath chair, the tiny car came with a lightweight shell and its engine allowed the car to accelerate up to 80 mph. It was substantial enough to be driven on highways, and small enough to be used on footpaths as well. Clearly distinguishable at a distance, and at one time quite ubiquitous, the "invalid car" made a strong statement for the government's sweeping new approach toward healthcare. Even its distinctive color was nicknamed "Ministry Blue" after the Ministry of Health. As journalist Tudor van Hampton insists, the "existence of invalid cars is a reminder of how far the British government once took its health care services" (Van Hampton, 2009: 8).

Oddly enough, while the invacar was highly visible on the roads and streets of the UK, the lowly wheelchair was of relatively little interest to the NHS. As scholars Brian Woods and Nick Watson observe, innovation came slowly to the NHS and more modern wheelchair designs seemed "a relatively small thing in itself at the time" (Woods and Watson, 2004a: 554). As it was, E&J's lightweight folding wheelchair began being imported only in the mid-1950s; collapsible, self-propelled chairs were not available through the NHS before that (Tremblay, 1996: 165). Instead, as the government was the industry's only client, in the years after the Second World War the Health Ministry maintained a near-monopoly over British wheelchair design and production (Woods and Watson, 2004a: 39). Through the 1950s, the government's hospital specialists (a group of physicians and bureaucrats who worked together to determine many of the NHS's policies toward disabled people) decided what types of wheelchairs were issued, and who was entitled to use them (Woods and Watson, 2004a: 556). For their part, these experts—especially those working in the Hospital Services Division—believed that wheelchairs were too expensive, overprescribed, and too often used as a nicety rather than for genuine need (Woods and Watson, 2004a: 564). To be sure, the

NHS could supply as many as twelve types of wheelchairs during this period (Woods and Watson, 2004a: 551). But most NHS issue designs were woefully out of date; several wood and rattan models remained little changed since the nineteenth century. At first, E&J chairs were regarded as a luxury, something like the "Rolls Royce" of chairs (Woods and Watson, 2004a: 562). Only in the late 1950s and early 1960s did UK wheelchair users begin to organize and assert that such chairs were a necessity (Woods and Watson, 2004a: 564). Special groups, especially invacar users who banded together as part of the Invalid Tricycle Association (ITA), argued that newer designs meant greater access, but the prolonged struggle for better wheelchairs continued in the UK through the 1960s. Little wonder, then, that Nugent's ideas about wheelchair access seemed earthshaking when Selwyn Goldsmith and others in the UK first heard them. At the same time, the British situation provided a different—and arguably much-needed—context in which to understand changing views of access (and the need for special signage).

The ideologies of "self-help" and "social welfare cultures"

By 1961, the year that Selwyn Goldsmith heard Tim Nugent speak on barrier-free architecture in Stockholm, there was already a division leading to two very different approaches toward disablement. On the one hand, Timothy Nugent was working in a world where the modern wheelchair was widely used. And he saw no fundamental difference between the disabled students who used it at Illinois, and other students at the University or in the world at large. Thus, Nugent took as his starting point the belief that conventionally designed buildings and facilities—not impairments—inhibited disabled people. If only the environment were more inclusive, he would argue, even seriously impaired persons could live lives like those of their peers. Given the right conditions, everyone, Nugent believed, was capable of taking care of his- or her self. Nugent was sweeping in his view, and strident in his idealism (Figure 3.6).

On the other hand, in Selwyn Goldsmith's world, disablement was treated thoughtfully as well, but in a more traditional and pragmatic way. Within Britain's social welfare system, there were a different set of attitudes. Until very recently, wheelchairs were meant for only the most severely disabled. In the early 1960s, lightweight, collapsible—modern—wheelchairs were only just beginning to be introduced; unsurprisingly, the institutional culture that hesitated to develop and widely distribute these designs focused little on changing public space. Instead, devices like the invacar were used to help disabled people adapt to the environment. Few people believed that it should be adapted to them.

FIGURE 3.6 The Chair of Champion Athletes (advertisement for Everest & Jennings' wheelchairs), 1963. Courtesy of University of Illinois.

When Goldsmith first heard Nugent's lecture in 1961, he found the approach breathtakingly different than anything he'd encountered in the UK to date. Nugent's ideas were so striking that, the following year, he was asked to speak to the Royal Institute of British Architects (RIBA) in London. Other listeners were equally transfixed. The wheelchair user Nancy Bull knew little of Nugent or the University of Illinois. But, writing in the Invalid Tricycle Association's newsletter the following year, Bull reported excitedly that

> I cannot speak, of course, for any other person who heard that lecture. I cannot know if it made the same deep impression on any other minds. I only know that it gave me, personally, an entirely different slant on the whole idea of disability. My world changed suddenly, in the kind of way, which sometimes happens through the exigencies of religion or love. (Bull, 1963: 12)

In a sense, Nancy Bull, Selwyn Goldsmith, and many others in Nugent's audience were converted. Looking back years later, Goldsmith called it "a landmark in the history of designing for the disabled in Britain and Europe" (Goldsmith, 1997: 7). After that talk, he explained, Nugent and the United States "set the mould for controlling the accessibility of the built environment on behalf of disabled people [and] Britain attempted to follow the path which America had taken" (Goldsmith, 1997: ix). Yet, over time, Goldsmith's conception of disablement would gradually change. Framing himself as a supporter of the welfare state, Goldsmith began to scrutinize Nugent's ideas, not to venerate and improve, but to revise and displace. By the mid-1960s, Goldsmith still approved of barrier-free access, but claimed that many of Nugent's assumptions did not translate to the UK. Goldsmith did not move methodically from one position to another. But, by 1965, he claimed two strikingly different ideologies of how society deals with disability, one based on ideas of "self-help" and the other on concepts related to "social welfare."

Goldsmith saw things as if across a great divide. On the one side lay the ramps, buses, and elevators mustered by Nugent, all meant to empower the disabled students at the University of Illinois' rehabilitation program. The whole point, Nugent would argue, was to help them help themselves. On the other side, there was a strong sense of mission and steady belief that society should help and protect its weakest members. As Goldsmith modestly insisted, "my decent English view ... was that disadvantaged people should be treated with concern, kindness, sympathetic understanding and compassion. Disabled people were individuals who were to be helped by dealing with their particular needs" (Goldsmith, 1997: 17). Of course, Goldsmith may have insisted that a deep chasm divided these views. But he probably exaggerated. Many questions of social responsibility, personal freedom, and political will all overlapped. But out of this friction, one new thing clearly emerged: the need for a universal access sign.

For his part, beginning in the mid-1960s, Goldsmith began campaigning for access signage with a surprising kind of obsessiveness. Less than ten years earlier, he'd been lackadaisical about his career. On graduating from

Cambridge, he began to work as an architect. After contracting polio in 1956, while on holiday in Italy, however, he became partially paralyzed. Goldsmith left professional practice and began working in the public sector. He made this choice at a remarkably good moment; in 1960 the British government launched a decade-long drive to build and fund a series of new hospitals around the country. Goldsmith joined the South-East Metropolitan Regional Hospital Board as an architectural advisor and researcher. He quickly discovered that designers had no experience with disabled people, especially those using wheelchairs. Britain's Polio Research Fund agreed. Goldsmith went to Stockholm in 1961, hoping to gather information for a treatise on architecture for people with disabilities. When he returned, he began advocating for an architectural guide on barrier-free access. The Polio Research Fund, along with the Royal Institute of British Architects (RIBA), commissioned Goldsmith's seminal study of accessible architecture: *Designing for the Disabled* (Goldsmith, 1963). In the end, this text was remarkably timely. In fact, the modern wheelchair was just being introduced in the UK, and Goldsmith's book was written with this technology in mind. But it was also the first practical application of Nugent's ideas and focused, unsurprisingly, on wheelchair access. Goldsmith's text spelled out the practical minutiae of wheelchair access, from forms of tactile paving to height criteria for building fixtures and fittings. Beyond disseminating information about how to widen doors and build ramps, Goldsmith's text also propagated Nugent's idea that persons with disabilities were very much like all others.

Before hearing Nugent, Goldsmith would recall, "It never occurred to me that anyone could be provoked and angered by [stairs], could insist that they were universally removable, could show how that was to be done and could assure me that he was not a crackpot" (Goldsmith Designing, 1997: 17). But Goldsmith, who came of age in the postwar period, was profoundly shaped by his training, his profession, and his own wheelchair use.[1] After hearing Nugent's Stockholm speech, and for several years thereafter, Goldsmith was one of the American's leading British converts. Yet, even after publishing *Designing for the Disabled*, Goldsmith's own occasional reliance on a wheelchair and also his acquaintance with other disabled people in Britain continued to nag. Nugent's work at Illinois didn't square with Goldsmith's own experience.

In 1964, at the small city of Norwich, Goldsmith decided to conduct the first-ever, long-term study of disabled wheelchair users. He hoped to learn more about their needs in advance of writing a British building code to mirror the US ANSI 117.1. What he found instead was "a wealth of evidence that to my mind made Nugent's stance insupportable" (Goldsmith, 1997: 20). Working off government information, interviewing users of government services, and collaborating with government officials, Goldsmith gradually developed a different picture of wheelchair usage than the one painted by Nugent. Over the course of his research, Goldsmith was welcomed into people's homes and he spent time with their families. He slowly discovered that most wheelchair users rarely went outside. In his study, he found only one person, a woman, would leave her home alone in her wheelchair—and that was to go to a neighborhood pub (McIntyre, 2015: 91). Goldsmith came to believe that these shut-ins, simply put, were "not independent" at all. Instead, he argued, they have acute needs, wanted "someone to push them around and help them in and out of the wheelchair when necessary" (Goldsmith, 1965: 971). In the end, he began to reason, most wheelchair users needed more help than Nugent's cohort of young and highly motivated college students. Furthermore, the Norwich study suggested that disabled persons would not benefit from barrier-free access accommodations alone.

To this day, Goldsmith's ideas remain controversial.[2] In retrospect, both his and Nugent's studies seem self-contained and hermetic. But also, it was as if they found complete opposites in the range of potential wheelchair users at the time. No doubt, Nugent's college students at Illinois were an exceptionally motivated and ambitious cohort. But Goldsmith's sample was notably restricted in other ways. Because he was working with local officials, Goldsmith limited his study to wheelchair users who received their chairs free from the British government. By definition, they had already passed a rigorous vetting process instigated by the government's medical establishment, were considered severely ill or impaired, and were almost always elderly. Indeed, the year before Goldsmith started his study, some 75 percent of people receiving NHS wheelchairs were over fifty-five (Woods and Watson, 2004a: 555). Furthermore, the nature of the NHS and its allocation of wheelchairs at that time must be taken into account; many of these stay at home wheelchair users were still using the older, more rigid, and antiquated chairs favored by the NHS. And the latter were so rickety and out-of-date, they almost proscribed any kind of use out of doors. At Illinois and across the United States, on the other hand, the E&J wheelchair was in widespread usage. Moreover, it was considered so successful that many semi-ambulatory people at Illinois were encouraged to use wheelchairs rather than crutches or other assistive devices.

But Goldsmith scarcely reflected on these subtleties; instead, he was struck by the obvious results of his research in Norwich. First, he chided Nugent for taking an overly optimistic point of view. Goldsmith admitted that even he initially felt the seductive pull of Nugent's "wheelchair students cavorting on the campus of the University of Illinois." After hearing Nugent's 1961 lecture in Stockholm, Goldsmith left the meeting understanding that there were "hundreds of active young paraplegics frustrated because architectural barriers stood in the way of their aspirations" (Goldsmith, 1997: 22). Certainly, the image of an active, fun-loving wheelchair user was embraced on the Illinois campus. As pictured in an E&J ad run in the Illinois program's annual newsletter, Illini wheelchair users were "champion athletes and brilliant scholars" (Figure 3.6). And, of course, what Goldsmith found in Norwich was something quite different. Neither accomplished sportspersons nor sage dons, most wheelchair users in Norwich were elderly and the vast majority relied on others to help them get around.

By the time Goldsmith issued a second edition of *Designing for the Disabled* in 1967, he felt his research in Norwich necessitated a different approach. Revising his earlier arguments, Goldsmith began by insisting that well-adjusted disabled people are dependent. In fact, he argued they must "accept the fact that they cannot be treated in the same way as everyone else." In this insistence, Goldsmith found a new voice. Calling American efforts "well intentioned but misguided," Goldsmith picked and prodded at Nugent's line of reasoning. He argued as well that the American Standard Building Code was "dogmatic" as well as "impractical and unrealistic" (Goldsmith, 1967: 388).

As a clear cleavage developed between Goldsmith and Nugent, the dispute was all the more bitter because the distance between the two men was still relatively small. Both men, for example, still agreed that special provisions like ramps in place of steps, wider doorways, and other accommodations for wheelchair users were important. But Goldsmith argued that disabled people and their supporters should recognize "physical independence is not a critical necessity" (Goldsmith, 1967: 387). It is clear, Goldsmith insisted, that society must "treat people differently according to their differing needs." We must, he argued, also offer "opportunities for dependence" (Goldsmith, 1967: 389).

Boiled down to mundane specifics, Goldsmith's argument revolves around the minutiae of daily life. Practical things, for example, public toilets, should accommodate disabled wheelchair users who arrive with an assistant or caregiver (Goldsmith drafted the British Standard building code as provisioning at least one unisex disabled toilet wherever there were public toilets; also, the latter was decreed nearly twice the size of its American counterpart) (McIntyre, 2015: 55). However seemingly commonplace, for Goldsmith these provisions carried a heavy moral weight. Architects, Goldsmith insisted, have "a responsibility to accommodate disabled people who are dependent as much as those who can be independent" (McIntyre, 2015: 55).

The most controversial matter at the time, though, was Goldsmith's insistence that special features not be hidden or denied; on the contrary, Goldsmith argued, attention should be drawn to them. On this point, Goldsmith admitted that "there are different points of view." But he held his ground, insisting that specially adapted or otherwise "suitable facilities should be brought to the attention of disabled people." If not, he observed, "the people for whom they have been designed will be unaware of their existence, and they will be valueless." To do this, disabled people needed specially designated signage. Seen this way, he reasoned, "the signposting of special facilities for disabled people is a rational and entirely appropriate thing to do" (McIntyre, 2015: 55). To refuse signage in favor of normalizing disability was, he insisted, a fool's errand (Goldsmith, 1967: 33, 34).

Breaking barriers

Even before Goldsmith made a formal call for signage in the second edition of *Designing for the Disabled*, the problem was clearly on his mind (Figure 3.7). In June 1965, he tracked Timothy Nugent down at a conference in Oxford and precipitated a full-blown confrontation. Face to face with the American, Goldsmith explained that "I could not sympathise—or empathise—with Tim Nugent's radical vision" (Goldsmith, 1997: 28). The two had a very public argument, culminating with Goldsmith suggesting that "not all disabled people were capable of doing wheelchair gymnastics" (Goldsmith, 1967: 389). But the rift that was developing between these two points of view is exemplified in two striking symbols that were almost simultaneously

FIGURE 3.7　The No Barriers logo appeared on the July 1962–July 1965 Architectural Barriers: Progress Report issued by the President's Committee on Employment of the Handicapped, 1965.

introduced in 1965. One, which appeared on a report issued by Nugent (Figure 3.7), strikes an oddly negative note. The other (Figure 3.8), designed for publicity materials for an international conference spearheaded by Goldsmith and held in Italy, is awash in optimism.

At the November 1965 meeting of the National Society for Crippled Children and Adults (NSCCA) in Chicago, Tim Nugent electrified the meeting when he delivered a report from the leading edge of the campaign against architectural barriers. But, while Nugent's work would form the basis for American building standards for a generation, a different discussion was taking place away from the main stage. Behind the scenes, Selwyn Goldsmith reported, there were discussions on the very real need for signage that could label these accommodations (Goldsmith, 1969b: 7). The convention's organizer, the NSCCA, already had a robust institutional culture in which complicated diseases and conditions were communicated to the public through modest, but powerful photographs and symbols. The group is perhaps best known for their poignant, annual fundraising campaigns featuring an impaired "poster child." And much of their financial support came from the simple, but religiously redolent, "Easter seal" stamps they sold each spring. Recognizing the power of a modest, effective symbol, the group used the distinctive, stylized lily logo for fundraising initiatives as well as its own literature. (They soon identified with this symbol so completely, the group even officially changed their name to the "Easter Seals Society" in 1967.) Perhaps unsurprisingly, when the group published Nugent's report for the 1965 Chicago convention (Slavitt and Pugh, 2000: 6), the organization dressed the report up, placing a symbol on its cover.

Two striking features emerge from this little emblem (Figure 3.7). First, the symbol was not tied in any way to the report's contents. Although thorough and exacting, Nugent's report made no mention of any form of visual frippery; nowhere in it is the graphic even mentioned. Second, although it represents a flight of four steps, the image remains remarkably vague. Depicted in skewed perspective, the step motif was published with a bold circle surrounding it. The most striking feature of the symbol, however, is the bar that runs across it, effectively stamping the stairs out. In handwritten letters the word "ACCESSIBLE" appears above it. While it would be too much to say that the rough little sketch was meant as a directional or wayfinding device, its anti-stairs motif did convey the spirit of the campaign against architectural barriers.

Simply put, the little no-stairs logo is confusing. Was it meant as a kind of "trademark" and intended to be used by supporters of the barrier-free architecture movement (Goldsmith, 1969b: 9)? Or was it developed as a visual illustration aimed at builders, urging them not to work with stairs? Goldsmith himself complained that it was not saying "positively 'this is a usable facility.' " Instead, he insisted, it could be read as the visual equivalent of a double negative. Rather than forthrightly stating what it is, the symbol announces "negatively 'this is not a facility which is not usable'"

(Goldsmith, 1969b: 10). Goldsmith tells us that this image was consistent with the rest of Nugent's philosophy; the image was meant to avoid "stigmatization" (Goldsmith, 1967: 389). But, he claimed, it was utterly useless. After making this brief appearance in Chicago, the "No Barriers" logo died a quiet death.

Prompted by Selwyn Goldsmith, and born in the rosy glow of Europe's developing welfare states, a clearer figure of disablement emerged on the world stage at the June 1965 conference "Disabled People and Architectural Barriers" (Associazione nazionale mutilate e invalidi del lavoro, 1965). Sponsored by two quasi-governmental groups based in Rome[3] and held at Stresa in the Italian Lake District, the conference drew representatives from the United States, Europe, and as far away as Chile and India. Germany's Parliament sent a special delegation. The chief architects from several Scandinavian ministries also attended. It should have been an international launching point for Tim Nugent's ideas. But Nugent did not attend and instead Edmond Leonard, from the US President's Committee on Employment of the Disabled, presented on ANSI 117.1 and the University of Illinois studies. Yet the notion of barrier-free architecture was overshadowed by Goldsmith's presentation of his own text, *Designing for the Disabled*. Though the second edition had not yet been published, he was already conducting his study in Norwich, and having second thoughts about Nugent's proposals.

Instead of following the US prescriptions in an ad hoc manner, Goldsmith insisted that attendees begin asking a new set of questions. For Nugent and his US supporters, discussion boiled down to one issue: just how much should the physical environment announce that it has been fitted to the needs of disabled people? At the Stresa conference, however, discussion took a different turn. Goldsmith and the other European delegates in attendance asked: how can the government better accommodate disabled people? Most attendees represented respective government ministries and their answers centered on housing, sports, and vacations for disabled persons. Here, the Americans were outliers. Most of the conference attendees were after a response to disability that mirrored the values and goals Europe's welfare states. Although the symbol was designed in advance of the conference itself, these discussions also provided the stage for a new representation: the disabled citizen (Figure 3.8).

Though seemingly straightforward, the figure introduced on the Stresa event's promotional materials does more than inform; it makes disability part of the visual landscape. In fact, placed on the meeting's public posters, the wheelchair user here was depicted as if part of a traffic sign; the image was placed on a pole, echoing the kinds of markers seen on the side of a road. Shown in silhouette, the figure sits in an oversized wheelchair; in a brilliantly humanizing stroke, the chair user leans forward and appears to be addressing us with a hand rising in salute.

FIGURE 3.8 A wheelchair logo was introduced at the 1965 International Conference on Barriers, held in Stresa, Italy, 1965.

Here was an admirable vision. Not only did the Stresa symbol give disablement a human form, but it also brought the image into dialog with broader communications systems that shaped modern design. In fact, the Stresa figure is also a pictogram and derives from a lexicon developed in the years immediately after the First World War, when international travel, trade, and communications forced the development of broadly legible visual language systems. Perhaps unsurprisingly, pictograms were identified as particularly useful. For instance, though the League of Nations had already, in 1931, introduced twenty-six designated road signs to facilitate global mobility, by 1938, they were proposing the first human figure (a silhouette of a motorcycle rider) during the Convention on the Unification of Road Signals (Schipper, 2009). In order to draw attention to the graphic, this figure was enclosed in a heavy black circle. Both the Stresa and the Chicago symbols pick up on this convention, as a way to draw attention to their respective icons and also to align with broader typographic and signage trends. But their resemblance ends there.

In fact, the Stresa symbol is torn in its allegiance, owing as much to politically charged graphics as the barrier-free architecture movement. Through the middle of the twentieth century, researchers began to study how abstract and pictorial symbols could carry meaning across language barriers (Baker, 2011). Then, in the postwar period especially, Europe's democracies pushed hard for a kind of a visual Esperanto (Bresnahan, 2011). At the same time, they aimed for forms of communications seemingly devoid of national or ethnic messages. The conventions advocated here, namely pictograms, form the core of the larger sign symbols systems we know today.

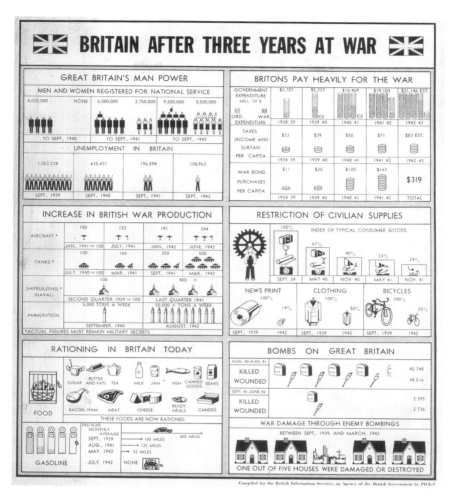

FIGURE 3.9 A Statistical Chart developed by the British Information Services for distribution in the United States. The chart uses abstracted human forms to demonstrate economic and social conditions in Britain during the first three years of the Second World War, c. 1942. Photo by FPG/Hulton Archive/Getty Images.

The Stresa figure, then, was a design that aligned with some of the most idealistic graphic design traditions in the twentieth century. Vanguard typographic movements, including De Stijl, Russian constructivism, Bauhaus, and New Typography, all rejected historical styles and embraced visual experimentation. But—most fundamentally—most aimed to discover universal signs and symbols that could help "achieve international communication and global peace" (Bresnahan, 2011: 7). The first extensive theorizing on pictograms began in the 1920 and early 1930s, steeped in the idealistic, science-inflected socialism of red Vienna. Here, the Austrian sociologist Otto Neurath developed a system of standard symbols meant to convey social statistics. But he was also aiming for a kind of clarity, something his collaborator Charles Ogden called "debabelization" (Ogden, 1931). Neurath even worked with the graphic designer Gerd Arntz to develop a series of easily comprehended stylized silhouettes that included a form of the human figure (Neurath and Kinross, 2009: 44). Steeped in ideas of scientific socialism of the period, the figure was part of a system Neurath called ISOTYPE (International System of Typographic Picture Education) (Figure 3.9). In Neurath's own words, he sought "a system of optical representation ... that would be universal, immediate, and memorable ... [ensuring] that even passers-by ... can acquaint themselves with the latest sociological and economical facts at a glance." (Neurath, quoted in Cartwright et al., 1996: 65)

Though development of such imagery came to a standstill during the Second World War, after the war these efforts were continued and expanded into public signage. Many graphic designers embraced the emerging pictographic language in the 1950s and 1960s, adopting its lessons to develop logos and corporate identity programs. Furthermore, a continuing engagement with the theory and practice of communication prompted, by the 1960s, a growing general interest in graphic symbols. In all, a steady stream of different international bodies developed symbol systems for vast governmental infrastructures, including highways, airports, hospitals, and many other services and products.

But signpost imagery like that evoked Neurath's simple figures and reflected by the Stresa figure was just beginning to be standardized in the 1960s. Only in 1963 did Willy de Majo, then president of the International Council of Graphic Design Associations (ICOGRADA), suggest developing a systematic "symbol language for directional signs in-doors and out" (Bakker, 2013). He played a pivotal role through his power and position, but it was behind the scenes that he first suggested further collaboration with professional organizations such as the International Chamber of Commerce and the International Union of Official Travel Organizations. The latter was especially interested in this effort as it impacted international trade and travel. Furthermore, these efforts were not limited to Europe. In the United States, the industrial designer Henry Dreyfuss was also interested. Indeed, his agency developed machine operation symbols as early as the 1940s, and he developed his own symbol sourcebook in 1972. Interestingly, however, while a number of designers plunged themselves into these practical systems, developing through the 1960s symbols for male and female figures, post offices and mail, restaurants and coffee, in these early symbol systems neither Dreyfus nor the European designers developed any kind of representation of access for disabled people.

Of course, there was every reason that these designers should be thinking in such radically new terms. The Stresa symbol was not simply a new image—it represented an entirely different way of thinking. By example, signs and symbols would follow, but the really remarkable development here was that a state of disablement was openly depicted on a public sign.

Notes

1 Later in life, in *Designing for the Disabled, a New Paradigm*, Selwyn Goldsmith explained his increasing reliance on wheelchairs. Essentially a hemiplegic, he underwent several hospital stays and used a wheelchair while convalescing. Over time, as he aged, he came to use chairs more and more.

2 Never afraid of controversy, in the course of his career, Goldsmith changed his position on the politics of wheelchair access several times. Although Goldsmith supported Timothy Nugent's ideas about environmental access initially, he changed his own opinions after his studies in Norwich in the mid-1960s. Nevertheless, later in life, Goldsmith would revise his opinions once again. For an account of his evolving ideas, see *Designing for the Disabled, a New Paradigm*.

3 These were the Associazione nazionale mutilati e invalidi del lavoro (National Association of Maimed and Disabled Workers and Invalids) and the Associazione Italiana Assistenza agli Spastici (Italian Association for Assisting Spastics).

4

Signs of Discrimination
(1965–1968)

"When they are planning buildings," asked Selwyn Goldsmith in 1967, "do architects continue to treat everyone in the same way, thinking of building users in "normal population" terms, with the result that people who are abnormal are not accommodated? Or do they treat people differently according to their differing needs, designing buildings not only for a normal population but simultaneously for a parallel abnormal population?" (Goldsmith, 1967: 389)

Goldsmith posed these questions in the *Journal of the Royal Institute of Architects*. By this point, Goldsmith had refit his entire career, becoming a full-fledged advocate for disabled people and arguing for separate, but equal, facilities for them. He even developed a special term for his approach, something he called "positive discrimination," and began using it in relation to access signs (Goldsmith, 1967: 388).

In the 1960s, the notion of "positive discrimination" was relatively new. Over several decades it had been used primarily in statistics, indicating a kind of winnowing process in which only the best kernels of corn or military recruits were found acceptable. But its meaning was never fixed. In the UK, "positive discrimination" took a surprising turn when it began to be applied to new educational initiatives in the 1960s. From "positive solutions" to "positive attitudes," the driving optimism of Britain's social democrats moved the term from numerical analysis to the very real world of schools and classrooms; it meant to discriminate in favor of people with certain characteristics (sex, age, religion, ethnic origins) rather than against them. But in the United States, the notion of discrimination, be it positive or not, carried a different set of associations.

As the Civil Rights movement gained momentum in the early 1960s, unequal treatment and segregation in the United States were increasingly criticized. In the midst of battles for voting rights and access to equal

FIGURE 4.1 Segregation signs like this, photographed by Esther Bubley at a bus station in Rome, Georgia guided people through the Jim Crow South, 1930. Courtesy of Library of Congress.

education, this movement proved a powerful model for disabled people. But the campaign for Civil Rights also brought into harsh focus an unequal form of discrimination that led to separate, but unequal, facilities in the segregated South. It also highlighted the power of prohibitory messages. Here, signs often served to regulate—not liberate—a visible minority (Figure 4.1). Jim Crow signs directed African Americans to backroom facilities and through hidden points of access. Separate treatment, like backdoor entrances, distinct water fountains, and basement toilets, haunted the North American social imaginary and built environment alike.

Long familiar with messages like "Whites only," "No Colored," and "Negro Entrance This Way," in the United States some disabled people and their supporters equated inaccessible spaces and barriers to access in a new way. For them, barriers in the environment seemed almost willfully designed to be unaccommodating. They signaled a different kind of unspoken segregation. To draw attention to the problem of architectural barriers, some persons with disabilities began invoking the specter of negative, prohibitory, and segregationist signage. Although no one was posting "no disabled" or "handicapped keep out" signs across the walls of North America, disabled activists argued that builders were actively designing inaccessible spaces. They might as well begin posting such signs. Writing in 1965, Charles Caniff, a wheelchair user active in the Paralyzed Veterans Association, found it hard to miss the parallels:

> At the present time there is an intensive campaign ... to eliminate signs and regulations in public buildings in one region of our country that restrict entry or use for certain people. Yet in every city and community in our country are buildings without signs, which have physical barriers preventing free access for millions of citizens and taxpayers. (Caniff, 1962: 14)

Similar concerns began to be voiced elsewhere. By 1966, the physician and rehabilitation specialist Howard Rusk compared lack of access with the Jim Crow South. He insisted that there may be "no signs reading, 'Handicapped Keep Out,'" but the "many thoughtless barriers—stairs, narrow doorways, revolving doors, and unusable restrooms and elevators ... have the same effect" (Rusk, 1966: 87). Newly empowered disabled students at Illinois used the same imagery when campaigning for local business to eliminate steps. When in 1965 senior Fred Fay visited a new shopping mall in Champaign, Illinois, only to discover 5-inch curbs at every entrance, he complained to the mayor's office. These new curbs, he argued, were "just as effective as a sign saying, 'Disabled, stay out'" (Fay, 1965: 22). In the United States, segregation signs were widely known and haunted the collective imagination of disabled people; they illustrated how written postings might be deployed to inhibit—not empower—disabled people.

Of course, signs forbidding access to disabled people were never posted. But, in conceptualizing the barrier-free architecture movement, Nugent and his supporters were themselves wary of the idea of "special" treatment and found the idea of discrimination of any sort worrisome. Certainly, from the very start, the groundbreaking program at Illinois never conceived the need for signage. But, as Goldsmith's case for access signs began to win followers on both sides of the Atlantic, the question of signage was more openly discussed. But it also revealed a simple truth. North Americans favored oblique, abstracting signage so enigmatic that its message of access seemed hidden or "secret" (Goldsmith, 1969b: 10; Tomlinson and Stevens, 1972: 108). Arguing for a form of "positive discrimination," in the UK, Goldsmith led the way for something different—access signs that were more robust and much clearer. Above all, he argued for symbols based on the human figure. In the end, the issue was seemingly swept aside in 1967, when the first professional designers began to address the signage issue. What emerged was not merely a simple directional sign—those existed before then. Instead, Paul Arthur introduced a disabled access symbol that fit into a larger system of communications for Montreal's Expo 67; but the problem of discrimination would return later, with reverberations to this day.

The secret signs of disabled people

In 1965, the Canadian Research Council, a part of the subcommittee on the National Building Council, introduced a circular form as part of its symbols for directional signage (Figure 4.2). Understood as one piece in the larger puzzle of designing accessible environments, this logo was introduced to the public in "Building Standards for the Handicapped," a set of guidelines intended to increase access in public buildings. Taken cumulatively, the Canadian guidelines are very similar to the American specifications first developed by Tim Nugent four years earlier. And, like the "No Barriers" symbol introduced in Chicago, this image graced the cover of a report. But there the comparison ends. While the "No Barriers" logo illustrated an architectural barrier (steps)—and blocked it out—the Canadian symbol effectively marked something different—an architecture of access. Its design

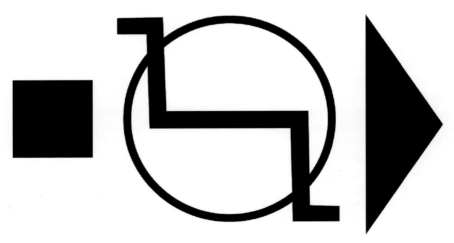

FIGURE 4.2 This abstract insignia was developed by Canada's National Research Council and adopted as part of the country's Building Code in 1965. It was first distributed in the government publication, *Building Standards for the Handicapped*, 1965.

relied on a stylized circle motif enclosing a zigzag line, and accompanied by a directional arrow. It was conceived to remedy a larger problem, and meant "for use as a directional sign to building entrances usable by semi ambulatory and nonambulatory persons." Most importantly, it was also intended to serve "as an identification symbol on all facilities provided for the handicapped" (National Research Council Canada, 1965: 2). And yet, it is oddly obscure. To the art educator John Sevens, its abstract nature put it in a class of symbols that "communicate only with the initiated" (Tomlinson and Stevens, 1972: 106).

Modestly referred to as an "insignia' rather than a "sign," the Canadian symbol's innovations are easy to overlook. But this insignia takes the image of stairs, and reduces the form to a simple zigzag. At the same time, the symbol is embedded in a directional arrow, allowing it to serve as a useful guide. Because it is non-representational, the insignia can be hung in a variety of ways, allowing the arrow to point in any direction. This aspect of the motif reflected a mixture of design cultures that was, in its own small way, revolutionary. On the one hand, it follows the advice of leading British access experts like Goldsmith. And it echoes the environmental signage exemplified by the Stresa figure when it was depicted on conference posters—that is, it functions as a signpost (and, of course, this idea reflected Goldsmith's advocacy for public signage). But it was hardly explicit in its referencing. The symbol is a little antiseptic—as it is, it includes nothing more than an arrow, the zigzagged line, and a circle. In this regard, it masks its meaning and hides the implication of special treatment. The Canadian insignia might suggest a sophisticated balance between the US and British approaches toward access and barriers in the public space. But it should also be seen against a backdrop of national ambition.

To be sure, at this same moment Canadians were deeply immersed in larger questions of symbols and their meaning. The entire country had only recently hashed through the "Great Flag Debate" of the early 1960s. Canadians were keenly aware of the power of graphic symbols when the country prepared to replace the Canadian Red Ensign, that is, the Union Jack and shield of the royal arms, with a new maple leaf flag; the latter was finally accepted in 1965, when it was introduced at an official ceremony in Ottawa. The building code insignia, in fact, shares its distinctly bold, graphic style with the maple leaf symbol. Both followed what the historian and designer of the Canadian flag, George Stanley, described as "simplicity—it should be clean cut and not cluttered" (Stanley, 1964: 3).

But, where the national flag was meant to be easily recognizable and iconic, the insignia was willfully covert. Its meaning, as one critic at the time complained, was "cryptic," and its vague symbolism presented itself as a form of secret knowledge (Tomlinson and Stevens, 1972: 27). Was the circle meant to represent a wheel? Was the zigzag line meant to connote steps? If so, asked Selwyn Goldsmith, why "represent steps which handicapped

FIGURE 4.3 The New York State Access Symbol began circulating in 1967 when it was introduced in the brochure "Outdoors Recreation for the Physically Handicapped," 1967. New York State Council of Parks and Outdoor Recreation, Albany.

people cannot manage? (If the latter is the intention it is not apparent whether the arrow is pointing to a location where there are steps or where there are not)" (Goldsmith, 1969: 9).

However puzzling its appearance, the Canadian symbol did fill a void. It could label accessible accommodations and it might also guide disabled people toward barrier-free routes and passageways. And it succeeded in attracting a following of sorts. By 1968, an informal market for the Canadian insignia stickers and placards developed in the United States. It was popular enough that groups like the Massachusetts Association of Paraplegics unapologetically began selling these as a "sign to indicate wheelchair facilities" (one was free, two or more, twenty cents each).

At the same time, in 1967 New York State adopted its own symbol (Figure 4.3). Officially issued by the State Council of Parks and Outdoor Recreation, this symbol was a pet project of Governor Nelson Rockefeller. It was quickly developed under the leadership of his younger brother, Laurence, who had only recently been made Council chair. Born dyslexic, the elder Rockefeller self-identified as disabled, and was an outspoken advocate for accommodations. With a vision that stretched from Lake Erie to the tip of Long Island, state parks bureaucrats introduced a symbol focused on circulation and access provisions for both wheelchair users and semi-ambulatory persons. To accomplish this, the 1967 park guidelines ordered eye-catching signs to be "located at the park entrances plus literature distributed at the entrance control station" to recreation areas (New York State Council of Parks and Outdoor Recreation, 1967: 4). The New York state symbol is a close cousin to the cryptic Canadian insignia. Resembling nothing so much as a spoked wheel, impaled by an arrow, it closely recalls the bicycle-like wheels common to wheelchairs at the time. Like its relative north of the border, its directional arrow could be shifted to point in different directions. It's worth noting that the New York symbol dropped the Canadians' puzzling zigzag line. But this didn't matter to Selwyn Goldsmith. Ever critical of North American attempts to introduce abstract symbols, he argued that the New York sign looked "less like a sign and more like the kind of 'lovers' graffiti' one could find carved into a tree trunk." Even "if a less frivolous interpretation is assumed," Goldsmith continued, the hapless symbol might indicate "archery and William Tell" (Goldsmith, 1969: 10).

For better or worse, these symbols never gained wide circulation. In the annals of graphic design, North America's curious engagement with public signage for disabled access might remain a strange footnote. But, from across the Atlantic, both symbols spurred dismay. And Goldsmith's consternation went beyond peevishness. A wheelchair user himself, he craved acceptance as much as clarity. Following trends in twentieth-century signage, Goldsmith insisted that someone, somewhere could do better: an access symbol needed to be clear, practical, and signal an open acceptance of disability.

Positive discrimination and the psychology of disablement

If he felt justified in critiquing the North American access symbols so harshly, it was because, with the 1963 publication of *Designing for The Disabled* in the UK, Selwyn Goldsmith immediately gained international stature as an expert on the subject of barrier-free architecture. Standing at the pinnacle of this growing field, he also embodied a kind of ideal—he was an engaged and active disabled person. No wonder, then, that his rethinking of these issues in the 1967 revision of *Designing for The Disabled* gained so much attention. When he recanted his initial support of Tim Nugent and the new barrier-free building code in the US, he called his earlier approach "a mistaken policy" (Goldsmith, 1967). The London *Times* went so far as suggest that Goldsmith's change of mind "unleashed an international controversy" (Anon., 1967c: 10). As one who was rapidly drifting away from what the *Times* called the "orthodox" American approach, Goldsmith made his case for something very different: "I want positive discrimination to accommodate severely handicapped and disabled people." But more to his original point, he aimed to align positive discrimination with what he called "the psychology of disablement" (Goldsmith, 1969: 11).

At the outset, it's important to recall that Goldsmith stressed one thing—there is no stigma to being disabled. Nevertheless, he insisted, "physically abnormal people must be provided with special facilities that are supplementary to those needed by normal people." He noted that "This special treatment is positively discriminatory but it need not mean stigmatizing treatment" (Goldsmith, 1967, 388). The examples he marshaled were clear enough: "people who use wheelchairs need ramps in place of steps; they need wider doors, larger lifts and larger w.c. compartments." More to the point, as Goldsmith supporters Nicholas Tomlinson and John Stevens editorialized several years later, "it is impossible to design facilities which are usable by everyone" (Tomlinson and Stevens, 1972: 108). Years later, Goldsmith explained his position more fully. As he saw it, the American ethos of independence—that is, of not accepting or needing help—was inconsistent with what he called the "social welfare" policies of the British government (Goldsmith, 1983). But Goldsmith also found the basic parameters of the US approach suspect. At best, he proposed, it exaggerates the problem. On the face of it, "the proposition that architectural barriers prevent disabled people from using buildings sounds plausible. It is ... easy to dramatize, for example, the incompatibility of a wheelchair and a flight of steps." But this ignores, according to Goldsmith, the obvious solution—ask for help. Take, for instance, staircases. Those who see steps as barriers ignore the possibility of outside assistance. It is, Goldsmith asserted, a "simple fact that a person in a wheelchair can be carried up and down steps" (Goldsmith, 1969: 14). But Goldsmith saw a darker logic at work here, too. He argued that the US approach fundamentally lacked moral authority. To Goldsmith's mind, "the architectural barriers campaign in the USA is being conducted not to enable all physically handicapped people to participate in community life, but only those who are of value—those who are potentially capable of contributing something of material account" (Goldsmith, 1967: 389).

Invoking his research in Norwich, Goldsmith maintained that many seriously disabled people simply could not be independent. Instead, "by using their initiative (which means requesting assistance) they are able to find their way into and around buildings" (Goldsmith, 1969: 14). Inspired by the ideals of the welfare state (which itself drew on attributes like mutual supportiveness, pragmatism, and compensation), he insisted upon suspending "judgments that one individual is worth more than another are out of place." Goldsmith felt that the job of architects is "to accommodate disabled people who are dependent as much as those who can be independent" (Goldsmith, 1967, 389). This marks a profound shift away from the US attitude. Nugent would have insisted that the abolition of architectural barriers would allow disabled people to live normal lives. But as Goldsmith told the London *Times* in 1967, independence is "only a relative value" (Anon., 1967c: 10).

As he began to stake out his claims, Goldsmith insisted that we care less about independence, and instead pay more attention to some basic principles of psychology. Goldsmith acknowledged that able-bodied people "attach immense importance on the attribute of physical normality ... [and] a common supposition about the way that people react to disability ... is that disabled people aspire to be 'normal' and constantly seek normality [*sic*] goals" (Goldsmith, 1969b: 12). By contrast, he argued, a well-adjusted disabled person may go through "an initial phase of self-consciousness" and be embarrassed by his or her impairments. But, if psychologically healthy enough, that person will become "accustomed" to it. In fact, over time, disablement would become "an integral part of the image which he presents to the world, and he looks upon it in the same detached fashion as people regard their spectacles or false teeth" (Goldsmith, 1969b: 12). For Goldsmith, acceptance of disability "without embarrassment, shame or self-pity" (Goldsmith, 1969b: 12) was essential. As Goldsmith's supporters put it, "if he is able to adjust to the limitations imposed by his disability as opposed to adopting a pretense of normality, a disabled man can cope very successfully—without any embarrassment or sense of inferiority" (Tomlinson and Stevens, 1972: 108).

The link between signage and this type of positive psychology was, for Goldsmith, clear enough. If a person were well adjusted, there would be no need for cryptic, abstracting, or "camouflaging" signs. As proponents of Goldsmith's position noted, the secretive approach suggests that physical disability is a "'tragic, calamitous and shattering experience' and supposes that disabled people must inevitably regard their handicaps in the same way." Such attitudes suppose that "disabled people must inevitably regard their handicaps in the same way—that they can best be assisted by pretending that the damage has never occurred" (Tomlinson and Stevens, 1972: 108).

The UK, Goldsmith insisted, needed a clear, practical access symbol that would signal a positive attitude toward disability. By 1965, Goldsmith developed one on his own and published it in the *Architect's Journal* (Goldsmith, 1965: 972), a publication that he helped edit. Complaining that the Canadian symbol was a "puzzle to many people," Goldsmith's introduction was entirely different—a silhouetted figure in a wheelchair. The symbol drew from the Stresa figure, but more clearly articulated both the human form and the chair on which it sits. When Goldsmith decided to publish a second edition of *Designing for the Disabled* in 1967, he went further, adding a new section devoted to "signposting of facilities for disabled people" (Goldsmith, 1967: 155–157). Here he introduced a newer, more abstract figure, who seems to roll along purposefully (Figure 4.4). This person pushes his or her own chair and looks directly ahead; as opposed to the friendly looking Stresa figure, this person advances toward some distant goal. At the same time, the depiction of this wheelchair is remarkably detailed, clearly articulating a newer, collapsible chair, complete with wheels—small in front and larger in back, seat, armrests, backrest, and push handles at its back and push rims on its wheels.

At the same time, for Goldsmith the discussion was not just theoretical; he meant to back his arguments up with solid facts. Careful research was important to Goldsmith, as was the funding, structure, and backing that came from the governmental and charitable support that his work received. Shortly after the first edition of *Designing for Disability* was published in 1963,

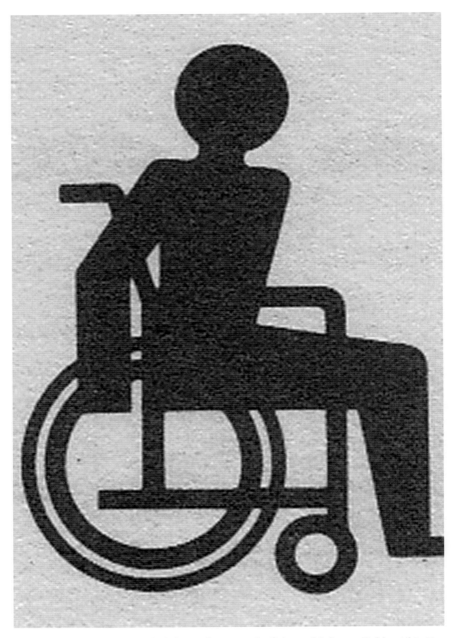

FIGURE 4.4 Access symbol from the second edition of Selwyn Goldsmith's *Designing for the Disabled*, 1967. 2nd edition. London: RIBA Publications Ltd.

Goldsmith moved to Norwich in 1964, where he began several research projects (among these was a study of disabled drivers in Norwich; another was a study of blind residents). But perhaps the most significant project was a "pilot signposting programme" that Goldsmith carried out in Norwich from 1967 to 1968. Subvented by the government, and administered through the National Fund for Research into Crippling Diseases, it was intended to concretize ideas of positive discrimination. As the London *Times* would later report, it aimed to replace "abstract symbols to identify special facilities (which are meaningless to the uninitiated) by pictorial signs" (Anon., 1967c: 10).

This "demonstration project" was run in collaboration with several local agencies and institutions, including the Norwich School of Art and the welfare and planning departments of the city government's Norwich Corporation. Their brief was to develop a system of postings analogous to road traffic signs; simply put, they aimed to "point the way to the whereabouts of specific facilities for disabled people" (Goldsmith, 1969: 18). The ambitious program aimed to put some thirty signs in public places, alerting the public to access in theaters and movie houses, as well as Norwich's Cathedral, main library, and the County Hall. There were also signs to indicate special parking spaces, as well as places that had wheelchairs available on loan to the public. Developments were grounded in a series of meetings between the designers (a class from Norwich School of Art led by Peter Rea, a professional graphic designer then teaching at the school as a visiting tutor) and a group of disabled people assembled by Goldsmith himself.

Goldsmith decided that none of the symbols then in place were satisfactory; the students were asked to develop "fresh" symbols and these would be presented to a group of about forty disabled people (Tomlinson and Stevens, 1972: 109). In the end, this group was asked to discuss multiple variations of what to depict, including an empty wheelchair, a crutch, a cane, as well as representations of people using chairs and crutches (Figure 4.5). The group spent the most time discussing a modular system, in which different pieces of information might be communicated. For example, individual panels might be printed with a single symbol, and the groups of symbols combined for different messages. Thus, a sign depicting a man might be placed next to a second panel that depicts a crutch and cane. This might indicate a facility appropriate for semi-ambulatory users. If a sign showing an empty wheelchair was added, the meaning would shift to indicate that the facility was appropriate for wheelchair users as well. Placed together, like words in a sentence, the composite of these three symbols would announce that a crutch, cane, or wheelchair user could access these facilities. The group also discussed three stylistic approaches to the images themselves. These included realistic photographs of men, women, canes, wheelchairs, and other assistive devices; a moderately abstracted set of forms, including a wheelchair

FIGURE 4.5 These preliminary studies were planned for a modular range of symbols designed by Selwyn Goldsmith, Peter Rea, and students at the Norwich School of Art, c. 1968.

somewhat reminiscent of the earlier *Architect's Journal* symbol and later reprinted in the second edition of *Designing for the Disabled*[1]; and a third group that veered closest, stylistically speaking, to the stylized silhouettes introduced by Neurath some forty years earlier.

As the assembled test group ran through these images, however, Goldsmith made several unexpected discoveries. First, the group indicated that persons with invisible disabilities like pulmonary or cardiac conditions ought to be included (Goldsmith, 1969: 20). Furthermore, although some prevaricated, Goldsmith reports that they preferred a "single symbol only to cater for all handicapped people, which would probably be a representation of a person in a wheelchair."[2] Goldsmith also found that, while he had proudly announced to the press that the signpost project would prove that there is no stigma associated with disability, some "sensitive" disabled people "do not wish to be reminded" of their disability and disliked any symbol that "focuses attention on the attributes which they are anxious to disguise" (Goldsmith, 1969: 11). Others in the group cared little about whether the symbol included a recognizable person or not, while at least one person liked the abstract symbols in use in the United States and Canada. Goldsmith treated the latter opinion as an outlier and rejected it wholesale. He explained that this point of view was advanced by a man who "had been severely handicapped since the age of two, had always displayed an aggressive attitude toward disability, was fiercely determined to operate as a normal person, and did not want to be associated with any stigmatizing emblem which advertised disability characteristics" (Goldsmith, 1969: 35). In many ways, this Norwich man was seconding the attitudes of reformers like Tim Nugent. But, according to Goldsmith's report, most of the group rejected the "secret" symbols outright. "There's no need for it to be secret," Goldsmith reports one participant stating. "There's no disgrace in being disabled" (Goldsmith, 1969: 20). Goldsmith agreed and believed an explicit symbol was the best way to make this known. But many in the test group believed that an empty wheelchair was enough, and that "the human figure was superfluous. They rejected it, not because they had any inhibitions or self-consciousness about personally associating themselves with it, but because from a practical point of view they felt that it was unnecessary" (Goldsmith, 1969: 22). This put Goldsmith in a bind, particularly because the presence of a person in the signage reflected his understanding of "positive discrimination." Ultimately, Goldsmith turned to what he called "the psychology of disablement" to deal with this.

For several years, Goldsmith had begun advancing the belief that "a pictorial symbol ... could make a valuable psychological impact on the community as a whole" (Goldsmith, 1967: 388). Of course he was not alone in this; Goldsmith's interest in the psychological aspects of disablement reflected broader trends in rehabilitation research. Indeed, as the fields of medical and vocational rehabilitation started to be infused with government funds after the Second World War, psychologists were increasingly consulted on a range of disability-related issues.[3] And so, in addition to the feedback he received from his test group of disabled people, Goldsmith consulted with a pair of authorities—two psychologists then practicing in Norwich. He was eager to find reinforcement for his idea that representing a human figure was psychologically important for a "healthy" acceptance of disability (Goldsmith, 1969: 23).

Goldsmith reports that the two local psychologists (the pair remain unidentified) each found the "without-figure" symbols "unsympathetic." Their critique was extended and troubling. One of the consultants determined that any kind of figureless symbol would be "ambiguous," "passive," and "non-informative." The other said that it was "totally negative, dead, and has no drive or motivation." Worse still, "unlike the with-figure symbol, [the empty wheelchair] will not promote positive feedback" from the general public. Instead, this expert continued, the figureless wheelchair symbol attempts "to neutralize physical handicap." They argued that it propagated the "secret" knowledge of disabled users, "and its role is thus analogous to reliance on the elimination of architectural barriers ... which also attempt to obscure disability characteristics" (Goldsmith, 1969: 23). Of course, Goldsmith had already determined to make a symbol worthy of "positive discrimination," a symbol that disabled people might identify with. And so, finding it "impossible to ignore [the] reactions" of these psychologists, he discarded the vacant wheelchair symbol (Goldsmith, 1969: 23). In his efforts to empower them, Goldsmith discounted the opinions of disabled people and considered instead what the experts, in this case psychologists, had to say.[4]

To this day, Goldsmith's methodology seems vague and how he arrived at his conclusions is sometimes elusive;[5] above all, his conclusions supported his belief that disabled persons were always in need of help. At about this time—midway through the process—he began to reconceive the program's purpose and decided to make the project something other than a "signposting system." Only rarely did disabled persons actually need directional signage, he concluded. Instead, they would benefit the most from "an information system communicating equally to the general public and the disabled people" where access—as well as helpful services like wheelchairs available on loan—could be found. Thus a single image—rather than the modular system combining different images—might work better (Tomlinson and Stevens, 1972: 110).

Once he reestablished priorities, Goldsmith returned to the project with new vigor. True, he allowed, "the whole character of the project had been radically altered" by the feedback that non-ambulatory and semi-ambulatory disabilities should be folded into a single figure; true, too, he now had to reframe expectations and accept "that the concept of a signposting system should be replaced by an advertising programme employing a symbol of group identity" (Goldsmith, 1969: 23).

But, after this initial study, Goldsmith now felt justified that he could "demonstrate the 'differentness' of disabled people, and ought not to attempt to disguise, camouflage or conceal the nature of disability or to pretend that disabled people are normal people" (Goldsmith, 1969: 24). The symbol, he insisted, could make disability visible without rendering individuals conspicuous misfits.

At the Norwich School of Art, students were given a new brief, and a submission by student Phil Bush was chosen, then developed and refined by the school's graphic design tutor, Peter Rea (Figure 4.6). It would concretize the idea of positive discrimination. Building off the Stresa and *Architects Journal* symbols, they worked with a simplified silhouette, abolishing the realistic details that Goldsmith himself described as nothing more than "fussiness" (Goldsmith, 1969: 24). This simplicity also lent the symbol a

FIGURE 4.6 In 1969 Selwyn Goldsmith, Peter Rea, and students at the Norwich School of Art finalized a symbol that depicted both crutch and wheelchair users, as well as those with pulmonary or heart conditions, 1969.

kind of "corporate identity," and could, he argued, embody an affirmative attitude toward disability itself. In a bid for inclusiveness, the symbol also comprises another man standing with a crutch. A circle in his chest is meant to symbolize cardiac and respiratory conditions. As it was, the wheelchair was reduced to a single large circle, with the figure in it slanted at a 5-degree angle "to enhance the impression that the wheelchair individual is exerting himself and is mobile rather than static" (Goldsmith, 1969: 25).

Goldsmith reported that his group of disabled interlocutors accepted the new symbol unanimously, as did the two psychologists he had consulted; with relatively little fanfare the new symbol was distributed around Norwich. But not everyone was satisfied. Some viewers were critical of its legibility. At the *Guardian* newspaper, journalists eagerly announced that several employees got hold of the Norwich symbol and conducted "a quick poll in the *Guardian* office." A total of seven people understood the Norwich symbol's significance immediately, "but the rest saw a variety of meanings in the design. These ranged from people playing stick and hoop to a man sitting in a car, and a man who has got so well after a hole in the heart operation that he is going to hit someone else with a stick" (Bendixson, 1968: 9). And yet although the *Guardian* picked at the symbol's clarity, the newspaper recognized its importance. Above all, they noted Goldsmith's insistence that the symbol should unabashedly "indicate special arrangements and special privileges for disabled people." Certainly, they acknowledged, Goldsmith wanted "to promote the status of the group" (Bendixson, 1968: 9).

Ultimately, Goldsmith's pilot project demonstrated that there are choices in representing disabled people, and these choices were shaped by more than legibility and convenience. The psychology of disability was also at play, as was a growing sense of group identity. But Goldsmith was not the only one learning these lessons. In fact, Goldsmith's signs were quickly overshadowed. At the same time, however, his ideas would persist long after the Norwich project was forgotten.

Toward a universal sign

As it was, even after taking stock of all Goldsmith's writings and research, his carefully calibrated symbols are hard to measure against Paul Arthur's almost simultaneous introduction of a wheelchair access symbol at Montreal's Expo 67 (Figure 4.7). Though the Canadian government introduced its own anonymously designed access insignia two years earlier, Arthur was the first professional designer to integrate an access symbol into a larger system of communication. But the very nature of this project was also significant. More than introducing signage for a world's fair, Arthur was sympathetic to the Expo planners' real aim—creating an ideal city. Although planned as part of this ambitious scheme, Arthur's symbol was developed and introduced rapidly; it was implemented after Goldsmith completed his research for the Norwich project, but before he wrote his final report. And though the two projects were never planned or conceived as competitors, Arthur's was better positioned for international attention. First, it received a great deal of press attention, primarily because it was part of a larger government-sponsored push to bring disabled visitors to the fair (Anon., 1967d: 12). But Expo 67 also provided something that Norwich didn't—an experimental site where the success of a coherent pictorial system was rolled out for a broader, polyglot public. And so, with the impetuousness of an outsider, Paul Arthur jumped headlong into the broader access signage debate.

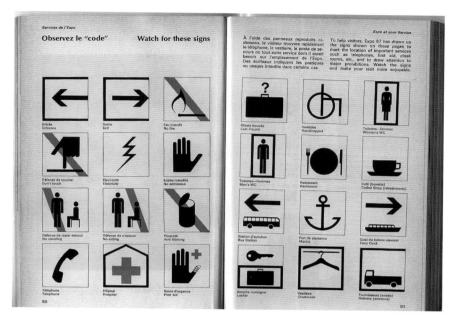

FIGURE 4.7 At Expo 67, Paul Arthur and Associates designed and issued a suite of directional symbols, including a wheelchair access sign. The groups of designs were issued to the public in a guide that urged viewers to "Observez le 'code'/Watch for these signs," 1967. From *Expo 67: guide officiel: 28 avril-27 octobre 1967, Montréal, Canada: chapitre spécial sur les fêtes du Centenaire.*

For his part, the Canadian-born Paul Arthur had been converted to the idea of universal of signs and symbols long before he joined Expo 67's design team. Arthur's seven years working as an editor in Switzerland during the mid-1950s left him well versed in Swiss multilingualism. But it also introduced him to the visual panache and universalist rhetoric of Swiss modernist typography. After returning to Canada in 1956, Arthur was credited with bringing a "European influence" back with him (Elder, 2005: 42). Stridently modernist and unflagging in his ambition, Arthur approached the fair's organizing committee on his own, after learning that the event would be held in Montreal. He presented them with a breathtakingly comprehensive directional and information signage system for the projected thousand-acre site. Arthur was lucky in finding that Expo 67's planners shared his vision. Norman Hay, for instance, coordinated design efforts at Expo 67. He was already known as "a design missionary" and celebrated for his clean, rational, and modernist work (Delaney, 1967: 21). His main goal was not merely to recruit professional designers into the project, but for a "unity" of design forms (Wainwright, 1967: 31). As the popular journal

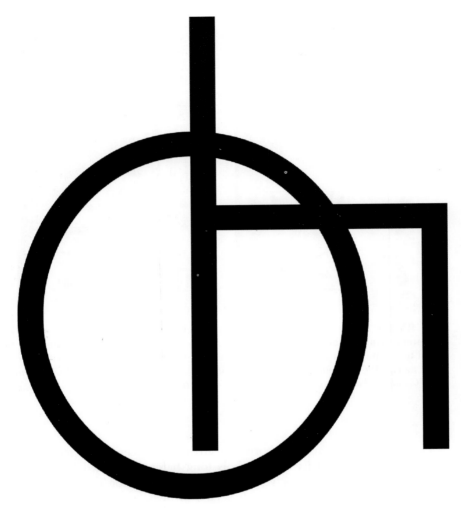

FIGURE 4.8 An abstracted depiction of a wheelchair was introduced by Paul Arthur & Associates for Expo 67's signage system, 1967.

Saturday Night gushed at the time, "Expo has developed a totally unified system of design that covers everything from wastepaper baskets to signs telling you where to park your yacht" (Delaney, 1967: 23).

For his part, Paul Arthur didn't aim to reach a yacht-owning elite; he wanted to create signage that was unified, but also legible. According to him, "A good symbol must be concise and simple, its form must be easy to understand and easy to remember" (Arthur & Associates, n.d.: 10). To develop symbols for the Montreal fair he sought feedback from experts, including Martin Krampen, a semiotician and professor at Michigan State University who had studied at Germany's renowned Hochschule fur Gestaltung in Ulm. Imbued with the school's rationalist ideology, Krampen argued that symbols should be created through a scientific method that identified a "common stock of signs" that would clearly be understood by both "sender" and "receiver" (Baker, 2011: 42). At Expo 67, Arthur applied these principles; by taking a more precise approach, he aimed for more than simply covering signs with words. "Typographic messages," Arthur insisted, "should be used when all other visual communication are inadequate" (Arthur, 1967: 50). Communications, he rationalized, are based on mutually agreed-upon conventions. They operate as a system of sounds and forms that could unify cities, regions, or countries. Symbols could be used to calm misunderstandings between nations, to facilitate the movement of goods, and to assist and advise both strangers and residents of vast cities.

With this in mind, Arthur and Associates quickly rejected the Canadian government's access insignia by simply arguing that "as this was an international exposition, Expo graphics had to conform to international standards and the existing symbol did not meet those standards" (Canadian Corporation for the 1967 World Exhibition, 1969: 2074). In fact, the Canadian symbol—like the New York State symbol and other abstracting access signage—was utterly out of step with the advice given by communications experts at the time: international signage, they urged, should be consistent with other symbols in use and also a degree of "recognizability."[6] By the time that was done, the Expo 67 access symbol bore no resemblance to its government-decreed counterpart (Figure 4.8). Where the Canadian Building Code insignia was completely abstract, Arthur's pictogram is representational, literally depicting a schematic wheel and stylized chair.

In effect, both Arthur and Goldsmith were astute enough to realize that the wheel was crucial to redefining modern mobility, and both build their symbols off it. Arthur and his team did not, however, aim to humanize their symbol. Nor is there evidence that they considered Goldsmith's reading and discussions of "the psychology of disablement." Instead, they developed a symbol reducible to logical, easily understood parts. Arthur may have been visually summarizing Krampen's arguments, but his symbol draws from commonly used verbal expressions found in multiple languages (Bakker, 2013: 43, 44). And so, in spite of Arthur's desire for nonverbal communication, the Expo 67 access symbol continues to reference words, albeit ones that exist in both English and French: it takes the word "wheel" or "rollant" and "chair" or "fauteuil" and presents a graphic form for each. Of course, this does not make for legibility at a global scale. Not all countries used the word "wheelchair" (nor, for that matter, were wheelchairs commonplace worldwide). But this approach was consistent with the broader system of geometric symbols that Arthur and Associates introduced at Expo 67. From their point of view, the brief was simple: to develop a series of forms capable of reducing a range of visitor services to pictures (Figure 4.7). A stylized square with triangle on top and red cross within, for example, marked the location of hospital services, a phone handset identified a telephone booth, and a simple cup stood in for a coffee shop. Parts of human bodies, like a raised hand, might indicate "stop." Alternately, the symbol for a first aid station was a hand with a bandaged thumb. All symbols were placed in a grid and mounted on signs. Directions were ordered by combining these pictograms with simple arrows. By the late 1960s, many designers agreed with Arthur—coherent systems of communication like this would lead to a more rational world.

Although Arthur could carefully justify this method, there is also something immensely conciliatory about his approach. It speaks to Canadian politics at the time, and stretches beyond the issue of multilingualism. Beginning in the 1920s, Canada's federal government began to create and administer a series of social programs. By the mid-1960s, Canada was unfolding its own version of a welfare state, covering employment insurance, family allowances, old-age pensions, and hospital and medical insurance; in many ways, these changes echoed those implemented in the European welfare states for the purpose of increasing social services. Expo 67 was originally planned to mark the centenary of the Canadian confederation; the writer Robert Fulford called it "the greatest birthday party in history" (Fulford, 1968: 201). But it was also meant to bolster national unity and advertise the nation's successes. For both Canadians and the world, Expo 67 represented, as historian Gary Miedema puts it, "a Canada that emphasized inclusion, not exclusion; impartiality, not ethnic or religious prejudice; unity and cooperation, not separation and division" (Miedema, 2005: 114). This vision also meant to include—but not highlight—disability. When integrated within a larger system of signage, the access symbol seems dispassionate and routine.

Just as Arthur created a disability symbol that fit within a larger design vocabulary, so too did fair overseers integrate access into the fair's most fundamental planning. Expo 67 made clear to even a casual observer that organizers had rolled "out the red carpet for handicapped visitors" (Saxton, 1967: 13). They aimed at 80 percent accessibility for visitors in wheelchairs. To achieve this, they distributed copies of the Canadian building code to all builders involved, and strongly encouraged pavilion planners to follow it (Francke and Francke, 1967: xxii); even seemingly inaccessible exhibits, like the Pavilion of Guyana and Barbados, didn't daunt visitors (Figure 4.9).

But most exhibits included a variety of accommodations and these were widely noted. And, a journalist at the time reported, the provisions drew "wide admiration." Fair organizers even had a special coordinator who led a small army of volunteers, "made up of Boy Scouts and women, many of them housewives, helping out on a rotating basis" (Anon., 1967b: 12). Some manned "La Balade," a special trackless train that provided transport around the park, while others served as escorts for disabled people. Working off the premise that there is no stigma to being disabled, planners

FIGURE 4.9 A wheelchair user passes in front of the Pavilion of Guyana and Barbados, Expo 67, 1967. © National Archives of Canada.

also installed special ramps, elevators, and transportation all reserved for wheelchair users. At popular exhibits, special privileges were given. For example, wheelchair users always went to the front of the line. At a public event where, as one disabled reporter explained, the "waiting time outside the better exhibits ranges from one to six hours (that's right—SIX hours— and sometimes in the rain) ... the privilege of going right into the exhibit halls turns the fair from a vast waiting room into a wonder land" (Anon., 1967e: 75). Taken as a whole, a different wheelchair user testified, Expo 67 was "much easier than negotiating any normal urban district of comparable size" (Compton, 1967: 39). By September 9, 1967, some 16,000 disabled people had officially visited the Expo (Anon., 1967b: 12). And yet, by the time the fair closed a month later, it recorded some 50 million visits. This does not imply that organizers efforts were in vain. By the standards of the day, its acknowledgment of disabled needs was forward looking; the impact of its design continued long after "La Balade" stopped running, and its Boy Scout guides went home. Arthur's wheelchair symbol was widely aired; in an October article on the fair's disabled access, for instance, the *New York Times* accompanied the feature with a depiction of the symbol itself. It was beginning to make visible a much larger—and hidden—problem.

That same success can't be applied to the rest of Arthur's Expo 67 pictograms. Most visitors were accustomed to a ragbag of public signage;

traditionally, North American signs were casually conceived and almost exclusively verbal. Arthur's pictograms were a new idea. Some visitors recognized in them a cheery echo of the contemporary art that sprinkled the fair grounds. Robert Fulford observed that "the Pop and Op art signs for things like hot dogs and souvenir stands ... became a kind of signature, a part of the mood of the place" (Fulford, 1968: 74). When Arthur's team introduced a system of animal silhouettes to appear on signs in the parking lot, all to help visitors remember where they'd left their car, many fair-goers were delighted (Figure 4.10). But some visitors were also mystified. In a few instances, illegibility generated multilingual confusion. Recounted by an Expo historian, Yves Jasmin, "One American visitor grew angry after asking an Expo employee to explain her animal symbol to her. As it happened, the symbol denoted a seal, and seal in French is phoque. The employee obliged but evidently forgot to translate. 'Madame,' he said, 'c'est un phoque.' The visitor gave him a hard slap across the face" (Yves Jasmin, 1997: 69). Instances like this suggest that in spite of Expo 67's utopian goals, the project of realizing a "universally legible" visual language was difficult.

Confusion was only exacerbated by symbols that represented human figures. Although almost universally understood today, Arthur used silhouettes to distinguish between men and women for washroom signage. There was precedent for this—pictograms differentiating men and women were first introduced at the 1964 Tokyo Olympics with little fanfare. Nevertheless, it was a novelty for North American audiences. Arthur's pictograms featured men in trousers, and women in skirts (their silhouette vaguely resembled the modest stewardess-like uniforms of Expo 67's own hostesses). But many found their space-age sheaths hard to read. Toronto's *Globe and Mail* almost gleefully reported that "Expo officials kept encountering that worried women [*sic*] who trotted nervously up to a restroom door, examined the pictograph with some puzzlement, reached for a handle, then retreated in blushing confusion as men appeared from inside" (Plumptre, 1967). In fact, as *Time* magazine reported, "The sophisticated silhouette pictograms intended to point the path to the lavatories were so esoteric that many people could not tell what they were, managed to find washrooms only after many desperate queries" (Anon., 1967a: 70).

Given the confusion around the pictograms featuring human figures, perhaps it is best that Arthur never even attempted to place a person in his wheelchair silhouette. But, when Selwyn Goldsmith saw the Expo 67 symbol, he remained deeply unsatisfied. When he looked at it in detail, he acknowledged that "aesthetically it is more successful than the official Canadian symbol" (Goldsmith, 1969: 10). And this was all very nice, he argued, but it was still too abstract. To Goldsmith's eye, the Expo 67 symbol remained too imprecise and "would be unlikely to be interpreted correctly by the uninitiated lay observer" (Goldsmith, 1969: 10).

FIGURE 4.10 Pictograms designed by Paul Arthur and Associates for parking at Expo 67, 1967. Courtesy of Royal Ontario Museum.

Goldsmith would later speculate that "Had the expo symbol been given the opportunity to obtain general adoption, it could have become widely accepted" (Goldsmith, 1969: 10). Arthur and the other representatives from the Expo 67 Design division actually did try to introduce their design beyond the precincts of Montreal's fairground. After their initial pictograms were drafted, Arthur and several other designers traveled to Ottawa in June 1966 to meet with Canada's Committee on Building Standards for the Handicapped; they hoped that the Expo wheelchair symbol might be adopted in place of the Canadian government's 1965 insignia. On arriving, they were told that many committee members actually "acknowledged that the [Expo 67] proposal was superior" (General Report, 1969: 2074). Like overburdened bureaucrats, however, the Ottawa government felt overcommitted to the 1965 insignia—it had already been published widely and could not be changed. In the end, Arthur's team learned a lesson. It is not enough to merely design a symbol; clearly, there had to be widespread institutional support for it as well. Similar bureaucratic pressures must be acknowledged. But at the same time, something else was becoming clear. Someone somewhere had to exert some kind of larger authority that transcended individual governments; the sheer multiplicity of access symbols at this point was becoming confusing.

Notes

1 The main change was that the figure was now made gender-neutral.

2 Goldsmith is not clear about the nature of this prevarication. At best, he asserts that all preferred a single symbol at first, but when presented with information that indicated how different disabilities call for different accommodations, he claims that the group changed its collective mind. He notes that later in the meeting, they revisited the question, and—although he does not explain why—they returned to their earlier opinion (that one symbol should stand in for all) (Goldsmith, 1969: 22).

3 After the First World War, the situation for impaired veterans returning home was different. There was a high casualty rate and seriously disabled soldiers had lower longevity rates. After the Second World War, many more survived. More and more psychologists recognized this and began working in the field. We can chart this rise with the flourishing of several international graduate rehabilitation psychology programs (Wright, 1989, 1993) as well as the founding of a number of professional organizations. These included, for instance, founding a special interest group within the American Psychological Association (APA) in 1949, which later became the National Council on Psychological Aspects of Physical Disability in 1958, and then the Division of Psychological Aspects of Disability in 1958.

4 Already in the UK, there were voices from within the disabled community who spoke up against the idea of the psychology of disablement. Speaking at a 1964 symposium, The Wheelchair: The User's Viewpoint, the founder and president of the UK-based Invalid Tricycle Association noted,

As one who goes about his daily life in a wheelchair I expect my chair to be strictly functional, and I am not so concerned with the appearance of the chair or the effect it has on others … I am delighted that this morning's panel of speakers does not include a psychologist to enlarge upon wheelchairs that scream "disablement," and the effect they have on wheelchair users, who either regress to dependent childhood patterns and demand help on all occasions, or become irascible and aggressive, refusing to accept any sort of help. (Denly, 1964: 42)

5 The main account of this process remains Goldsmith's own 1969 book as well as an article by Tomlinson and Stevens, written in 1972. Both leave holes in their discussion, particularly as they report the feedback from the test groups of disabled users.

6 The problem of forming an international system of signage was under extensive discussion at this time, especially in graphic design circles. (For more on this see Bakker, 2013.)

5

A Design for the Real World?
(1968–1974)

Sunday morning, July 28, 1968, readers of Sweden's biggest newspaper, *Dagens Nyheter*, opened the weekend edition to find a full-page, centerfold spread that showed a man in a wheelchair falling down a subway staircase. Directly below that alarming image, readers were confronted with the provocative question, "Is there democracy for wheelchair users?" ("Miljö för alla?" or "Is the environment for everybody?") (Anon., 1968c; 4)

That same morning, art students were gathering at Stockholm's prestigious school Konstfack, taking time out from vacation to attend a radical, two-week-long summer seminar. They, too, were asking if democracy could truly accommodate its disabled citizens. And so, too, just 20 minutes to the north, in the leafy suburb of Bromma, the same question was being chewed over at the new Institute for the Handicapped, a government-funded institution that had opened its doors just four weeks earlier. This highly focused interest in the intersection of design, disability, and social justice that summer in Stockholm led to the earliest iteration of the access symbol. It was so influential that it is still used today (Figure 5.1).

By 1968, as the barrier-free access movement had spread across Europe and North America, it prompted a deeper reckoning of ideas of citizenship. This also led to a proliferation of access symbols. Some were abstract, some descriptive, some used wheels, while others showed wheelchairs, people in wheelchairs, and others still represented persons using canes. Some were intended as wayfinding, that is, to guide people by helping them find accessible routes to where they wanted to go. Others were intended to label accommodations. In the face of this variety, Norman Acton, Secretary-General of the charitable organization Rehabilitation International (RI), would later recall, "a number of different symbols were beginning to appear and several of us could see a messy situation" (Groce, 2002: 52).

Taking into account the proliferation of interest in acknowledging and accommodating disability, it is perhaps surprising that no universal approach

FIGURE 5.1 An abstracted wheelchair served as the basis for the access symbol designed by Susanne Koefoed at a 1968 summer seminar organized by the pan-Scandinavian Design Students (SDO). The meeting was held at Konstfack in Stockholm in July of that year, 1968.

toward access had yet developed. But professional graphic designers began engaging ideas around access, disability, and their relevance to design only in the late 1960s. At Expo 67, Paul Arthur introduced an access symbol that was part of a larger communications system. The next year, a variation on that symbol was developed by students in Sweden, under the influence of designer and critic Victor Papanek. Responding to this cacophony of signage, in 1968 Rehabilitation International (RI) stepped forward to develop a single symbol. This long-standing charitable organization was founded in 1922 as the International Society for Crippled Children.[1] To date, it focused largely on educational and employment efforts for disabled persons.[2] Nevertheless, the symbol project was prioritized and pushed quickly through the organization. The final design incorporated a series of unacknowledged, but implicit, tensions, but it was heavily promoted by RI and quickly accepted internationally; it was officially accepted by the United Nations in 1974.

This, of course, is the symbol still in use today. Few observers realize it, but today's wheelchair figure represents a rough and sometimes contentious compromise. Acton authorized a committee within RI, the International Commission for Technical Aids (ICTA), to rapidly develop an official International Symbol of Access (ISA) that could be presented at the group's 1969 World Congress. The resulting image—essentially a schematic wheelchair with a circular "head" placed on its back—unwittingly embodies a series of culture clashes; first and foremost it awkwardly expresses a conflict between the goals of the student-activist designers who authored the symbol, and the long-standing and rather conservative organization promoting its use. A Danish design student—Susanne Koefoed—may have developed the original, but before it was introduced at the 1969 Dublin conference, her figure got a curious refitting. Koefoed's empty wheelchair design was "fitted" at the last minute with a "head" or circle added to it. This change is unintentionally provocative. The urgent question of access, it suggests, is bound in conflicting social priorities and practices. Nevertheless, when the loosely organized but sprawling Rehabilitation International adopted it, the symbol was rapidly implemented on a global scale. In this sense, the wheelchair figure is itself a compromise between the "real world," and the ideals that it represents.

A technical aid

In order to clean up the chaos created by multiple access symbols, Acton turned to Karl Montan, a Swedish bureaucrat who headed the ICTA. A serious and level-headed bureaucrat, Montan's life work was developing better medical and technical aids for disabled people. As a thinker, Montan often provided modest answers to modest questions. His genius lay in navigating entrenched bureaucracy while also creating change. By the summer of 1968, after persistent lobbying by Montan on behalf of the Swedish Central Committee for Rehabilitation (SVCR), the government created the Swedish Institute for the Handicapped. The latter group was tasked with research and development of technical aids for disabled people, as well as their testing and marketing. With Montan at its head, the institution would become an influential organization for years to come.

But Montan's engagement with issues of disability was both professional and deeply personal. Montan identified instinctively with disabled persons. At age 11, he was involved in a tram accident in his native Helsingborg, Sweden, and had a midfoot amputation. Drawing on what he called "lifelong experience," he would later profess "a sincere interest to find an optimal medical and technical service both for myself and the disabled" (Montan, 2000: 85). Montan focused his early career on the development of prosthetics, but gradually got more and more involved in administering services for disabled people on a national and international scale. In the early 1950s, for example, he became active in Rehabilitation International, and beginning in 1951, he served as the official secretary at the Fifth World Congress of Rehabilitation International held in Stockholm. Montan easily fit in, negotiating between engineers and doctors, bureaucrats and government ministers. Throughout his career, Montan maintained a strong interest in rehabilitation engineering, and most notably in prosthetics and orthotics; his was a deep lifetime engagement with what he called "technical services," as well as evaluating their "shortcomings and successes" (Montan, 2000: 85).

But Montan was more than a specialist in prosthetics. Over time, he also became deeply enmeshed in a drive to bring disability to the attention of Sweden's growing social welfare initiatives. He was aided in this pursuit by the fundamental ideology that motivated Selwyn Goldsmith as well— the promise of equality and societal support for all. In fact, by the late 1960s, Sweden was considered a leader within "the Scandinavian model" of postwar state support delivered to those with physical and mental impairments. In the two decades between 1951 and 1971, the amount of money the government dedicated to these projects grew by more than 450 percent (Montan, 1974: 103). This growth reflects, in part, the country's deeper and deeper engagement with the social welfare of all its citizens. But it also reflects the highly effective lobbying of bureaucrats like Montan and the work done by the Institute he founded in 1968. Of course, policies and programs intended to benefit disabled people weren't entirely new. As early as the 1950s, adapted housing was being designed for wheelchair users. Beginning in 1964, the Swedish Fokus Society, a nonprofit organization funded by the Swedish government, began to provide disabled people with barrier-free apartments, as well as environmental and technical aids. Local governments also began to provide disabled people with health services and regional medical and social centers.

In many ways, Montan's Institute for the Handicapped was itself deeply enmeshed in the politics of the Swedish state. It was formed specifically to carry out oversight, and tasked with developing and distributing technical aids for the physically impaired. Reporting directly to the Swedish Parliament, the Institute was meant to operate largely as a central coordinating agency, but also conducted basic research (Montan, 1974). Technical aids for disabled people were, at least in principle, free to all individuals, as was their maintenance and repair. But a bureaucratic organization like the Institute, the reasoning went, was necessary in order to "observe developments in the field," as well as to test and distribute them to the public (Montan, 1974: 4).

The Swedish Institute for the Handicapped was deeply enmeshed in a wide range of technical aids and assistive devices designed to help disabled people negotiate a world not built for them. Considered within this context, a symbol meant to guide the mobility impaired to accommodations was less a piece of graphic design than it was a technical aid akin to hearing aids and prostheses. All three attempt to integrate disabled people into the physical world around them. They also evince the Swedish government's serious and strong mandate to help disabled people. From Norman Acton's point of view, selecting Montan to determine the first international access symbol must have seemed straightforward enough: Montan was to act as a bureaucrat, a man capable of marshaling and coordinating design experts, helping them shape a technical aid.

But the status of graphic design and its very conceptualization was also beginning to shift during this period. By the 1960s, designers were laying claim to their proficiency and technical knowledge; they were more than commercial artists. The International Council of Graphic Design Associations (ICOGRADA), established in London in 1963, clearly staked out a professional space as experts in the field, arguing that symbols in the public space should aspire to a degree of clear, visual coherence (Baker, 2011: 39). The group strove "to encourage the better use of graphic design as a means toward the advancement of humanity," and to "raise the standards of graphic design and the professional status of graphic designers" (Middleton, 1963: 12). Many people in architecture and design, as well as government, began to listen. In fact, Paul Arthur's success at Expo 67 indicates the rising professional profile of designers in organizing public information symbols.

At the same time, neither Montan nor Acton knew much about this, nor about graphics more generally. That is not to say that either man was incapable of understanding the power of graphic design nor intuiting the multiple meanings foisted on visual forms; but the development of technical aids and the design of graphic imagery were generally recognized as distinct endeavors that, for reasons of time, effort, or training, were difficult to balance. Furthermore, neither man fully grasped the extent to which Swedish design in particular was undergoing a period of soul searching and experiencing a groundswell of change.

Man and the environment

This groundswell of interest in design for disability represents a clear and significant shift in the discourse around Scandinavian design. After an initial flush of postwar enthusiasm for furniture, clothing, and other consumer items, by the mid-1960s the taste for Scandinavian design was fading as patterns of consumption changed (Fallan, 2011; Lie, 2014). Many were beginning to question the character of "Nordic design." This included the pan-Scandinavian student design organization or SDO, an activist group founded in February 1966 at a Stockholm meeting of student council representatives from a number of different design programs in Scandinavia.[3] The group pushed for a radical rethinking of design curricula in schools, aiming to introduce more activist, anti-consumerist models and theories into the academy (for more on these activities at Konstfack, see Widengren 1994). But they also wanted to develop practical solutions. To this end, in the late 1960s they sponsored a series of annual summer seminars intended to supplement teaching at conventional design schools.[4] Led by forward-thinking designers and theorists like Buckminster Fuller, the seminars were marked by talks and also workshops that took up social issues. And it was here, during the 1968 seminar held at Konstfack in Stockholm, that the access symbol came into being.

The SDO's 1968 Konstfack seminar seemed to reverberate with a kind of electric charge felt around the city that summer. Victor Papanek, the charismatic American design educator and reformer, set the tone for the conference; almost immediately after arriving, he transfixed students and the Stockholm design press alike. *Dagens Nyheter*'s design and fashion correspondent Rebecka Tarschys interviewed Papanek shortly after he arrived in Stockholm, and introduced him to her readers as a design "prophet" (Tarschys, 1968: 7). Voluble and clearly excited by a recent visit to Finland, Papanek told Tarschys about the portable play space for children with cerebral palsy that he helped innovate there. Papanek even gave the paper a photo of this portable gym, which Tarschys' editor chose to run alongside the interview. Prior to this interview, Tarschys' writings focused on couture dress. But the interview with Papanek prompted the paper to publish its unflinching expose on the state of access and disability in Stockholm soon after (Anon., 1968c: 4). At a moment when the Swedish state was rapidly increasing its commitment to aid people with disabilities, and when Karl Montan was establishing a government-funded institute devoted to the needs of disabled people, the timing could not have been better.

At the SDO's Konstfack seminar, Papanek was one of a number of speakers invited to lecture on the theme of "Man and the Environment." The roster of speakers focused on constituencies overlooked by commercial design, including developing countries, medical patients, and the poor. Different than in their regular classes, students looked to radicals like Che Guevara for inspiration, and sought activist approaches to shape their work. But to solve practical design problems, the assembled students also split into smaller groups to work on practical projects revolving around six working themes: morally and socially responsible design, housing, communications, the environment, and disability. In many ways, the multilingual, multinational SDO event was the perfect place to develop an international symbol.

The focus of the group working on disability was carefully delineated from the outset. In its early publicity for the event, SDO organizers described their object in great detail, promising that this "team" would work to produce a variety of "clothing and technical aids" (Anon., 1968b: 323). They expected the students who eventually enrolled in this group to come from a variety of backgrounds and, the SDO coordinators stressed, they were expected to draw on their respective areas of expertise. Those studying textile design, for example, were asked to create clothes that could be easily worn and removed by disabled people. Furniture design students would work on a line of furnishings and fixtures accessible to wheelchair users. Industrial design students were asked to create kitchen utensils that were easy to hold and use. For a radical student-run workshop, the SDO's disability group was pointedly practical in its focus.

In fact, this was not the first time design and disability had been discussed at Konstfack. Several months earlier, Montan had participated in a three-day seminar on the theme "Design for Disabled Children." Participants included psychological and ergonomic experts as well as several private groups, including Montan's SVCR (Swedish Central Committee of Rehabilitation). Of course, the character of the SDO and Montan's Institute could not have been more different. The Handicap Institute was a government-funded organization, while the SDO was a scrappy start-up that characterized itself as a radical group formed in opposition to formal educational and bureaucratic structures. (By the following year, at the 1969 meeting in Copenhagen, the student group collapsed under accusations that it was "an inefficient organization with neither objective nor a long-term program" [Lundahl, 1969: 372].) But the SDO seminar's emphasis on the development of "technical aids" for disabled people echoes Montan's broader project. This focus helped the Konstfack group coalesce. Very rapidly, and of their own volition, the student group moved to approach the problem that Montan had only recently been assigned by Norman Acton— access and signage.

The SDO's 1968 working group on disability had its own tensions, but it was also more productive than most of the other workshops held that summer. When *FORM* magazine sent a correspondent to "Man and the Environment," the reporter found that most of the discussion remained "abstract, utopian and inclusive" (Anon., 1968b: 323). As it came to actual practice, however, things became more diffuse. The reporter observed that the members of the Communications group, for example, spent much of their time arguing. With "major differences in educational background, social aims, awareness of social roles," the participants struggled to find common ground (Anon., 1968b: 323). Meanwhile, *FORM* magazine reported, the students in the disability workshop watched several educational films about disability, and dismissed them as too optimistic in outlook. The students rapidly moved to a broader and more critical discussion, and experts—including a psychologist, a doctor, and an industrial designer, as well as a disability consultant—not only joined them, but also introduced them to recent work on access and signage. Norwegian sociologist and educator Olav Dalland also recalls intense sessions of sharing. At one point he described his evening job as an attendant at a rehabilitation clinic. He outlined for the group just "how complicated it was to take disabled people to a shopping center, a cinema, a theater or a restaurant. At the opera we had to use the lift behind the stage" (Dalland, 2014). Similar personal experiences were incorporated into the discussion, as was the need for coherent signage that could direct people to hidden accommodations.

With their focus on tangible results, the group kept returning to the problem of access and technical aids. Dalland recalls Danish graphic design student Susanne Koefoed "drawing sketches" during their sessions (Dalland, 2014), and soon she asked to work with another student to develop some kind of symbol that would quickly identify wheelchair access. Enrolled at the time in Copenhagen's Art Industrial School for Women (later to become the Danish Design School), Koefoed was one of the few in the group who specialized in graphics. As she recalled later, the girl Koefoed was assigned to work with became ill, and Koefoed "had to create a solution alone. Very quickly I got the idea for the sign/symbol" of the wheelchair (Koefoed, 2012) (Figure 5.2).

FIGURE 5.2 Poster created by Susanne Koefoed (and others) for an art exhibition held at Konstfack at the end of a summer seminar held by the pan-Scandinavian Design Students (SDO), 1968. Courtesy Veryday.

In the end, Koefoed's symbol was hardly unique. Because wheelchairs were still so new, and since they encountered so many barriers in the built environment, they were already represented on the proposed signage introduced by Selwyn Goldsmith and Paul Arthur. Koefoed's symbol was, however, closer to Arthur's than to Goldsmith's. Introduced just one year earlier, Paul Arthur's wheelchair symbol for the 1967 Montreal Expo was widely publicized at the time. Koefoed's solution bears at least a passing resemblance to that symbol—a schematic depiction of a simple wheelchair. Both Koefoed and Arthur ignored the older "trike" wheelchairs (with two big wheels in front a small one in the back) and focused on the skeletal structure that to this day defines the modern wheelchair. Like Arthur's image, Koefoed's figure is dominated by a large rear wheel (the hallmark of modern folding wheelchairs). And both combine the wheel with a structured seat, legs, and upright back. But with its clearly articulated seat and back, as well as its foot and armrest, the Koefoed chair symbol is more legible. Furthermore, Koefoed's design simplifies the chair form even more than Arthur's, and placed the chair's back and leg rest at a slight slant. Finally, in a more realistic depiction of a wheelchair, it also includes the armrest and footrest common to most modern wheelchairs.

Koefoed sketched the symbol on her own, presented it to the disability and design group and then, in her own words, "cleaned it up" (Koefoed, 2012). The chair image was highlighted at a final exhibition at Konstfack, mounted at the end of the SDO seminar's final day. Drawn on a hastily prepared poster, the presentation embodies the radical, activist nature of the SDO seminars themselves. Despite its later significance, the chair is nearly upstaged by the slogans around it. Shunted to one corner, the wheelchair symbol pictured next to the handwritten question "VAR FINNS ENTOALETT JAG KAN ANVÄNDA?" ("Where can I find a toilet?"). Considering the institutional power that it would soon carry, the scrappy, improvisational nature of Koefoed's symbol is all the more striking (Figure 5.2).

Koefoed's design began receiving widespread attention in Sweden almost immediately, and was featured prominently in *FORM*'s December 1968 special issue on "Living with Disability." Koefoed's symbol appeared on the journal's cover (Figure 5.3), and was then used again to illustrate the editors' opening statements. And yet, even as the symbol was being endorsed in the popular media, behind the scenes some were angling to alter it. Ultimately, it was a variation on Koefoed's design that was finally accepted by rehabilitation professionals worldwide.

A misfit head

In 1969, Rehabilitation International unveiled an access symbol at their World Congress in Dublin. The icon was based on Koefoed's design, but it had been subtly altered in a significant way. A small circle had been added to

FIGURE 5.3 The wheelchair symbol created by Susanne Koefoed in 1968 appeared on the cover of Svensk *FORM* magazine later that year, 1968. Courtesy Swedish Design/Centre for Business History.

Koefoed's image of a wheelchair. Depicting a side view of the wheelchair, and elegantly linking the wheel with armrest, Koefoed had introduced a carefully calibrated pictogram. Encompassed in a single line, too, the chair back, seat, and leg rest articulated a simple and direct symbol. Small as the change may seem, setting a circle atop the chair's back made the wheelchair into a person.

As Koefoed relates the story, she had nothing to do with this change (Koefoed, 2012). In fact, once the SDO's Konstfack summer seminar ended, she was never told that the symbol was entered into Rehabilitation International's competition. According to Rehabilitation International's own records, Koefoed's symbol was presented to an international jury of nine professionals, and selected from a field of six entries, all of which were already in use.[5] Alongside the Koefoed symbol were two Canadian candidates— Paul Arthur's design for Expo 67 and the 1965 access code insignia; two American entries—the New York parks symbol and a variant submitted by a Pennsylvania-based organization, Open Doors for the Handicapped; and, finally, Goldsmith's Norwich design. The group chose the Swedish entry, but its acceptance was provisional; Karl Montan, committee chair, suggested that a head be added (ICTA, 1969; Ben-Moshe and Powell, 2007: 492).

Montan's addition was officially explained as an act of simple, bureaucratic pragmatism. In its official report, the competition committee expressed concern that Koefoed's original icon was too abstract. The problem, they suggested, was "the equally thick lines," which "may give an impression of a monogram of letters." In response to this, which Montan deemed but "a slight inconvenience," he added the circle (ICTA, 1969). In his stolid march through the committee proceedings, Montan's intervention is significant. He is, in effect, the uncredited coauthor of this landmark design. And, through it all, it is important to remember that Montan's engagement with issues of disability was deeply personal. An amputee, Montan himself used a prosthetic foot. But he was also a specialist in technical aids for others, specifically specializing in the fitting of prosthetics and orthotics. Much of his career was spent researching and developing arms and legs, hands, and feet—all meant to be assistive devices for impaired bodies. Of course, he'd never before developed a prosthetic head. But, by choosing to change the wheelchair—effectively adding an appendage to it—he essentially added a prosthetic to the graphic symbol in question. Indeed, if we follow one line of thinking to its logical end, disability itself can be cured by simply adding something on and making up for a perceived lack or deviance from normality. Essentially, he created a design misfit.

For those who argued for the professional integrity of the field, Montan's design intervention seemed hubristic. With the insertion of that small circle, systems of graphic rationality clash with the more emotive realm of human identity, and practical needs run up against idealized design conventions. Koefoed's earlier, starkly schematic form speaks the language of international modernism. But the circle on its top subtly changed its formal impact and the geometric harmonies implicit in the original figure. The new "head" is disproportionately small when compared to the rest of the "body," and it rests awkwardly forward atop the wheelchair itself. By adding the circle, Montan also forces viewers to reconceive the rest of the wheelchair shape. The footrest becomes a foot, and the leg support reads as a lower limb. Nevertheless, if the armrest becomes an arm, it has no hand to balance the foot. Not only does the final iteration compromise the integrity of Koefoed's original design, it also represents a compromise between a series of formal questions and the desire to "humanize" the figure, giving it social and psychological resonance. In the end, it's neither an abstracted symbol of the idea of access, nor is it an entirely recognizably human figure.

Koefoed has largely been forgotten as the designer of this symbol. Though she received an award "for inspired leadership and outstanding achievement on behalf of the handicapped around the world," at Rehabilitation International's 17th World Congress, held years later, in 1992 (Rehabilitation International, 1993: 45), the symbol is typically identified with RI. This is not only because of Montan's amendment to Koefoed's design. It also owes to the fact that RI was uniquely positioned to promote the wheelchair figure on a global stage. And, as it turned out, developing an international icon of access started, rather than ended, the process of introducing barrier-free architecture worldwide.

A positive step forward

In April 1970, Norman Acton announced that this would be "The Decade of Rehabilitation." In the London-based *Guardian*, he wrote that society must "awaken rising public interest in the growing problems of disability and in the economic and social advantages of solving them" (Acton, 1970: 17). He anticipated that Rehabilitation International would lead the way. In some ways—most notably the acceptance of RI's new symbol of access—he was right. Times were changing. But this was not entirely as Acton had envisioned them. Rather than characterizing the new decade as one of rehabilitation (a notion that was increasingly under fire), he should have predicted that the 1970s would be the decade of the ISA. The symbol rapidly gained credence and visibility worldwide. When the Canadian Rehabilitation Journal introduced it to a disabled audience in Canada, they unironically called it a "positive *step* forward" [italics mine] (Anon., 1970a: 6). Ultimately, the symbol took on a life of its own, becoming an object of identity, especially for persons active in the Disability Rights Movement. It began to evolve far beyond what Acton, Goldsmith, or any other early proponents could possibly have imagined.

When the symbol—and the structural changes for access that it represented—first appeared, many people who knew nothing about disability took note. In the years immediately after its introduction, the ISA was more and more embraced as a success. From Braille numbers on office elevators, hearing aids on public telephones, as well as wheelchair ramps and curb cuts, the idea of disabled accommodations gained currency through the 1970s. Moreover, in tiny, far-flung towns across the United States and Europe, the ISA spoke to a linked world of access.

However, not everyone accepted the symbol. Key figures in the design community objected to it. Peter Kneebone of the professional group

ICOGRADA immediately registered the profound design "misfit" of the head, remarking on "the wrongness" of the symbol and the method in which it was designed. In the long run, he believed that "the situation is sad" (Kneebone, 1969: 73). Selwyn Goldsmith called it "a crude device with none of the graphic merit" of Koefoed's original (Goldsmith, 1969a: 45). It's difficult, of course, to evaluate the sincerity of this critique, and to what extent it was motivated by the hope of having one of his own designs adopted in its stead. In fact, even after Rehabilitation International announced its acceptance and promotion of the new, "universal" symbol, designers continued to introduce new symbols. Only in 1969, with the publication of his *A Symbol for Disabled People* (Goldsmith, 1969b), did Selwyn Goldsmith, for example, unveil his final version of a symbol. Goldsmith's symbol had the advantage of being based on the laborious user-based studies he had already conducted in Norwich from 1967 to 1968. And yet, he lacked the backing of Rehabilitation International and his symbol was quickly forgotten.

After introducing the wheelchair figure in Dublin, Rehabilitation International pledged to do "everything possible" to get the word out (Anon., 1970a: 6); in so doing, it effectively pushed aside all other claimants. The successful adoption of this symbol internationally rests almost entirely on RI's global ties and persistent advocacy. The group leaned on its professional authority and its network of affiliated organizations worldwide. From Delhi to Helsinki, RI instructed its regional partners to make copies of the symbol available to the press and television networks. RI also recommended to its affiliates that they provide it to architects, town planners, and others interested in using the symbol. Many countries mounted a national accessibility campaign through their branch of the international Red Cross. In Belgium, for example, the group sent thousands of questionnaires in French and Flemish to provincial, postal, and tourist offices, asking them to self-evaluate their accessibility. ISA decals were awarded to those meeting minimal criteria (International Society for Rehabilitation of the Disabled, 1975: 11).

The symbol was also promoted widely in American and British professional rehabilitation, nursing, and medical journals like *Nursing Times* (Anon., 1970b: 674). Popular medical journalists like Dr. Walter Alvarez, who then wrote a medical column syndicated across North America, also took up the cause. In the United States, Fenmore Seton, a sign manufacturer and later president of RI, donated signs printed with the symbol, as did the Minnesota-based 3M Corporation (which fabricated self-adhesive decals and distributed them free of charge) (Rehabilitation International, 2017). In 1972, the Electric Prosthesis unit of America's Institute of Electrical and Electronic Engineers spent the fall distributing to its 400 affiliates special "information kits" that "contained information on the international access symbol, the minimum criteria necessary to display the symbol, and instructions on how to give the symbol as wide publicity as possible" (Jackson, 1973: 30). And in 1976, officials at Rehabilitation International launched a letter-writing campaign to US government officials requesting that postage meters in offices across the country print postage in the form of the ISA (Council for Exceptional Children, 1976: 237).

Rehabilitation International wanted more than to simply disseminate the symbol; they wanted the wheelchair figure to be commonplace worldwide. At the time, there were only two groups capable of setting international pictogram standards: the International Organization for Standardization (ISO) based in Geneva, Switzerland, and the United Nations. Even before Acton had assigned Montan to the project, he had been in discussion with the ISO. But the organization was primarily focused on construction, mass manufacture, and engineering. Founded in 1947, their original mission was to facilitate commerce and safety by ensuring standardized measurements and the quality of commonly used parts including, for example, aircraft and electronic equipment. Though the group began to discuss symbols in the 1960s, it wasn't until the early 1970s that they started to focus on signage, after a majority of member countries asked the group to identify and maintain a standard for public information signage (Bakker, 2013: 45). They would finally adopt and register RI's symbol as part of their Graphical Symbols in 1984, as ISO Standard 7000 (ISO 7000. Graphical Symbols for Use on Equipment, 1984, 1989, 2004). The United Nations, on the other hand, issued a more rapid response. In 1974, its Centre for Social and humanitarian Affairs sponsored an Expert Group Meeting on Barrier-Free Design. The meeting resulted in a publication, "Barrier-Free Design" (International Society for Rehabilitation of the Disabled, 1975), and also the symbol's adoption by the UN.

With its carefully hewn strategy for promoting the symbol, RI had every reason to think that the 1970s would be the decade for rehabilitation, especially in the United States. Already in 1968, a commission chaired by former American Institute of Architects President Leon Chatelain, Jr. had presented a three-year-long project report, "Design for All Americans" (U.S. National Commission on Architectural Barriers to Rehabilitation of the Handicapped, 1968). Based in part on Nugent's barrier-free access proposals, the Commission urged action. The same year, Congress translated its recommendations into law, adopting the Architectural Barriers Act. And a number of states sent representatives to RI's 1969 Dublin conference. Many of them were on a fact-finding mission, hoping to understand how to enact the new federal law and even extend it on the state level. Through the early 1970s, individual US states passed a series of new laws that addressed issues of mainstreaming in schools and non-discrimination for jobs. In 1971 alone, 899 bills for education of disabled persons were introduced and 237 passed into law (Mental Health Law Project, 1973: 43; Stick, 1976: 638). They were followed by the 1973 Rehabilitation Act, which prohibited discrimination on a national basis.

people are asking about...

displaying the symbol of access

FIGURE 5.4 The President's Committee on Employment of the Handicapped aimed to promote the Rehabilitation International's new wheelchair symbol in brochures like "People are asking about displaying the symbol access," 1977.

Some states and cities had their own accommodations already in place, and they continued using them for several years after these national efforts were mounted. New York City, for example, and the state of New Hampshire presented disabled drivers with a written card for their car's sun visor and granted them access to parking (Ranzal, 1973: 39). Similar privileges were granted in California, where disabled people were given special license plates that could be identified by police but not the casual observer (Anon., 1975). Supporters of this system argued that criminals would be more likely to prey on disabled drivers and thus their car marking should be as anonymous as possible (Anon, 1977: GB6).

Especially in the United States, where secret knowledge had long dominated disabled access, the new symbol was deployed to guide users to accommodations, but also to raise awareness of the problems disabled people faced in public spaces. Selwyn Goldsmith had long argued this point. Describing the Norwich Symbol to journalists from the *Guardian* newspaper in 1968, Goldsmith insisted, "One of the purposes of the symbol is that it should indicate special arrangements and social privileges or disabled people. What we want overall is to promote the status of the group" (Bendixson, 1968: 9). Although RI did not adopt Goldsmith's symbol, it agreed with his proposition. This line of thinking insisted that "the more it is used and seen, so much more will the general public become aware of the problem that design barriers present" (President's Committee on the Handicapped, n.d.: 4). For a time, the multiple goals for the symbol perplexed designers, officials, and the public. Was the symbol meant to label facilities? Did it function as a wayfinding device? Or was it meant to increase disabled people's visibility? ICOGRADA's Peter Kneebone said as much in his critique of the symbol. Beyond what he deemed the ICTA's jury "arbitrary selection method," he also noted that they lacked "an extensive brief on the purpose of the signs, and information on any research of findings relevant to the signs" (Kneebone, 1969: 73). Even after the President's Committee on the Handicapped published a promotional brochure, "People Are Asking about … Displaying the ISA" (Figure 5.4) which clarified the purpose, placement, and usage of the symbol, larger problems loomed.

Notes

1 In 1939 it became The International Society for the Welfare of Cripples. After the Second World War, in 1960, in an attempt to include veterans and other adults, it was retitled The International Society for the Rehabilitation of the Disabled. In 1972 the group was renamed Rehabilitation International.

2 After this division, the locally oriented branch renamed itself The National Society for Crippled Children and Adults, later changing its name to The National Easter Seal Society. The international segment kept as its name The International Society for Crippled Children.

3 The original participating members were from Oslo's Statens Håndverk-og Kunstindustriskole (SHKS), Bergen's Kunsthåndverksskole, Copenhagen's Kunsthåndværkerskolen, the Konstindustriella Läroverket in Helsinki, Göteborg's Konstindustriskolan, and the Konstfackskolan in Stockholm. Later, Beckmanns in Stockholm and the Kunsthåndværkerskolen of Kolding would join (Lie 2014, chapter 3).

4 The first large SDO event was held in the summer of 1967 at the international design festival at Jyvaskyla, Finland. The next, held in July and early August, 1968, was split between Suomenlinna, Finland, and Konstfack's College of Arts, Crafts and Design in Stockholm. The final event was in Copenhagen in 1969.

5 These included the Swedish Typographer Bo Berndal; William P. Cooper of the World Veterans Foundation; Manfre Finke, of the Fédération Internationale des Personnes Handicapées Physiques (FIMITIC), Educational Rehabilitation professor Alexander Hulek of Poland; the British cartoonist Peter Kneebone, representing the International Council of Graphic Designers Associations (ICOGRADA); Finn Esko Kosunen of the Krigsinvalidernas Brodraforbund; William P. McCahill, head of the US President's Committee on Employment of the Physically Handicapped; French physician Alain Rossier, representing the ICTA itself; and Austrian architect Karl Schwanzer for the International Union of Architects.

PART THREE

A Mark of Identity
(1974–Today)

6

Signs of Protest (1974–1990)

In 1981, a group of disabled people wanting to use a public bus in Los Angeles discovered that, although the United States could lift men to the moon, city buses couldn't lift a wheelchair a few feet into a bus. Twenty-odd wheelchair users gathered at a bus stop to stage a protest. In an event covered by the local press, Jynny Retzinger positioned her wheelchair in line with the rear doors of an arriving Rapid Transit District (RTD) bus. Marika Gerrard, a *Los Angeles Times* reporter, noticed that Retzinger was carefully aligning herself "in front of the blue decal indicating access for the handicapped. The doors slid open. 'Can I get on?' she asked. The doors slide shut." Gerrard noted that, although the door was marked with the access symbol, and installed with a "specially designed lift built into the two-week old General Motors Corp. bus, it was apparent that no wheelchair rider would be able to board. An annoyed driver stepped to the sidewalk. Retzinger repeated, 'Can I get on the bus?' With reporters watching, the driver testily replied, 'No you can't' " (Gerrard, 1981: D3). Although the city had just purchased a fleet of 940 new General Motors buses, their wheelchair lifts were determined unusable; they took too long to use, and they would throw the buses off schedule.

The International Symbol of Access (ISA) was, of course, adopted by the United Nations in 1974, but recognition of the symbol and the access it was meant to ensure was something else entirely. In the United States, after years of discussion, and the passage of many local and state laws adopting the building code initiated by ANSI 117.1, federal legislation affirming barrier-free access as a civil right finally became law in August 1968. The US Architectural Barriers Act required all new buildings constructed with federal funds to be accessible. This included government-owned buildings like post offices and federal museums like the Smithsonian, as well as National Parks, federal prisons, and courthouses. It also applied to public housing and mass transit systems that received federal funding. These laws were written to ensure disabled persons' access to buildings and the public services available there. And the symbol was deployed here as a way to guide disabled citizens toward these points of access. In so doing, the wheelchair figure came not only to label accommodations but, we might argue, also visualized a kind of "fit" between citizens and the environment. Where the symbol appeared, access was guaranteed. Or so was the promise.

In fact, the United States was progressive in conceptualizing the idea of access, but here as elsewhere actual change came slowly, if at all. Though federal law required accessibility, there was little effort to enforce it. There were no inspections, nor were there any fines. Moreover, many types of new construction, from private housing to public retail, were not covered by the legislation. And older buildings and other facilities that predated the law were not required to be retrofitted. Hugh Gallagher, an advocate for disabled access and the congressional aide most responsible for the 1968 law, summed up the palpable disappointment. In 1974, the year the UN adopted the symbol but also six years after the US Barrier-Free Access Act had been passed, he observed how few federal buildings were accessible. In a letter to the *Washington Post* he pointed out that many Smithsonian museums, the Lincoln Memorial, and most other public buildings in the nation's capital remained off limits to disabled citizens. "It is all very frustrating," he wrote. "More than that, it is thoughtless and stupid. It is cruel" (Gallagher, 1974: A31).

When Jynny Retzinger and nineteen other activists staged their 1981 protest at the Los Angeles bus stop, the problem was still quite common. By this time, a second law, the Rehabilitation Act of 1973, had also been passed. In that case, however, government officials moved slowly to implement key parts of its legislation. This Act, for example, carried with it a watchdog Architectural and Transportation Barriers Compliance Board, but enforcement was still largely piecemeal. Retzinger's protest marked a different route to achieving access. Over the prior decade, many disabled people staged protests modeled after the campaigns of the Civil Rights movement. As Daryl Lembke wrote in the *Los Angeles Times* in 1975, "a new political force is on the march in California and nationally, although many of the marchers cannot even walk" (Lembke, 1975: B1). And the symbol of access played a significant role in these actions. In some cases, like that of the Los Angeles bus protest, it signified a promise made, but not kept; it guaranteed to users a kind of environmental fit that was, in fact, unavailable. But in many other situations, the access symbol was beginning to serve as a mark of identity and solidarity. Disabled people with very different impairments rallied around the design. They embraced its visibility and used it as a symbol for self-representation.

"The Selma of handicapped rights"

Jynny Retzinger's bus stop confrontation in Los Angeles was by no means unique. She was inspired in part by activists in Denver who, three years earlier, had protested the lack of wheelchair-accessible buses citywide.

Denver had a small but active disability rights community centered around Atlantis, an independent living community founded in 1975 by Wade Blank, a former civil rights demonstrator and the Presbyterian minister who would go on to form the activist group ADAPT (Fleischer and Zames, 2011: 82). In Denver, reporters witnessed protests reminiscent of those led by Martin Luther King a decade earlier; one journalist went so far as to call them "the Selma of handicapped rights" (Tim, 1982: 54).

But the situation in Denver was symptomatic of both a broader problem and the nature of the growing disability rights movement. Disabled people began these protests in response to legislation that was unevenly implemented and rarely enforced. In 1975, for example, an internal government audit conducted by the General Accounting Office (GAO) admitted that not a single "building inspected was completely free of barriers." The report made a laundry list of problems, which included curbs too high to negotiate, steps to climb, restrooms with unusable toilet stalls, and elevators with controls beyond the reach of wheelchair users. In sum, the report admitted, the "Architectural Barriers Act has had only minor effect on making public buildings barrier free" (GAO, 1975: 8). The GAO found a variety of reasons why the law was not followed. Many offices were exempted through loopholes in the law, which covered only government-owned buildings, not those which had been leased. But also many architects, government officials, and police didn't understand the new regulations or were reluctant to implement them.

These bureaucratic tangles had major ramifications for disabled people. In the winter of 1979, wheelchair user Katy MacKay took a *New York Times* reporter with her to go Christmas shopping. She chronicled a range of obstacles at every turn. Stopped on the sidewalk, she remarked, often "the people who put these curb cuts in don't know why they're doing it ... so they make them unlevel with the street and make them basically useless" (Smolowe, 1979: 26). Old construction remained unchanged, and even in new buildings contractors often ignored, misconstrued, or simply did not understand what access meant. In Los Angeles, a new restaurant provided a wheelchair ramp to its main entrance, but its door was too heavy for a wheelchair user to open (Ward, 1975: SG1). In Chicago, the Furniture Mart installed ramps and removed bathroom doors so Rehabilitation Institution (RI) could hold a conference for thirty handicapped persons on site. But when the conference ended, the ramps were moved and the doors replaced (Oppenheim, 1975: 35). In New York, a newly constructed state university built a music complex, which, as one reporter noted, "complied with the law by constructing a long rambling ramp that led to the front doors where—do you believe it?—wheelchairs were blocked by stairs!" (Little, 1977: 486). A new, little known agency, the Architectural and Transportation Barriers Compliance Board, was charged with ensuring that equal access was possible in all federal facilities. But it was small, ill-funded, and only acted on noncompliance cases specially brought to its attention. In a 1976 article on the Architectural Barriers Act, the *Washington Post* reported that "the law has no teeth in it, so most architects and bureaucrats ignore it" (von Eckart, 1976: B1).

Even when access was provided, builders often didn't understand how to use the ISA or frequently forgot to post it. Describing a new downtown building, the Broadway Plaza in Los Angeles, in 1977 a local politician and advocate for disabled people complained that "Technically, on paper, it complies with the law ... but a handicapped person needs an Indian guide to get in. There's a special entrance—but who knows where it is?" (Green, 1977: 14). Of course in some instances, like that of Los Angeles' bus fleet in the early 1980s, the access symbol was displayed even though accommodations did not exist. This type of misuse happened often enough that a 1977 brochure published by the President's Committee on Employment of the Handicapped was obliged to remind the public that using "this symbol improperly or indiscriminately where a building is not genuinely barrier-free is to play a cruel hoax on millions of persons" (President's Committee on Employment of the Handicapped, 1977).

This persistent and pervasive problem sparked protests across the country. Many activists would argue that architectural barriers did more than deny access. They also deprived disabled people of the full panoply of protections and duties of citizenship. To be clear, such concerns were simply not discussed earlier in the century. The disability rights protest movement is important not only for connecting civil rights to barrier-free access (with serious ramifications for physical mobility), but also because people with disabilities were claiming the right to participate in the public sphere, as well as to protections that they had long been denied. The symbol was not just a functional disseminator of information about where there were access points. It was also a marker of growing visibility.

Rights and protest

Jynny Retzinger's 1981 stand-down with the RTD bus driver is only a small part of a much broader history of disability rights activism. But many other groups embraced a graphic symbol and deployed it publicly. Anti-war demonstrators quickly co-opted the familiar "peace symbol," for example, from the Campaign for Nuclear Disarmament (CND). Meanwhile the Black Panthers adopted two symbols—the clenched fist and the silhouette of a prowling panther—to disseminate their cause. Just as major corporations increasingly relied on a strong visual identity for corporate communications and advertising, so too did late twentieth-century activists. Ultimately the ISA filled a similar need for the nascent disability rights movement.

After the ISA was introduced in the 1970s, it came to play a curious double role. On the one hand, it functioned as a wayfinding device, labeling accommodations and pointing out routes of access. But it also stood in as a kind of visual shorthand, reminding disabled people and others of society's commitment to barrier-free access—that is, to the idea that disabled people could be "fit" into contemporary society. For Jynny Retzinger and many others, the wheelchair figure sometimes functioned as a "false" symbol, advertising access that wasn't actually available. The disconnect between promise and reality pushed the symbol into a newer, more contentious direction. In this latter mode, Retzinger's protest is emblematic of a larger culture of demonstration and protest fostered within the disability rights movement.

The drive for equal rights—and a good social fit—was hardly monolithic, and began long before Retzinger's confrontation in 1981. Most histories of the disability rights movement point to the catalyzing efforts of a small group of disabled students at UC Berkeley who gathered around the polio survivor Ed Roberts. In 1962, after resistance from that campus' administration, Roberts was finally matriculated as a student but still was considered too disabled to live in university housing. Instead, he was asked to take up residence at the university's student health facility. Roberts' admission to Berkeley gained national attention, and other disabled students joined him, living in the dorms as well as student health services building there. This loose group, self-styled "the Rolling Quads" after their wheelchairs, began advocating for access across campus and in the city of Berkeley as well (Shapiro, 1993: 45–49). By 1972, these students had joined forces with other disabled people around the Bay Area to establish the Center for Independent Living. Their efforts to gain greater autonomy and control in their own lives became a model for similar efforts in both the United States and Europe.

To be reductive, what these disabled people wanted most was a better "fit," that is, to participate more fully in society itself. In order to achieve this, they asserted their rights as citizens and, like African Americans active in the civil rights movement and women involved with women's liberation, demanded the ability to live and work free of social discrimination. By the early 1970s, several explicitly political groups of disabled persons began to organize. The California Association for the Physically Handicapped and Disabled in Action formed to address housing and transportation inequality as well as civil rights issues and questions of political self-representation. At the same time, activists were beginning to adopt change strategies like demonstrations and sit-ins—all modeled on the civil rights movement a decade earlier—to draw the public's attention and force government action.

Particularly forceful in this, Disabled in Action (DIA) (a group of students at the Brooklyn campus of Long Island University) formed in 1970, to advocate for the rights of people with disabilities. As an activist organization, DIA was cast in a different mold from older "service" groups like the March of Dimes, Easter Seals, and the American Foundation for the Blind. The group also positioned itself as cross-disability (that is, inclusive of people with vision or hearing impairments, and persons with mental disabilities as well), arguing that older groups fostered overprotectiveness and insensitivity.

Back in California, Gerald Belchick from the state's Department of Vocational Rehabilitation began working with the Rolling Quads and quickly noticed how the technical aids around disability could themselves be deployed as political symbols. In the nascent disability rights movement, as protesters began to agitate together, he observed something powerful. Berkeley's disabled students helped make

> a very visible cause. It was everything—it would be an organizer's dream—because you didn't have to depend on rhetoric; you could just depend on what you could show. And, of course, this panorama of all [of] them in wheelchairs ... made all the papers, and it made it in grand style. (Belchick, 1998; 189)

But it wasn't just that the chairs themselves were gaining visibility (Figure 6.1). As the embodiment of the right to access, the wheelchair symbol was gaining a different kind of prominence; the disability rights movement began using the access figure itself, as part of their own activism. At early DIA rallies, the symbol became a unifying icon of protest. Founder Judy Heumann was already active in Civil Rights circles and understood how demonstrations functioned. "If we were going to have them," she later argued, "we wanted fliers,

FIGURE 6.1 Senator Harrison Williams addressing protestors using wheelchairs on the steps of the Capitol, Washington DC. Flanking the group is an American flag, with its stars rearranged in the shape of the wheelchair access symbol, 1970. Bettmann/Getty Images.

we wanted things that you could give to people that they could understand" (Heumann, 1998–2001: 194). The wheelchair symbol helped them do this. When, for example, disabled protestors converged on Washington DC on May 5, 1972, for a rally and to mark "Advocacy Day for the Disabled," they reimagined the American Flag with the ISA figure in place of the traditional fifty stars. The group, comprised almost exclusively of students, carried this modified flag when they met with NJ Senator Harrison Williams, then head of the Labour and Public Welfare Committee, on the Capitol steps. This revision of the American flag became a standby at disability protests for years to come. (One group, Americans Disabled for Accessible Public Transit, or ADAPT, used it so frequently that in later years, it became known as the ADAPT flag.) In this context, anchored in patriotism but also a set of political ideals, the wheelchair symbol became a reminder of a constitutional promise—as US citizens, disabled people were entitled to a series of legal rights. In effect, they should "fit" into society better.

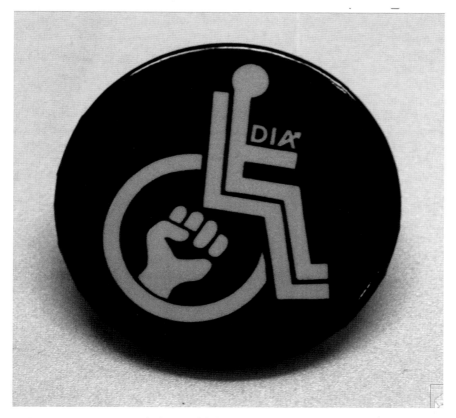

FIGURE 6.2 Button with the Disabled in Action logo, c. 1974. Courtesy American History Museum Gift of Carr Massi.

But Heumann's DIA branch in New York also developed an entire logo that used the ISA differently. Pat Figueroa, a DIA board member and part-time graphic designer who used a wheelchair, designed a logo for the group, riffing on the familiar ISA. Instead of placing a circle on the top of a wheelchair, however, he articulated a stick figure that sits in—but is distinct from—the chair. The imagery is somewhat reminiscent of Selwyn Goldsmith's, or that of the Stresa logo, in which humans are clear and distinctly present in their chairs. The figure is separable from the chair, whereas in the ISA symbol, the figure *is* the chair.

At the same time, however, Figueroa also added a second, more provocative clenched fist to the image. It references the strident militancy of radical activist groups in the late 1960s like the Black Panthers. The clenched fist was a powerful image throughout the period. The Panthers especially used the image as a powerful statement of self-assertion and autonomy. The boldness of the fist helps redefine the seated figure. It fundamentally breaks with earlier depictions of persons in wheelchairs. In the past, to talk about disability almost always meant engaging ideas of weakness and dependency.

In this context the access symbol, and its evocation of individual identity and independence, began to resonate with the larger goals of the disability rights movement. Some protesters agitated for better access in urban spaces. At Berkeley's Center for Independent Living, for example, Hale Zukas and others created a wheelchair-accessible route through the town of Berkeley, linking the University of California's campus to the greater community (Zukas, 1998: 165, 166). Networks of young activists, often wheelchair users with university connections, began to form advocacy groups in larger urban areas like Boston, St. Louis, San Francisco, and New York. Their first efforts may have focused on the removal of architectural barriers, as at Berkeley, but disabled persons and their advocates moved rapidly to other forms of autonomy, including the deinstitutionalization of disabled people, the formation of independent living communities, and a range of broader, access-oriented initiatives. Some asserted pressure via lawsuits, and other forms of legal action. Still others mounted activist campaigns, using the ISA to invoke society's promise of a better social "fit."

Of course, the ISA's official status made it an especially useful symbol of protest. With RI's aggressive and widespread promotion, the wheelchair symbol was becoming rapidly and widely known. But in the United States, it also began to serve as a reminder of the series of legal reforms that promised access, but then failed to make good. With hand-scrawled drawings on cardboard and stickers affixed to poster board, disability rights protesters claimed the symbol as their own. When in 1974, for example, disabled people in Denver gathered outside the Colorado statehouse to advocate for funding for independent living, they carried placards proclaiming "We need your support ... we count too!," emblazoning their signs with the ISA (Figure 6.3). They went so far as to use in their protests the same stickers and signage issued by RI itself. In one sense those stickers carried with it a kind

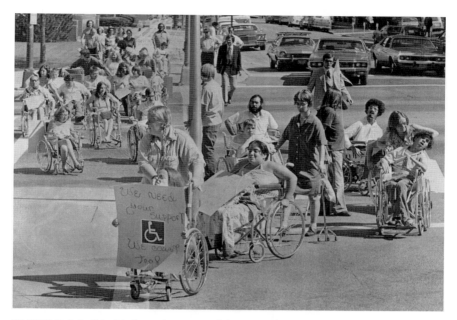

FIGURE 6.3 Disabled youths, most of them in wheelchairs, protesting inadequate housing provided by the state, 1974. Bill Peters/Denver Post/Getty Images.

of official authority. The preprinted blue and white sticker was standard issue and meant to mark restrooms and ramps across the country. Employed at these early protests, its meaning was subtlety changed. Instead of marking access, it worked to remind officials of their promise to help disabled people fit into society as a whole.

Had political events not turned out as they did, this legacy might have passed unmarked. That changed in 1977, when a series of groups coordinated a nationwide push to have the Rehabilitation Act of 1973 implemented. The law, which prohibited discrimination on the basis of disability by any public or private entity using federal funds, was slow to be adopted. By 1977, four years after Richard Nixon signed the original bill into law, the Carter administration was still delaying implementation of its strict non-discrimination regulations (outlined under section 504 in the original bill). By early April of that year, a national coalition of disabled people formed and began mounting protests and sit-ins in offices of the Department of Health and Human Services across the country. In San Francisco, protestors staged a twenty-five-day sit-in at the local office of Health, Education and Welfare, while others marched outside, carrying pickets reading "Sign 504 Now!" (Figure 6.4).

The protests brought together a broad-based coalition of disabled people, representing, for example, the interests of vision and hearing disabled

FIGURE 6.4 Protest 504 poster drawn by activist Ken Stein and used at the twenty-five-day occupation of the San Francisco HEW Building, 1977. Courtesy Ken Stein.

persons, as well as those with mobility impairments. And, for the first time, national television reports broadcast images of these protests, bringing the rhetoric—and images—of the disability rights movement into living rooms across the country night after night. This coverage also introduced the general public to many variations on the ISA. Some were idiosyncratic and whimsical. At least one of these posters was distinguished by a wheelchair figure that fills the "0." Painted by Ken Stein, an early activist and advocate at the Berkeley-based Center for Independent Living, his "Sign 504 Now!" poster carries a subtler visual pun. Not only does the "0" duplicate the ISA symbol, but it also carries its own sign reading "NOW" (Stein, 2016). Other placards were more militant, incorporating, for example, the ISA with the militant clenched fist of the DIA logo.

The Section 504 protests succeeded in so far as HEW Secretary Joseph Califano signed into effect the regulations stipulated by the 1973 bill. But they also helped establish the ISA as an emblem in cross-disability protest; the question of visibility—and the fundamental issue of social and environmental misfit—was forcefully brought into public view for the first

FIGURE 6.5 Wheelchair users in Denver demonstrate the lack of access citywide by making their own curb cuts at street corners and traffic intersections. As the protestors arrived, they carried with them homemade placards bearing the wheelchair access symbol, c. 1978. *The Denver Post* via Getty Images.

time. It also made clear that large numbers of disabled Americans with a variety of impairments could wield more power if they worked together. As one organizer told the *Los Angeles Times* in 1979, "The idea of a coalition of groups of different disabilities is a new one—it used to be that people grouped around a specific disability" (Cimons, 1979: B8). But, as grassroots coordinator Fred Fay realized after 504 was passed, it was clear "how much more effective we could be informally if we could act in coalition on different issues" (Fay, 2001: 48).

Amid this bigger picture, of course, individual groups would develop their own protest symbols. On the one hand, the wheelchair symbol continued to hold relevance, particularly for mobility-impaired demonstrators. When, in 1980, demonstrators protested the lack of curb cuts in Denver, for example, they brought picks, hammers, and handmade placards embellished with the wheelchair figure (Figure 6.5).

But other groups began to develop more specialized symbols. For example at Gallaudet University, the only higher education institution in the United States devoted to people who are deaf or hard of hearing, students developed protest emblems that depict a signing hand. In 1988, when students protested the appointment of a non-deaf president of the university, students developed a picture of a clenched fist next to a schematic depiction of a human ear (Barnartt and Scotch, 2001: 209). After these successful protests, the clenched fist symbol continued to be used within the Deaf

Power movement. But in cross-disability protests in particular, the successful lobbying efforts in 1977 helped cement the ISA as a unifying symbol for the disability rights movement's loose network of supporters and affiliates.

The dynamism of the US disability rights movement (shaped in the wake of the American civil rights movement) sometimes overshadows similar events elsewhere. But the question of disability and human rights was percolating throughout the industrialized West at this time. In 1970, for example, the British Parliament passed the Chronically Sick and Disabled Persons Act. Unlike its US counterpart (the 1968 Barrier-Free Architecture law), this legislation specified that "where any special facility was available for a handicapped person, it had to be signposted prominently." The clear mandate for signage here might be attributed to Selwyn Goldsmith, who of course advocated in the UK for special signage for several years before that. But Goldsmith's arguments for a uniquely "welfare state approach" toward disability and his support for positive discrimination—along with a kind of blunt, straightforward "tactlessness"—"brought him unpopularity in some government circles" (Anon, 2011). Furthermore, Rehabilitation International's pull was strong and the British government never adopted the access symbol that Goldsmith arduously developed while doing research in Norwich. Instead, the ISA was heavily promoted throughout the country and quickly adopted as an all but official symbol (Hodgson, 1972: 9) (Figure 6.6).

FIGURE 6.6 By the late 1990s, public signage for accessible accommodations for wheelchair users was common not only in the United States, but across Europe. Photo by Nitschmann/ullstein bild via Getty Image.

All the same, British persons with disabilities began to chaff at the 1970 Act, arguing that it "won greater advances for professionals and specialist services than for physically impaired people themselves" (Anon, 1981: 2). As disabled activist Vic Finkelstein noted in 1975, "recognition of the need for disabled people to be involved in their own affairs has by no means been fully accepted by the medical profession" (Finkelstein, 1975: 32). As in the United States, activists argued that disabled people should be de-institutionalized and also given equal access to education, housing, and a host of other rights. In 1972, Paul Hunt, a wheelchair user, invited disabled people to join him to challenge the "patronising assumptions" being made about them (Hunt, 1972: 5). Hunt proposed a Union of the Physically Impaired Against Segregation (UPIAS) and the group quickly began using a logo that imaginatively reworked the ISA to include the initials of the newly formed British group. With the "U" turned on its side, the letter turns into a wheel, while its "P" forms a body's neck and head. Its "I," "A," and "S" become the figure's arms and legs.

In other European countries, the ISA and barrier-free access were also rapidly adopted, but they were sometimes co-opted by activists there as well. In postwar Germany, a number of laws focused on the comprehensive rehabilitation and employment of disabled people (Geist, 2003: 563). But, by the early 1970s, student-led human rights activism began to challenge long-standing social stereotypes and indirect discrimination toward disabled persons (Poore, 2007: 274). Here, too, the ISA was deployed as a unifying symbol of protest. When, for example, in 1980 a group of disabled persons organized to protest a Frankfurt district court ruling, they made banners and pins depicting the wheelchair symbol. The legal judgment allowed a local woman to sue the German travel company that booked her Greek vacation. Claiming that the agency placed her at a hotel where a large number of cognitively disabled Swedes were vacationing, she argued that the experience ruined her vacation. The court agreed, noting that "there is suffering in the world, and this cannot be changed. However, the plaintiff is justified in not wanting to see it during her vacation" (Poore, 2007: 277). Protestors gathered to assert what they felt was a dehumanizing ruling. And, filling the streets to dispute this ruling, they gathered in front of the court, at the city's Fountain of Justice wearing handmade badges decorated with the ISA or carrying signs and posters graced with the same image (Poore, 2007: 279).

Of course, the rapid and global adoption of the access symbol in the early 1970s remains a notable achievement. But the scale of its adoption tells a second story. Ultimately, the symbol escaped RI's control. As late as 2000, Acton still felt personally responsible for "shepherding the International Symbol of Access through its conception, design, approval and legitimatization." Even after he'd retired, he still worried for its "promulgation, promotion and defence against abuse." Violations of "the approved design," he claimed, became "a major challenge over the years," and Acton more and more found himself forced "to defend the integrity of the design against deviations which, if permitted would (and in some cases have) escalate to levels that destroy the universally recognizable symbol that is so important" (Acton, 2000). Acton may have worried that the ISA was being used to sell soap, furniture, and other commercial products. But he also saw activist appropriations that staked out a political position very different from Rehabilitation International itself. The organization's leaders considered applying for a patent for the design, but remembered that patents must be enacted in individual countries. Moreover, patenting the image would limit its usage—something that members wanted to avoid. Ultimately, they decided to think of the symbol as "a gift to mankind" (Rehabilitation International, 1978).

By the 1980s, the seed of an idea—access—grew in soil tilled by the previous decade's activists. As the idea slowly matured, it branched out, touching in new ways law, education, health services, and also design. For some time activists and experts alike argued that disability could result not from impairments per se, but rather from society—and, by implication, design itself. By the late 1970s, the rights advocate, architect, and professor Ronald Mace began arguing that architectural and design barriers could disable people If only architects and designers would design for a wider range of human bodies and abilities, Mace insisted, disability might be neutralized. With his consulting firm, Barrier Free Environments, Mace was one of the first architects to actively argue that accommodations for disabled people were more than an add-on for a small minority. Himself a wheelchair user, Mace noted that features like curb cuts, automatic doors, and elevators benefit a wide range of people, including those using strollers, rolling luggage, carrying bags, and joining in a host of other activities. Larger numbers of users—disabled or not—find easy access valuable.

Of course, earlier proponents of these design accommodations had, from time to time, made a similar case. When Tim Nugent reconfigured the lecture halls, dormitories, toilets, and buses of the University of Illinois, making the campus more accessible to people with disabilities, he noticed that many non-disabled students used—or even preferred—these accommodations. For his part, Mace made access a cornerstone of his practice; by 1985, he finally began calling the broader idea "Universal Design" (Mace, 1985: 148). As a way of thinking, Universal Design deeply engages ideas of access but, Mace argued, the "focus is not specifically on people with disabilities, but all *people*" (emphasis his) (Mace, 1998). While Mace never addressed the access symbol directly, the Universal Design movement spread a similar ideology of inclusiveness. As scholar Amie Hamraie demonstrates, "Builder's magazines, newspapers, textbooks, and conference workshops began to tell a new story about Universal Design: that this approach was not about accessibility for disabled users at all, but rather about a common sense approach to 'good design' for everyone" (Hamraie, 2017: 7). Universal design in architecture and industrial design insists that buildings, public spaces, and products should account for the widest possible range of functional capacities as possible. Mace himself helped draft the 1988 Fair Housing Amendment Act and the 1990 Architectural Guidelines of the ADA. Mace himself focused primarily on building design and construction, but his understanding of Universal Design extended to design that impacted all aspects of life, including transportation to homes, businesses, and schools. The broader spirit of these ideas animated a variety of consumer products and services in the late 1970s and 1980s; Marc Harrison's original Cuisinart DCL 7-PRO to Smart Design's OXO Good Grips line of kitchen tools began to spread the idea of universal design far beyond the movement's original roots (Williamson, 2012).

In many ways, these ideas culminated in the early 1990s with a series of acts and legislation. In the United States, the ADA was signed into law in 1990; in the UK, the Disability Discrimination Act (DDA) was passed in 1995. In the case of the ADA, no other federal law aimed to reshape physical space so completely. As a vehicle for change, the ADA was sweeping in its vision, born of the political drawing together of cross-disability activists over the previous two decades. It showed what activism could achieve. Less directly, it was also a sweeping endorsement of architectural access as broadly embedded in the Universal Design movement. But the law's posterity (sometimes called "the post-ADA period") (Hamraie, 2017: 198–199) would also prove the biggest challenge to the access symbol yet.

Passing the ADA: Compliance and defiance

On January 26, 1992, much of the signage used throughout American office buildings became instantly obsolete. Or so Richard Ellseby reported in the trade journal *Office Systems* (Ellseby, 1995: 6). Of course, he exaggerated. But there was more than a grain of truth here. Two years earlier, George Bush had signed the ADA; at the time, it was lauded by many observers, and even described "as the most decisive human rights legislation since the Civil Rights Acts of the 1960s" (Busch, 1995). But it was—and remains—an unusual piece of legislation. The idea of access is woven through the warp and weft of this new law. Access to buses and trains, the enjoyment of parks and pools, entry into stores and classrooms, the law covers huge swaths of the world around us. The law also assumes that something would mark the accommodations being legislated. In this way, the figure in a wheelchair holds a prominent place in the design guidelines developed for this legislation. Marking accommodations and/or pointing the way toward them, the symbol itself was catapulted into the public consciousness with new vigor. Little wonder that legislators gathering together for a photo shortly after the new bill was signed were given T-shirts bearing the wheelchair logo (Figure 6.7).

FIGURE 6.7 Shortly after the Americans with Disabilities Act (ADA) was signed, United States legislators paused for a photographer. The gathered together, holding T-shirts printed with the International Symbol of Access, 1990. The LIFE Images Collection/Getty Images.

For many longtime activists in the disability rights community, the new regulations were liberating. But for others, including a number of designers, the legislation seemed challenging at best and superfluous at worst. Until this point, design for persons with disabilities was conceived as specialty work. The new laws, on the other hand, insisted otherwise. In theory, many of the accommodations shaped by the ADA draw from the Universal Design movement. But the law also demonstrated how the general public was unfamiliar or uncomfortable with broader ideas of access and accommodation. From facilities managers and small business owners to many architects and designers, these regulations sometimes felt like a creeping disease or, as one observer remarked, one long and continuing "headache" (Doherty, 1995: 18). For at least one construction industry trade journal, *Buildings*, it seemed more like "an epidemic." Worse still, the magazine continued, the problem "could take thousands of dollars to cure" (Madsen, 2004: 94). The tumult was significant enough that, at one point in 1994, the *Wall Street Journal* asked, "just how open are Americans to people with disability?" (Pierson, 1995: B1). Many professionals grumbled about the legislation; the boldest suggested it boiled down to a question of compliance or defiance (Madsen, 2004).

To the casual observer, the passage of the ADA would seem rather unnecessary for Americans with disabilities. Long before it was passed, several significant pieces of legislation mandated barrier-free access in the United States. Through the 1960s, dozens of state and local laws aimed to make the physical environment more accessible to disabled people. In 1968, the Federal Architectural Barriers Act made access mandatory for buildings constructed with federal funds. The Rehabilitation Act of 1973 (amended in 1974) reinforced the 1968 legislation by introducing a watchdog, the Architectural and Transportation Board, to hold hearings and issue orders to ensure compliance. But the ongoing question of access also highlighted the country's uniquely conflicted position on disability rights; while national legislation was liberal in asserting the civil rights of disabled people, there were surprisingly few legal, social, and medical structures to ensure and support those rights. Implementation and enforcement remained spotty at best. Throughout the 1970s, architects and disabled people alike admitted, "citizen attitudes and lukewarm or uninformed enforcement of codes dilute the legal breakthroughs already attained" (Kliment, 1975). As Jynny Retzinger demonstrated when the "accessible" Los Angeles transit bus refused to pick up disabled riders proved in 1981, the various laws issued until then were only of limited success. When it was passed in 1990, the framers of the Americans with Disabilities Act were pushing for the kind of universal barrier-free access first envisioned by reformers in the 1960s.

In fact, the ADA reached farther into American life than the older legislation that preceded it. For years after the protests involving section 504, the language of unity knit disability rights activists together. With the goal of broadening access, the medical understanding of disability, as well as its legal definition, was shifting. The new law acknowledged this change by encompassing both "physical or mental impairment." Furthermore, disability was defined as a condition "that substantially limits one or more of the major life activities (that is one's hearing, walking, speaking, seeing, breathing, and learning)." Essentially a civil rights law that forbade discrimination in employment and housing, the ADA promised equal rights to services and programs. But these assurances were predicated on physical access to the spaces that all able-bodied citizens used.

Though the changes promised by the ADA were sweeping, it took time to develop specific regulations for reconfiguring the built environment. By the middle of 1991, the Department of Justice published guidelines called the Standards for Accessible Design (SAD). These went into effect on January 26, 1992. They covered a host of specifics, including public areas and institutions, but they were also applied to privately owned ones, including hotels and motels, offices and commercial facilities, entertainment and healthcare facilities. Furthermore, they applied to all new construction as well as the old, all "to the extent readily achievable" (defined as "easily accomplished without much difficulty or expense"). They addressed access for the mobility impaired, as well as for the hearing and visually impaired. Indeed, many of the provisions focused on eliminating communication barriers. Some types of signs, for instance, had to include Braille, while others required a sharp contrast between characters-letters, numbers and symbols, and the background.

When the guidelines were introduced, larger businesses, corporations, and employers found it easier to absorb the costs of building ramps, changing the grading of inclined paths, lowering water fountains, and attending to other legislated changes. But many smaller businesses found the SAD regulations hard to understand and expensive to follow. "After all," opined one industry magazine editor, "what *exactly* (italics theirs) is meant by 'readily achievable' and 'no undue hardship'?" (Leibrock, 1994: 56). Few challenged the rules in open defiance. But so, too, did "few, if any, facilities managers talk openly about how their organizations are complying with Americans with Disabilities Act (ADA)." Expecting a rush of new clients, in the early 1990s some lawyers, architects, and designers formed consultancies specifically meant to advise and oversee the expected scramble to comply with the new law. They misjudged. Most builders, planners and designers affected by this legislation "seemed to be ignoring it, almost hoping they would go away" (Leibrock, 1994: 56).

Perhaps unsurprisingly, design professionals—even those who supported disabled people's right to access—also faced the new guidelines with trepidation. When, in 1994, design journalist Akiko Busch interviewed practitioners who embraced the new law, she "found that nearly all designers initially greeted the ADA with everything from irritation to outright hostility" (Busch 1994: 44). Resistance to barrier-free provisions was hardly new to the worlds of architecture and design. In the 1970s, many professionals dismissed ramps, elevators, and other accommodations as both unattractive and stifling to the creative process (El Osman, 1975; Morgan, 1976; Williamson, 2012). When the ADA was passed, this feeling was only exacerbated. For design professionals, "access is a byword for ugly, cluttering up lean pure spaces with hospital hardware, like grade-rails stair/chair lifts and ramps" (Milner et al., 1991).

While some resisted the new regulations for aesthetic reasons and cost, others were more practical in their concerns. Some questioned the most basic premise of the barrier-free architecture movement: physical access would lead to better opportunities for disabled people. Philadelphia designer Virginia Gehshan voiced this uncertainty when admitting, "I have mixed emotions about it ... I'm not sure it was well researched. And even with the best of intentions, it's hard to legislate a social issue." (Busch, 1995: 45) Others believed in the spirit of the law, but felt these new regulations were too bureaucratic; in the end, they failed to take practical considerations into account. Remembering when the ADA was first passed, the designer Roger Whitehouse "groaned about more mindless legislation" (Busch, 1995: 45). Some observers went further, complaining that the laws were illogical, "put together largely by well-intentioned bureaucrats rather than users" (Busch, 1995: 45). Many dreaded the 1992 deadline when ADA compliance went into effect. Some architects even rushed to get any and all new work finished before they would be held accountable to the new legislation (Busch, 1995: 45).

The new law may have posed major problems for architects, but it also raised a number of questions for graphic designers. Before the ADA was passed, graphic design had rarely been regulated, and few practitioners had ever been forced to follow sweeping governmental regulations. But the new law placed unusual emphasis on public signage, insisting that all "permanent areas such as restrooms, lunchrooms and conference rooms must be identified by signs that use internationally recognized visual symbols" (Ellersby, 1995: 6). As designers started to examine the SAD guidelines more closely, they discovered that parts contradicted popular design wisdom. Paul Arthur railed against rules that "fly in the face of 'what we think we know' about legibility" (Arthur, 1993a: 16). As Roger Whitehouse recalls, they "were nonsense." That is, to his practiced eye, they literally "made no sense" (Whitehouse, 2016). While some designers voiced generalized fears, other concerns coalesced around specific worries. Arthur, for example, derided "the insistence" on raised letters (and Braille) on signage for the visually impaired when, he asserted, only a "tiny percentage of visually impaired people ... can actually make practical use of them" (Arthur, 1993a:16). He also complained that these guidelines were poorly written, and used "terminology that no one understands." Arthur drew particular attention to awkward neologisms like "simple serif" type styles (Arthur, 1993a: 16).

In the early 1990s, unhappiness with the government's SAD strictures swelled alongside resistance to the ISA itself. Of course, long before the legislation was even conceived, some communication designers harbored a particular antipathy toward the wheelchair symbol. Now charged with bringing it into widespread and consistent usage, architects and graphic designers balked. Of these, some continued to bridle at the symbol's hacked origins. Robert Probst, a designer teaching at the University of Cincinnati, called its odd assemblage of parts little more than "a life-less committee job" (Pierson, 1995: B1). Publicly, Paul Arthur, who himself created the stylized wheelchair symbol used at Montreal's Expo 67, questioned its design integrity (Arthur and Passini, 1992: 174). Privately, Arthur was more specific, focusing his ire on Karl Montan's last-minute addition of "the extraordinarily ugly head" (Arthur, 1993b). At his most dismissive, Arthur referred to the ISA as a "pollywog in a wheelchair" (Arthur, 1994a).

Some professional organizations, for example, the Society of Environmental Graphic Designers (SEGD), took preemptive action and tried to arm their members with comprehensive explanations of the new SAD regulations. Of course, their members' livelihood depended on introducing signage into the built environment, and they were hired for their knowledge and expertise. Above all, SEGD's constituency was expected to produce designs in keeping with current legislation. The SEGD took the new law as a call to action. The group introduced a regular column in the organization's quarterly newsletter and also offered members an ADA hotline to help answer questions. The SEGD's then-president, Roger Whitehouse, even authored a white paper advising colleagues on how to deal with the new signage needs. In retrospect, he calls this a "pre-emptive" action, meant to intervene before the government dictated further strictures. But he quickly found openness at the Department of Justice and elsewhere; they too didn't know how to enact the new laws (Whitehouse, 2016). In the end, the SEGD tried to bridge the divide between the ADA's government-mandated design regulations and professionals in the field.

But these actions left many designers still unsure what to do with the wheelchair figure itself. Even among those who reviled it, the symbol's sheer ubiquity made it difficult to tinker with. As Paul Arthur related to a colleague at the time,

> whatever you think of Susanne Kofoed's [sic] symbol of accessibility, screwed around with as it has been by the addition of a tadpole at the top, it is not something [designers] should be wasting ... time on redesigning. I hate it, you hate it, but it's there and neither you nor I nor anyone else can "undo" it. (Arthur, 1994b)

Yet, not everyone shared Arthur's frustration and weariness. Some designers thought it was time for a redesign. SEGD members and others began to toy with the access symbol. So too did disability rights groups. In fact, as definitions of disability were beginning to change, many people with impairments were reappraising the wheelchair figure, arguing that it was an inadequate representation of disability. In the years after the ADA was passed, designers and activists alike began to reject the ISA.

7

A Critical Design? (1990–Today)

In 2013, Victor Calise, New York's commissioner of the Mayor's Office for People with Disabilities, announced that the city would replace the International Symbol of Access (ISA) with a new sign. Identifying the 1969 ISA as "stagnant," he told reporters that it was too passive and lacked "movement." Worst of all, he claimed, "It makes people seem like they don't do much with their lives"(Baskin, 2013). This view, he suggested, could be changed—and a more up-to-date vision of the wheelchair figure could do it. Furthermore, Calise already had a newer symbol at the ready. Fusing the dynamism of wheelchair sports (Figure 7.1) with the subversiveness of graffiti art, the revised symbol seemed to break new ground (Figure 7.2). But really, over the past two decades, the older ISA was on a collision course with change.

FIGURE 7.1 Louise Sauvage joins other wheelchair atheltes competing in a 10-kilometer road race on Australia Day in Sydney, Australia. 1999. Corbis. via Getty Images.

FIGURE 7.2 Brian Glenney and Sara Hendren hold their design, a new version of the wheelchair symbol, 2011. *The Boston Globe* via Getty Images.

It's a sign of how universal the ISA had become that Calise cared enough about the symbol to even consider changing it. After the UN ratified the symbol in 1974 and the United States passed the Americans with Disabilities Act (ADA) in 1990, the symbol became ubiquitous. From parking lots to parks, airports to children's schools, the ISAs mark accommodations on a global scale. Its staggering proliferation suggests a good social, cultural, and environmental fit.

But, while all of this helps explain why the ISA flourished as a global symbol, it doesn't reflect changing views of disability itself. In the early 1990s, the ADA and a series of similar laws were enacted globally. At the same time, just as the access symbol gained new authority, its imagery seemed increasingly dated. Some critics even questioned the role, meaning, and relevance of such signage at all. Of course, the symbol's meaning had evolved over time. Although it was introduced in 1969 as a directional or wayfinding device, it quickly became a symbol of visibility and a marker of identity. But it was still found wanting.

The access symbol continues to embody a series of internal compromises and tensions—neither really a wheelchair nor fully a human figure, the symbol remains a profoundly awkward figure. Moves to change or even replace the ISA speak to a new criticality in both design and disability circles. In the last twenty-five years, the "cold," "rigid," and vaguely "mechanical" figure adopted in 1969 has undergone two serious makeovers in the United

States (Hendren, 2013). Even so, it has not kept up with expanding notions of disability itself. Furthermore, the wheelchair figure was developed and introduced by a charitable organization; the access symbol has never fit easily within larger systems of visual communications developed by professional designers. But also, unlike most wayfinding symbols, it bears a heavy burden. Not only must it be highly functional but it is also a symbolic and representational form.

Like it or not, with the passage of laws like the 1990 ADA (and the subsequent tightening and enforcement of its compliance guidelines), the symbol is an unavoidable fact of life for many architects and designers. Keeping these facts in mind, Victor Calise participated in this ongoing discussion, but was strategic in his approach. He proposed a plan in which the City would gradually, not to mention unceremoniously, phase in a new symbol. When old signs decayed, they would be replaced with new ones featuring the updated symbol. After Hurricane Sandy hit New York in 2013 and destroyed a great deal of infrastructure, the timing seemed good. Perhaps more fortuitously, when New York introduced a new fleet of accessible taxi vans, the new symbol (showing a revised wheelchair figure hailing a cab) was placed on the vehicles' hoods. As word got out, other cities—large and small—took the lead. But, opposition also began to mount. Critics objected to the cost of replacing the old symbol, as well as its legality (the newer figure had not been vetted by the International Symbols Organization). Others questioned the newer figure's legibility and meaning. In the end, New York's state government eventually bulldozed through the discussion; rather than fretting about whether the symbol might be used in the City, two lawmakers co-sponsored a bill that made the symbol legal throughout the entire state. Nevertheless, the nature of these changes and the ideologies behind them remain very much in question.

A cry for help

By the time New York embraced its newer, more dynamic access symbol, many members of the disability rights community asked, "Why didn't we do this before, it makes so much sense?" (Baskin, 2013). In fact, since its inception, professional designers have quietly updated the symbol over and over again. But the 1990 passage of the ADA provoked a more fundamental rethinking of the symbol's design. The ADA's tough new strictures regarding graphic design caught many designers off guard.[1] In what he called "A Cry for Help," Paul Arthur appealed to his fellow designers, asking them to conduct their own research and determine what kinds of signage best accommodates persons with disabilities (Arthur, 1993a: 16). Brendan Murphy, then a student at the University of Cincinnati, took up that charge. But, in place of a single image of access to replace the ISA, Murphy developed a series of symbols fitting better with rapidly changing views of disablement, actual need, and identity.

FIGURE 7.3 Access symbol developed by Don Meeker and Associates, for the
National Parks Service, c. 1985.

Murphy's redesign built on earlier efforts. When, for example, Don
Meeker developed a pictographic signage system for the US National Park
Service in the mid-1980s, he and his team created signs that could wordlessly
guide visitors to activities and unify facilities scattered through large and
dispersed, not to mention often remote, park settings (Figure 7.3). Using a
unified aesthetic, they also aimed to visually link their signed vocabulary.
Meeker's team didn't accept the unbendingly rigid figures commonly used in
international signage at the time; instead they used the parks service signage
as an excuse for envisioning a series of schematic, yet congenial figures who
use their rounded bodies, legs, and arms to busily enjoy the outdoors. In
addition to figures biking, skiing, and swimming, this applies equally to
Meeker's variation on the ISA figure; the parks service figure bears a close
familial resemblance to its athletic brothers and sisters. Where the older

symbol is little more than a stick-like figure resting on a wheel, Meeker's wheelchair user stands apart, with a more rounded, limber, and fluid body. But there is one subtler, more profound difference: the parks service symbol clearly distinguishes between user and chair. Meeker's team never intended the redesign as a statement in itself. Brendan Murphy took up that task.

An Irish-born graduate student in graphic design, Brendan Murphy studied under Robert Probst and Alan Chewing, two designers with deep ties to the professional community and particularly to the Society for Environmental Design (SEGD). Even if Meeker had redesigned the ISA, Paul Arthur's "cry for help" made it clear that the symbol needed a more ambitious makeover. When Murphy began to search for a thesis topic, his instructors pointed out the problem of the ISA. The complaint wasn't simply that the ADA was mandating a vast system of accommodations, but that the access symbol that announces them is ungainly and misleading. Murphy recalls how his teachers at Cincinnati "encouraged me to do research, to dig into it" (Murphy, 2016). He was given an SEGD scholarship to support this effort, and a board of advisors drawn from the tightly knit design community including renowned logo and environmental designers like Lance Wyman, Roger Whitehouse, and David Vanden-Eynden. All he had to do was design a new symbol (Figure 7.4).

Murphy found the whole process "liberating" (Murphy, 2016). As a research project, he saw that "there were no rules ... my job is to push the boundaries" (Murphy, 2016). Rather than focusing exclusively on disability signage, his own research was largely based on a broader study of symbols. After "three or six months of digging into the history of symbols and looking at the broader cultural landscape," he also became "much more aware of how society uses labels ... [and how] a symbol can be a form of labelling." For example, the designer points to the culturally specific meanings of the Red Cross, which may mean humanitarian aid today, but "which in 1665 symbolized the presence of plague" in a particular parish or district (Murphy, 1993: 2). Moreover, the deeper he dove into cross-cultural symbolism, the more Murphy noted that symbols in one society shift meaning in another. A finger tapped to the head may mean madness in one context, and signify the use of a telephone in another (Murphy, 1993: 4).

Publicly, Murphy identified his touchstones as largely personal. That it derives from Murphy's Irish heritage was emphasized in press accounts at the time. The very fact that he drew from stories of an impoverished life in Dublin helped shape the discourse around his design. He would also recall Christy Brown, the disabled Irish poet and close neighbor, who was the subject of the Academy Award–winning film *My Left Foot* (1989). Murphy admired how Brown "fought to be seen for his artistic and intellectual abilities, and not to be defined by his physical disabilities" (Murphy, 2016).

But more privately, through his research, Murphy also came to learn of a shift in thinking around disability itself. For almost a decade, activists

FIGURE 7.4 While at the University of Cincinnati, Brendan Murphy proposed a revision of the International Symbol of Access, 1993. Courtesy of Brendan Murphy.

and scholars, fueled by feminist theory and identity politics, were recasting disability; arguing that social forces could debilitate impaired people, the larger disability rights community was undertaking a transformation of thought. Rather than focusing only on medical assessments of how the body functions, discussion turned toward the social factors that contribute to disablement. The point, they argued, is that lack of education or employment opportunities can profoundly shape disabled people's access to spaces and resources.[2]

While Murphy chose to play this more politicized discourse down when he introduced his design, it should be understood as part of a broader, rapidly evolving discussion of disability in the media. In 1993, the year it was designed, a growing debate centered around depictions of disabled persons on television and in film. Comedian Jerry Lewis' yearly Labor Day Telethon was particularly targeted; disability activists launched a critique of these annual appeals, arguing against "the paternalism, reflected in the telethon: the attitude that stresses that no matter what one does, life is meaningless in a wheelchair" (Johnson, 1992: 232). The power of these accusations intrigued Murphy, who worried that the comedian "has perhaps unwittingly crossed the line from being a patron into being patronizing" (Murphy 1993: 3). Echoing the arguments of disability rights activists, scholars, and theorists—and their contention that disability does not signify an empty, impoverished, or defining condition—Murphy began to experiment with the wheelchair figure. As Murphy put it, "the person's identity is not the chair" (Murphy, 1993: 7).

With this point in mind, Murphy decoupled his figure from its chair, but he also pushed the ISA in a different direction (Figure 7.5). Murphy made the symbol more human, but Meeker already did that, with the parks service signage, a decade earlier. Murphy gave his figure agency. The very fact that he made his figure less "rigid and helpless" illustrates a broader rethinking of disability (Murphy, 1994: 15). Murphy's working process and sketches show a move from a static figure into someone "no longer imprisoned by the chair" (Murphy, 1994: 15) (Figure 7.5). Murphy's thumbnail sketches set out to establish by experiment which factors in the symbol might create dynamism. Thus, he experimented with adding a hand and a foot to the seated figure. Although he would reject these two details, he also aimed for a more dynamic and less passive form. In the end, Murphy focused these ideas on the figure's positioning. To imply movement, he developed the figure on a diagonal and moved its arm backward. The angle of the torso and the "pushing position" of the arm were essential to portraying an active, independent person. Implicit in these changes was Murphy's idea that "designers can play a major role in how impaired individuals view themselves and are viewed by the public" (Murphy, 1993: 5).

Noting the global ubiquity of the ISA—and its easy fit into built environments—Murphy aimed not to undo the wheelchair symbol, but rather to "evolve" its awkward appearance—effectively remaking its misfit design (Murphy, 1993: 6). For one thing, even though it rejects the official design, Murphy's wheelchair symbol still takes the ISA as its starting point. But by reworking the established symbol, Murphy's may be tied to an alternate tradition. Although he did not quote Selwyn Goldsmith directly, Murphy's bid for a humanizing symbol echoes Goldsmith's call for an image that that could echo the precepts of the postwar welfare state. Both Goldsmith and Murphy embraced values of universal healthcare, support for the unemployed, and a host of other services and supports for people with disabilities. For Goldsmith, these values were all bound up in a figurative, non-abstract symbol that would speak for itself, making it clear "that they are people with special needs, and that someone is sufficiently concerned to be doing something to help them" (Goldsmith, 1967: 389). Murphy claimed

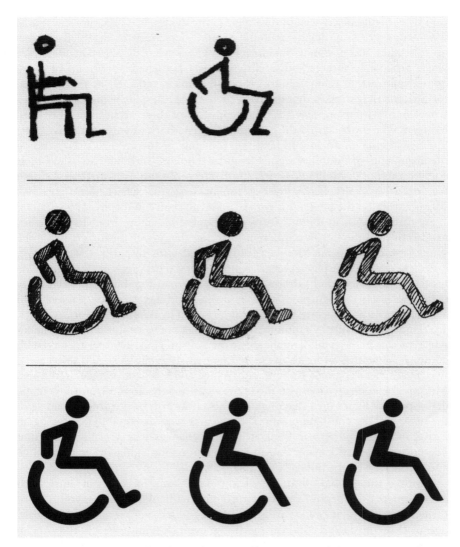

FIGURE 7.5 Early drafts of Brendan Murphy's revision of the International Symbol of Access, 1993. Courtesy of Brendan Murphy.

a similar set of values, readily asserting that his "access point is different and socialist" (Murphy, 2016). But Murphy's sense of inclusivity is, in fact, different from anything Goldsmith anticipated.

After settling on this project, almost immediately Murphy identified a second, more complex misfit. He observed that the image of a wheelchair had little relevance for the vision or hearing impaired. In other words, there was a basic misfit or gap between the symbol's message and the varied contexts in which it might be used. Murphy realized that the entire construct of disability

FIGURE 7.6 I am visually impaired button, 2017. Courtesy trend badges.

was expanding, and becoming more and more capacious. Of course, as scholars Ben-Moshe and Powell have noted, the wheelchair serves as "the prototypic representation of disability in Western societies" (Ben-Moshe and Powell, 2007: 497). Yet it really does denote just one kind of disability. Selwyn Goldsmith shared a similar concern, but he was never quite able to shape his experimental 1969 Norwich symbol to express different ambulatory, respiratory, and cardiac disabilities. It is possible to address this problem, Murphy reasoned, but he needed more than a redesigned wheelchair symbol. Murphy's mentors, Robert Probst and Lance Wyman, encouraged experimentation, saying, "let's see how can far we push the idea" of access. They asked of the wheelchair symbol, "Is this good for showing ALL access? What about others?" (Murphy; 2016). Suddenly, as Murphy began to work on this project, the wheelchair became but one symbol in an expanded series of glyphs, each separately addressing the needs of sight-, hearing-, speech-, and mobility-impaired persons (Figure 7.7).

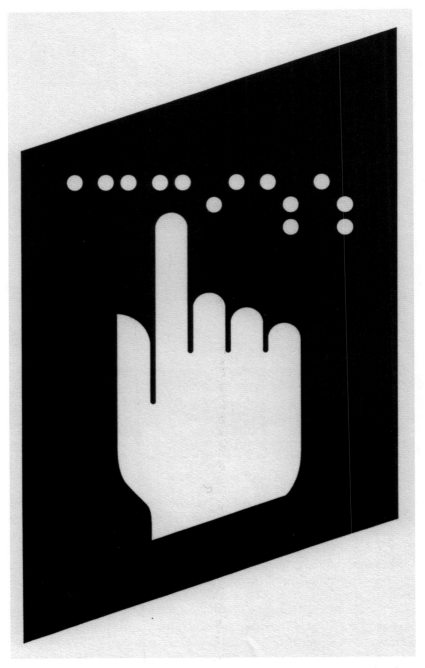

FIGURE 7.7 Brendan Murphy designed a suite of signs, all meant to be alternatives to the wheelchair sign, 1993. Courtesy Brendan Murphy.

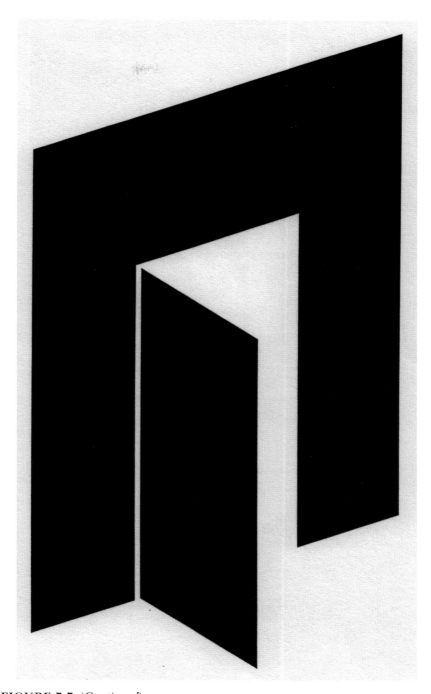

FIGURE 7.7 (*Continued*)

FIGURE 7.7 (*Continued*)

Murphy conferred respectability on the idea that three different symbols might better serve disabled people, but he offered a curious fourth image as well. The first three are, in fact, relatively straightforward, including not only Murphy's reworking of the ISA wheelchair figure, but also a hand signing the motion OK, and a finger touching a dotted Braille script. But the fourth glyph—a pictogram of an open door—represents a newer line of thinking in terms of access and usage itself. This was, in fact, unrelated to any recognizable disability. It was meant, instead, to suggest a "welcoming" or "barrier-free" environment in a "strong, positive, symbolic connotation" (Murphy, 1994: 15). Originally, Murphy thought to use a large letter "A" for "Access" letter (recalling the "H" used to denote Hospitals). But, he soon realized that such a symbol would resonate only with English speakers (Murphy, 2016). But also, with the Open Door symbol, Murphy's image also recalls the earlier destigmatizing access symbol first introduced in the United States during the 1960s. Of course, a number of North American designs, including the Canadian building code "insignia" and New York's wheel and arrow form, also avoid reference to specific disabilities. Although Murphy was unaware of these forerunners, his thesis advisor Robert Probst described the open door symbol as "neutral" and even expressed the hope that it "would not stigmatize and would not categorize the abled from the disabled" (Johnson, 1995: 37).

The public unveiling of Murphy's symbols was very different than the highly orchestrated introduction of the wheelchair symbol at Rehabilitation International's conference in 1969 Dublin some twenty-five years earlier. Murphy was invited to Seattle and took to the stage at the SEGD's national conference in August 1994. The reception to Murphy's designs was mixed. Many members concurred with Lyn Jeffery, SEGD's education director, who rushed to praise "a more sensitive and practical set of symbols" that seemed to be "going in the right direction" (Busch, 1994: 45). But many more were guarded. Susan Mampre, the SEGD's communication director at the time, was circumspect about the entire suite of symbols. "Some people think they're great," she observed. "Some people think they're not going to help. But people are interested at the very least" (Johnson, 1995: 37). At the same time, Murphy never stipulated how any should be used. Ultimately, the suite of symbols failed to gain traction.

Perhaps unsurprisingly, Murphy's rendition of the more conventional wheelchair symbol received the most attention. Whether part of the original suite of symbols or not, Murphy's moving wheelchair gave a conscious nod to newer ideas of active disablement. Soon after it was introduced, this updated symbol was adopted by a variety of organizations, from the camping and outdoors outfitter REI to the city of San Antonio, Texas. But the symbol's reception was not that simple. Almost immediately, questions about its message and efficacy were raised. When Belinda Carlton, director of the Coalition of Texans with Disabilities, polled some fifty representatives of disability groups across the state, she found solid opposition to Murphy's active wheelchair figure. Many of these professionals were caught off guard, and openly worried that the new "symbol's not going to change society's image about people with disabilities." Even at the state's architectural barriers office, staffers agonized that "it has taken this long to get the public to recognize the current symbol. Why go through this again" (Pierson, 1995: B1). Other critics were concerned that having "two symbols for a long period of transition ... could be confusing—people may think they are intended to convey two different messages" (Pierson, 1995: B1). And still others worried

> that the proposed symbol appears an attempt to separate the user from the wheelchair, perhaps suggesting the user has a choice of whether or not to use the chair. It does not ... suggest movement of chair *and user* but whether mobility of user apart from the chair, as if the chair were something to be ashamed of and escape from. (Pierson, 1995: B1; italics in original)

In the end, as concerns around Murphy's symbol mounted, his sponsors at the SEGD decided that the group could not endorse its acceptance. The part played by Murphy in this unfolding narrative is relatively minor. And, where Rehabilitation International actively pushed for the acceptance of the ISA, the SEGD was reluctant to promote Murphy's revision. Murphy gave the group the legal rights to his image, but the SEGD was squeamish;[3] worried that they would be held responsible for circulating an unapproved variant of the ISA, the organization's legal counsel advised the SEGD to issue a disclaimer each time it was contacted by persons interested in the newer symbol (Society for Environmental Graphic Design, 1994). The statement acknowledged that Murphy's symbol deviated enough from the official version that, if users adopted it, they might be charged with failure to comply with the ADA. Effectively, the law was written referencing use of the ISA, and only the ISA (Murphy, 2016).

Paul Arthur also repudiated Murphy's design, though in a less public manner. Focusing on the guidelines issued by the government in the wake of the ADA, Arthur sought more "human factors research." Essentially, he wanted more research on specific problems related to disability and communication. What typeface, for example, is legible to vision impaired and fully sighted people alike? How practical is Braille lettering when only 5 percent of blind people read it with ease? Murphy didn't investigate these types of questions. Instead, he offered a symbolic representation of disablement itself. In a letter to Murphy, he wrote that the new symbols "are backsliding into pure decorativeness. You seem with these symbols at least, to be becoming less interested in effective communication and more in being pretty" (Arthur, 1994b). To some extent, Arthur was correct. Murphy made the symbol less rigid, more rounded and organic; generally speaking, he harmonized the inelegant ISA, making it work more congenially with other symbols in use at the time. The newer symbol was made more appealing for the broader design community who, broadly speaking, found it ugly. But the effort to "prettify" the access symbol must also be seen in relation to the larger political climate of the period. Murphy's symbols, and especially his reworked wheelchair figure, were more than mere aestheticization. States of disablement had long been stereotyped publicly as ugly, and even unfit to be seen.[4] For this misfit symbol, a gesture toward beauty was, in itself, a meaningful act. Disability, the revised symbol seemed to insist, could be a dynamic, purposeful, and even graceful state.

Though some organizations, including Williams College and Wal-Mart stores, have adopted Murphy's symbol, its greatest legacy is, perhaps, its influence. For instance, a well-received version was adapted for the Museum of Modern Art's 2003 revised signage system. It would also have a profound influence on a second redesign, introduced in 2010 less as a design than as a form of guerrilla art. But the latter pushed further, challenging not only the ISA's appearance, but also the symbol's fit in public space.

A twenty-first-century makeover

While this discussion slowly unfolded in the design community, casual observers began to take note only when, in late 2010, a Harvard design student and a philosophy professor from nearby Gordon College began defacing the International Symbol of Access throughout the Boston area. Placing a transparent but bright orange sticker over the familiar wheelchair figure, the pair said this defacement could capture "the social power of the urban street." They printed a thousand transparent window decals and quickly began distributing the sticker to anyone who asked (Vanhemert, 2013). In that respect, it could be interpreted as an example of what its instigators alternately called "guerrilla activism" and a "graffiti art project." As such, this sticker brought a new level of scrutiny to the ISA (Baker, 2013: A1). But the narrative is not that simple. For a start, when it was featured in a 2011 *Boston Globe* article (Baker, 2011), disabled people, including Victor Calise, began agitating for the sticker symbol to replace the older, officially recognized wheelchair symbol. By 2013, the *Globe* breathlessly announced that the project "has gone from an artistic statement to a global movement" (Baker, 2013: A1). But this new image was not designed by Brendan Murphy, the SEGD, or any member of the professional design community. In fact, the image that finally seemed poised to replace the ISA was not, at first, even presented as a work of design.

The so-called Accessible Icon Project (AIP) had higher aims (Figure 7.8). Sara Hendren, one of the AIP's creators, acknowledges that the redesign does edit the older symbol. But it also presents "a much bigger question to ask about who is abled and who is disabled and what we think about dependence and need" (Baker, 2011). In effect, it forced the ISA to undergo "a 21st Century makeover" (Deque Systems, 2013). But has the redo finally redressed the symbol's fundamental misfit?

FIGURE 7.8 The Accessible Icon Project, developed by Sara Hendren and Brian Glenney, 2010. Courtesy Sara Hendren.

Like Murphy's 1993 remake of wheelchair symbol, the AIP gives a nod to the older International Access Symbol, but only as a point of departure. Thus, while it still uses a wheelchair to symbolize access, the seated figure is in dynamic motion. It also highlights the maladroit misfit of the original design—to this day, the ISA remains a schematized depiction of a modern wheelchair, with a circle placed on its back. But in this case, the question of context is key. Understood as an activist or street art campaign, the transparent orange sticker overlay was used as an act of defacement; it challenged the ubiquitous presence of the symbol—its very "fit" in the built environment—as well as the message that it carries. It also transcends its material setting. Instead of relying on official channels of distribution, the Accessible Icon merges social networking, the web, and the evolving rhetoric of disability rights. The new figure attracted global attention. As Hendren relates, "It outpaced our expectations … We heard from a doctor at a big rehab hospital at Delhi and he'd changed the official signage there. People in Italy, people in Sweden, people in Canada. I could go on and on" (Vanhemert, 2013). But it is also meant to challenge ideas of disability and fitness itself.

With this in mind, the AIP carries a casual, unembarrassed assertiveness that transcends earlier images and debates around the access figure. Fifty years earlier, designers, disabled people and their advocates grappled with the symbol, even debating how "secret" any form of access signage should be. This new revision makes no apologies for its public presence. Instead, it presents a powerful and dynamic wheelchair user on the move. In stylistic terms, it builds off Murphy's 1993 figure. The chair and the user are distinguishable. But the AIP's aggressive dynamism exaggerates the sense of movement introduced by Murphy; were the two in a race, there's no doubt who would win. In a restless age, where everything is moving faster and faster, the AIP remake is dynamically slanted, inexorably moving forward as if racing through traffic or over a finish line. For its makers, the significance is clear. For one thing, the symbol focuses on the abilities of the wheelchair user; by emphasizing the motion of the individual, the disabled person is the driver. As explained on the AIP's website, the wheelchair user asserts his or her "active status of navigating the world" (Accessible Icon Project, 2013).

Even more specifically, to Hendren's collaborator, philosophy professor Brian Glenney, the new icon was different from the unworldly, inexpressive wheelchair user conceived back in 1969; this newer sticker figure most closely approaches the street-savvy grace of the skateboarder. In fact, skateboarders have long shared spaces with wheelchairs, both using curb cuts and ramps if to different ends. Looking for equivalents, Glenney recalls a favorite wheelchair athlete, Aaron Fotheringham ("Wheelz"), a 21-year-old from Las Vegas who uses his wheelchair at skate events. When Hendren developed the final design, Glenney recalls how "I felt good about the symbol … I knew it could represent Wheelz" (Phelps, 2012).

Glenney and Hendren are not the only ones to rethink and question the role and appearance of the wheelchair figure. But, while no one claims that more access is a bad thing, some observers believe that signage is not the best means to this end. To some critics, the wheelchair symbol translates as a form of paternalism. As early as 1977, architects Charles Moore and Kent Bloomer complained that access signage forces a kind of "childhood status" on disabled people. In this way, they observe, "over emphatic graphics" can be too much. Alarmingly, plastered around an urban environment, they "scream that this is a safe place for the handicapped" (Moore and Bloomer, 1977: 7). Other critics have focused on the question of segregation. In seeking a benevolent approach toward disability, Selwyn Goldsmith argued for a form of "positive discrimination" that might grow out of Britain's postwar welfare state. But Goldsmith never fully convinced the British design establishment and—by the late 1970s—he found himself increasingly under attack.[5] Instead, a number of critics gave new urgency to the South African activist Vic Finkelstein's argument. Architectural critic Rob Imrie spoke for many when he worried that "current urban planning is inscribed by a 'design apartheid' where urban planners, architects, and related officials are guilty of constructing spaces that exclude disabled people" (Imrie, 1996: 24). For the same reason, scholars Liat Ben Moshe and Justin Powell note, some activists and critics feel ambivalence toward any symbol that "directs persons needing accommodations to 'special,' often segregated, locations. If universal design principles had been carried out fully we would have no need for such a symbol, because places and objects would have been designed from the start for a diverse population" (Ben-Moshe and Powell, 2007: 494).

If these critics argue that access signage is counterproductive, others have leveled visual critiques at actual access signage itself. In the UK, artist Caroline Cardus, for instance, created a collection of self-authored road signs she called "The Way Ahead." Conceived as a traveling exhibition that opened on October 1, 2004, the day that the UK ushered into law its new Disability Discrimination Act,[6] Cardus designed a series of symbols that quietly send up existing signs. One reads "Warning! People Using Sign Language Ahead." Another announces, "disability is not a choice— your attitude is." More recently, in the US artist Park McArthur devised a series of blank blue signs that imitate the traditional rectangular format of disabled parking signage (Figure 7.9). These signs eliminate the troublesome wheelchair figure entirely. On the other hand, the point of Hendren and

FIGURE 7.9 Artist Park McArthur's *Blanks* suggests an alternate reconsideration of the International Access Symbol, 2014. Copyright Park McArthur.

Glenney's sticker was to embed critique into the world around us. Presented as street art, affixed to signage already in place, and introduced into the built environment, it was integrated into daily life.

But the active wheelchair figure also sits at a curious intersection between graffiti art and design, digital networking, and political identity. In late 2009, when Hendren and Glenney first conceived the revised symbol, they were already at work on a device that might help blind users perceive colors by listening to sounds. The spirit of cross-disability practice and theory, however, led the pair to push off into a different direction when Hendren saw a variant of the Murphy design and wrote about it on her blog. Observed on the door of a local department store, she snapped—and posted—a photo, comparing it to the ISA. Her first thought was of design and disparity. To begin, she noticed, "The difference between two icons like these was so striking to me that I couldn't believe the second one (and others that are closely similar) wasn't used more commonly" (Accessible Icon Project, 2013). The same was true for Glenney, who quickly offered a proposition: replace the old signs. Glenney's part in this unfolding story is significant. He had a background as a graffiti artist and suggested something that would evoke the subversiveness of graffiti tagging. By designing an "overlay" sign, placed on top the original ISA, they could emulate graffiti artists' sticker campaigns (Accessible Icon Project, 2013). He found the possibilities exciting. The same was true of the press, who would refer to the campaign as "a guerrilla street art project" (Baker, 2013: A1)

But it is misleading to present the finished sticker as a completed thought, much less a rash act. The process for creating their icon more closely resembled designers' working methods. For one thing, Hendren began by developing a sticker in the shape of a stand-alone orange figure, and applied it to outdoor ISA signage around Boston (Figure 7.10). But, after consulting a group of friends and colleagues, Hendren and Glenney discovered that it lacked clarity. So, too, viewers' feedback indicated that the new figure looked more like a person getting up and out of a wheelchair than someone at ease in one. Instead, they tried a different approach. Since the early 1970s, US access signs have been blue and white, following the international norm for roadside signage. Glenney and Hendren made their own version of the blue and white symbol, the better to blend in. But this was misleading. For one thing, the new signs went unnoticed. They hoped that their revision would spark vigorous discussion and debate, but it went entirely unrecognized. People pay little attention to the access figure; they simply didn't notice when the new stickers were applied.

For the final iteration, they made a transparent sticker with their new symbol printed on it in orange (Figure 7.11). All the better to make the revision clear. The color made it difficult for observers to miss the image overlaid on the older symbol. And because the original sign was still visible under the newer sticker, the gesture invited what Hendren wanted all along—a visual comparison. Hendren would later point out that "this

FIGURE 7.10 An early version of Brian Glenney and Sara Hendren's Accessible Icon Project (AIP) uses red sticky vinyl figures which could be placed on top of the official International Symbol of Access, c. 2010. Courtesy Sara Hendren.

image feels like the heart of the project: a clear-backed sticker that shows the newer figure—here in red and orange, leaning forward 'italicized,' while the original image shows underneath" (Accessible Icon Project, 2013). There was no mistaking the static older figure for the dynamic newer one. This is the figure that finally got public attention.

FIGURE 7.11 A later version of Brian Glenney and Sara Hendren's Accessible Icon Project uses a transparent red sticker. This allows the official symbol of access to continue being visible under it, c. 2010. Courtesy Sara Hendren.

Of course this imagery was a more critical edit or "correction," of the ISA's original—and maladroit—misfit. Whatever would come next, it is important to note that the original sticker campaign functioned as a form of critique. That is, it comments on the original design's fitness. This criticality has often been overlooked. The sticker symbol was introduced not as a replacement for the ISA, but rather as an attempt to spark a kind of visual debate. Glenney and Hendren did not design the project as part of a protest movement like those held in the 1970s by Disabled in Action or by the Atlantis community in Denver. According to its makers, the newer wheelchair figure was designed to raise questions, not push for answers.

If, as its makers claim, the newer symbol reflects current discussions around the nature of disability, its appearance was particularly timely. Beginning in the 1990s, activist and academic circles began to rethink disability as a constructed cultural category. Seen this way, theorists note, disablement might be deemed not only worthy of reflection and study but also, much like gender and race, as a broader concept open to discussion and critique (Garland-Thomson, 2013: 916). Of course, this discussion was just beginning to take shape when Brendan Murphy launched his 1993 remake of the ISA. But, unlike Murphy, Glenney and Hendren did not claim to present a design solution to these questions. Instead, they pitched their sticker as a loose reflection of these broader intellectual currents. Placed around the city of Boston, they claimed, the image was meant to extend an ongoing conversation about society's stereotypes around disability, agency, and change. Academic writing and intellectual discourse have an appropriate place, Hendren argues, but that's not enough—"people need to see it" (Hendren, 2015). In the end, "framing this work as a street art campaign allowed it to live as a question, rather than a resolved proposition" (Accessible Icon Project, 2013).

Whatever its theoretical resonance, the red decal overlay was itself a kind of misfit. Hendren explained its sheer oddity as part of the strategy; it was "like drawing a circle around the change in the design that we were trying to do, and pointing to that change" (Baker, 2011). Reflecting on Murphy's symbol and other variants, the pair observed, "we knew that better icons already existed." As they reconsidered Murphy's symbol, however, they presented their stickers a kind of commentary, all the while capitalizing on the ISA's pervasive presence. It is so common today, the ISA has become, in Hendren's words, "invisible" (Hendren, 2015). In some ways, that very ubiquity made the ISA a perfect platform for raising "questions about disability and the built environment, in the largest sense. Who has access—physically, yes, but moreover, to education, to meaningful citizenship, to political rights?" To ask this question, the pair began distributing stickers to friends and to Glenney's contacts among graffiti and sticker art networks; they began plastering the image around Boston (Baskin, 2013).

Whatever the symbol's resonance today, this kind of critical design has a healthy history. Take, for example, the Italian Radical Design movement of the 1960s. Though this period is perhaps best known for launching postmodernism, the Italians also saw design as a form of intellectual discourse rather than a consumer-driven practice. (This discourse was rooted in the culture around the Italian magazine *Domus*, which launched a series of provocative design statements.) More recently, "critical design," a term first used by British designer Anthony Dunne (Dunne, 1999), has extended this tradition. The attraction of this approach led Dunne and, later, Fiona Raby to reject design that affirms the mainstream corporate culture of consumerism—what they call "affirmative design." But Glenney and Hendren deployed their critical design differently from Dunne and Raby. Where the earlier pair placed their work in gallery and museum settings, the Boston duo relied on networking savvy and social media to push critical design into the twenty-first century. This approach is especially meaningful given the context and history of disability signage, where large institutions and governmental authorities have largely controlled access symbols and signs, dictating how, when, where, and why it is put into use.

Yet, the notion of design as critical provocation was entirely absent from the processes surrounding earlier iterations of the access symbol. Most official access symbols designed in the 1960s stressed one form of assimilation or another. That was more or less the approach of Selwyn Goldsmith, whose symbols were meant to address what he called "the

FIGURE 7.12 Artist Shepard Fairey affixing a sticker on a parking sign in Los Angeles, 2005. Getty Images.

psychology of disablement" (see Chapter 5). What mattered primarily to Paul Arthur was that his Expo 67 pictogram fit within a larger symbol system. In many ways, the 2010 sticker makes a statement similar to that of the 1993 symbol designed by Brendan Murphy. Both aim to present disability as an active and dynamic state. But Hendren and Glenney's sticker campaign took a different shape and employed an unusual means of distribution. It was, they admitted, "mildly transgressive" in "altering public property." But what mattered primarily was that its means of distribution caught attention, especially because of what Hendren has referred to as "media interest in graffiti's legality." More to the point, the pair capitalized on a recent exhibition in Boston, featuring the career of sticker and graffiti artist Shepard Fairey. That artist was already well known for posting enigmatic stickers and posters throughout Boston and beyond (Figure 7.12). Not only did the art exhibition bring attention to his work, but he was also arrested at its official opening: he had outstanding warrants for damage to property at two Boston locations. Fairey's transgression made headlines when the artist arrived at the opening, only to be arrested by the Boston police as his cab neared the museum. For publicity purposes, the timing was perfect.

With such headline-grabbing precedents, the pair gained more and more space in the press. They also found they could "shape our interviews to our own agenda: the politics of disability, access, and inclusion" (Hendren, 2015). For models, Hendren points to the Austrian collective WochenKlausur, an activist group of artists that has been successfully carrying out social projects since 1993, and writing about them. She relates, "When I read this it was like the oracle speaking" (Hendren, 2015). WochenKlausur are typically invited by art institutions to develop and realize proposals which are small scale but concrete for identifying and improving local sociopolitical problems. Their first attempt was at the Vienna Secession, where they took over an exhibition space and used it as an office (one will search in vain for a work of art). The group designed and launched a mobile medical unit that aimed at serving the local homeless population. Their name WochenKlausur or "weeks of closure" describes the time they set aside to work on a problem, usually in closed session working spaces and often limited to eight weeks. And their work is in fact not about conceptual or expressive autonomy, but rather issues often related to social design and public policy.

Like WochenKlausur, Glenney and Hendren's work slides between easy definitions of "art" and "design." The slippage is most prominent in Hendren's understanding of WochenKlausur's tactical use of the media. Hendren observes that the Austrian collaborative works in areas normally understood as the realm of urban planning and design. Contemporary art provides a useful umbrella for social practice, at once attracting publicity, but also opening the public sphere to issues ripe for confrontation and speculation. "Call something art or culture," Hendren notes, and "you will get more attention" (Hendren, 2015). By naming their practice as art, WochenKlausur was able to engage in a level of cultural critique and critical discourse normally alien to design. This is also important for posing questions about disability. Much like the ubiquitous International Access Symbol, disability is common enough in most people's lives, but it and the stereotypes around it are rarely probed and discussed at any length. The new symbol was presented not as a definitive design, but rather as a piece of guerrilla art and thus an object of discourse. But it also brought the Boston project considerable press coverage. In the end, the design received glowing reviews in the American press, including extensive coverage in the *Boston Globe*, *Washington Post*, *New York Times*, and National Public Radio. For inspiration, Hendren again points to an early WochenKlausur project. When, for example, that group's 1993 grant ended, they used the threat of press coverage of the closure to scare politicians and cashier the project permanently. As Glenney observed, "If she were to make this thing domesticated, it wouldn't have that social power" (Baker, 2011).

In fact, as it gained more and more attention, there began a separate campaign for it to substitute for the ISA. In Boston, where the sticker campaign began, Triangle, a nonprofit disability services organization, began to advocate for widespread adoption. From its inception, the access symbol has cast and recast different strategies for dealing with a continuing problem—the very public misfit between disabled bodies and the built environment. In the mid-twentieth century, accommodations were often hidden, and forms of secret knowledge were favored. When professional designers finally began to consider the problem of how to disseminate information about access, they focused primarily on how to fit it within larger systems of public communication. Hendren and Glenney's guerrilla action and tactical use of the media suggest an alternate, and arguably more effective strategy for design distribution. That said, it was ultimately fitted to existing standards.

Hendren and Glenney worked with a professional designer, Tim Ferguson Sauder, to bring the icon in line with international signage standards. Complying with the Department of Transportation's ISO DOT 50 standards meant bringing this renegade symbol in line with a series of pictograms originated in 1974 and spearheaded by Roger Cook and Don Shanosky. The symbol was transformed from a transparent orange figure meant to clash with the blue ground and white image under it, into a single, cohesive image that erased the older, static figure. Sauder immediately understood this difference; the revision was "an approach that, in many ways, opposes Sara's original goal." Revising the figure's dimensions, line width, and other details helped Sauder regularize the new symbol. The aim was "to make it feel like it's part of that family, so an airport in France, Russia, or Greece will consider using it, to extend the conversation to those countries, so people will notice the difference and think about it. It's a tension that we've talked about quite a bit" (Kirkwood, n.d.). By 2014, the symbol was in use in parking lots and buildings across the state of New York, and had entered the collections of the Museum of Modern Art as a critical design. As Glenney observed at the time, "What was 'against' the law is 'becoming' a law in just three years" (Gordon College, 2014).

But what did disabled people themselves think of the new symbol? Some of the earliest advocates for the AIP are themselves disabled, and many see the new symbol as an opportunity to revise stereotypes and misconceptions. Brendan Hildreth, a wheelchair user and a former volunteer at Triangle's headquarters outside Boston, praises not only the symbol, but also the advocacy around it as a mark of empowerment. Says Hildreth, "I hope people understand that this project is about more than just a picture. People look at me differently just because my muscles don't work the same as theirs, but my disability does not change the fact that I am a leader ... Anyone can be a leader, and bring positive change" (Hicks, 2013).

Hildreth's remarks gesture at the ways in which the new symbol has drawn attention to our shifting attitudes toward disability, and encourage discourse. However, the symbol has also struck up debate around issues of disability and identity. According to some activists, its dynamic portrayal of impairment still follows a kind of "ableist" logic. Activist Stephen Mendelsohn has noted, "The new symbol conveys a profound prejudice against those of us with severe disabilities who need things like power wheelchairs, attendant care, breathing support, and feeding tubes. The message being sent is that while it is cool to be 'able disabled,' having a severe disability causes one to be a 'burden' " (Haigh, 2015). Others identify with the older symbol. Protestor Cathy Ludlum prefers the original ISA which has been described by detractors as "blocky and rigid." "I AM blocky and rigid!" Ludlum has said (Haigh, 2015). Others see it as beside the point. Scholar Kelly Fritsch, for instance, wonders why we continue to define disability in terms of wheelchairs at all (Frisch, 2013). Perhaps more comprehensively, others have complained that the new symbol is not part of a larger signage system, and fails to integrate with those already in place (Whitehouse, 2016).

Nevertheless, the fate of the AIP symbol looks more promising than that of Brendan Murphy's 1993 design edit. In 2015 the US Justice Department informally declared that it could be used in place of the ISA.[7] But the series of critical questions posited by the AIP's creators remain unanswered. Why is a symbol still needed? What meanings does the symbol have for those who are disabled and for those who are not? Does the current symbol facilitate or hinder inclusion?

Notes

1 Murphy was initially drawn to the topic after his instructors at Cincinnati directed him to Arthur's article (Arthur, 1993a).

2 For more on this see Finkelstein (1975), Groce (1985), Eisland (1994), and Oliver (1990).

3 In the end, Murphy gave the rights to his symbol to the SEGD, with the caveat that it never be used in conjunction with the word "handicapped." But the Boston-based group only released it along with a legal disclaimer noting that they couldn't "endorse" the symbol (Pierson, 1995: B1). Instead, their statement noted, "We advise environmental graphic designers, fabricators and their clients to proceed with caution and seek the advice of an attorney regarding ADA compliance and symbols liability" (Society for Environmental Graphic Design, 1994).

4 A fuller consideration of these issues, and the laws surrounding them, is available in Schweik's (2009).

5 Goldsmith's approach was increasingly attacked in the 1970s. His third edition of *Designing for the Disabled* (1977), for instance, continued to focus almost exclusively on mobility-impaired persons; it provided little consideration of architecture for hearing and vision impaired persons, and even less for those with developmental disabilities. But more specifically, Goldsmith's ranging meditations on the benefits of dependency were also found wanting. As one critic put it, his philosophical stance was out of date, introduced poorly explained concepts like "interdependence," and most generally "plagued with contradictions that will confuse rather than enlighten the reader" (Ripley, 1977: 26).

6 The 1995 Disability Discrimination Act made it illegal to discriminate against disabled persons in most capacities of day-to-day life. It also made provisions for the employment of disabled persons, and established the National Disability Council.

7 The Accessible Icon Project, that is, the group formed after Hendren and Glenney gifted the rights to this image to the nonprofit organization Triangle Inc. That group has encountered its own problems. When supporters of the new symbol requested that the Massachusetts Architectural Access Board support its use in that state, it was rejected because of concerns about a financial conflict of interest. In fact, Triangle Inc. sold stickers and parking stencils of the symbol from their website. To date, most legislation has focused on continuing acceptance of the older ISA—in tandem with recognition of the newer symbol.

Epilogue

The Beginning of the End?

In September 2013, Ontario's Lieutenant-Governor David Onley announced that it was time to replace the familiar wheelchair symbol. In tandem with Ontario College of Art and Design University's Inclusive Design program, he agreed to co-sponsor an international Reimagining Accessibility competition. Although Onley himself uses a power chair, the competition guidelines explained that "less than three per cent of persons with disabilities in Ontario use a wheelchair or electric scooter for mobility purposes" (Inclusive Design Research Centre, 2013). The contest's goal was to revise and extend ideas of disability, finding a symbol effective across multiple, global cultures. Recalling the year when the ISA was first developed, Onley tweeted, "So much has changed since 1968: TVs, phones, computers. But the wheelchair symbol has stayed the same despite our evolving attitudes and understanding of accessibility" (Inclusive Design Research Centre, 2013).

When the competition closed in October 2013, over 100 designs had been submitted, including entries from Brazil, Columbia, France, Germany, Mexico, the United States, the UK, and Iraq. A panel consisting largely of North American designers gathered to winnow the field.[1] They narrowed the competition to forty, and then six, before settling on a final two. And then the competition stalled. The panel's eleven members were unable to reach a consensus and select a winner. In the end, the two finalists were each awarded honorable mentions. One, conceptualized by students Taghreed Al-Zubaidi, Julie Buelow, Yijin Jiang, and Arief Yulianto, introduced a series of stylized "affinity" symbols, each in a different color or value (red, blue, yellow, and gray-scale) and indicating a different need (Figure E.1). The other, student Dalton Hadwen's blue and white representation of an opening door, was set inside a circle. Onley called both new symbols "brilliant."

Logo Application

4

FIGURE E.1 A range of symbols were created by a student design team for the Reimagining Accessibility contest. One of two designs that earned an honorable mention, this project features an infinity symbol in red, blue, and yellow. Stylized symbols, representing a variety of individual disabilities, can be placed within the larger design, 2013. Courtesy Julie Buelow.

But he also remarked that they still did not represent the complex needs of people with disabilities. That, Onley admitted, was "far more complex than we thought" (Reiti, 2013). More ambiguously, when his competition co-chair, Sophie, the Countess of Wessex, addressed the award winners she noted, "Even though you have not come up with the exact replacement, what you do see here is the beginning of the end of the traditional symbol" (jgeboers, 2013). But is this really the end of the older symbol? If so, what is going to replace it? At the same time, who will decide what message the replacement will send?

As this book has shown, it is simply not possible to reduce the development of the access symbol to the work of an individual, a movement or industry. From the outset, the symbol was debated and, one might even say, *designed* by many different powers. It is the same today. Some critics like Frank Bowe argue that "our objective now should be to abolish the symbol of accessibility. America should have no need for it: a barrier free America would require only a symbol of non-access to designate special-purpose areas that are not accessible" (Bowe, 1978: 106). Others, meanwhile, see the access symbol as an important opportunity to shape public perceptions of disability. They argue "that representation matters; that public portrayals of disabled people have effects and consequences which—though slippery, diffuse and difficult to trace—are nevertheless ubiquitous and capable of powerfully shaping disabled people's lives in innumerable and very tangible ways" (Sandell and Dodd, 2010: 3). This debate is not new. It turns on the same issues that years ago drove early advocates for barrier-free access like Timothy Nugent and Selwyn Goldsmith.

Of course any access symbol designed today must bear a heavy weight. Designing a perfect symbol—a symbol that can be all things to all people—is close to impossible. Officials at the ISO claim that any new symbol must meet rigorous design standards. As one authority insists, "changes must undergo extensive human factors testing to ensure adequate levels of comprehension, recognition, and legibility for optimization in a roadway environment" (Lindley, 2015). Because of this, international authorities are reluctant to make even slight changes to the ISA—even though its original design was haphazard at best. The symbol may be imperfect, it may be a misfit, but the authorities seem to suggest, it is what it is.

In 2013, the same year as the Reimagining Accessibility competition, the *Boston Globe* approached Joseph Kwan, the current chairman of Rehabilitation International's Commission on Technology and Accessibility (ICTA) (that is, the group headed by Karl Montan and responsible for the original design). What, the Globe asked, did he make of recent attempts to redesign the access symbol? Kwan was quick to dismiss these efforts, claiming "there will always be people who wish to redesign [images] to satisfy their creative urges" (Baker, 2011). Barry Gray, chair of the ISO's committee on graphical symbols, was similarly dismissive. He homed in on the Accessible Icon Project's wheelchair figure, critiquing it for the very reason that others embraced it. Noting that the new figure was too dynamic, he insisted that it "has to work in static situations. Part of its job is to mark wheelchair spaces in public transportation or indicate refuge in emergency situations, as well as lifts and toilets" (Choksi, 2014). Gray's position (that the image should literally reflect the kind of function it describes) reflects the long-standing policy of the ISO. Seen from this perspective, the two great advantages of the ISA are its static neutrality and its sheer ubiquity.

But this hasn't stopped designers, organizations, and corporations from proposing alternatives. Some have proposed a linguistic symbol. For instance, several submissions to the Reimagining Accessibility competition proposed a giant A, though these were quickly eliminated because the letterform was judged too limited; the press was told that only five languages convey the idea of "access" using words that begin with the letter "A" (jgeboers, 2013). In recent years, other alternatives have been recommended. Microsoft marks

FIGURE E.2 In recent years, designers have struggled to develop an access symbol that transcends the wheelchair image and remains applicable to newer technologies. From DigitalVision Vectors, Getty Images.

accessible computer programs, usable for those with hearing and vision impairments, with an "Ease of Access" symbol; similarly, Apple has launched a blue and white symbol that resembles a squat, friendly Vitruvian man. The latter has been imitated widely and billed as a "Universal Access" image. Nevertheless, in the material world the wheelchair motif remains unrivaled.

At the same time, although the ISA is now posted all around the world and indicates a shared commitment to access, as a symbol it remains flawed. Taken literally, the figure suggests access for wheelchair users alone (Figure E.3). Indeed, nearly every disabled person who is not a wheelchair user can recall at least one occasion of being denied access simply because they don't look like the figure depicted on the symbol. Scholar Kelly Fritsch, for example, tells how her disability meant she could not climb the steep steps of an accessible bus. But the bus driver would let her use the lift only if she were seated in a wheelchair. "I found myself in the position of being both disabled and not disabled enough, or not disabled in the right way," she says. "When I pointed out this contradiction to the bus driver, he shrugged his shoulders and commented: 'Why don't you just get a wheelchair' " (Fritsch, 2013: 136). On the other hand, she notes that when she uses a tandem bicycle (riding with a partner "who does most the pedaling"), she has been told not to bring it on a rail car specially adapted for disabled users to walk or roll through the door (and avoid the steep steps at the entrances of many North American trains). When asked, a train worker insists "No bikes allowed," while "pointing to the blue and white icon of the wheelchair mounted on the train walls" (Fritsch, 2013: 136). After she told these stories at a scholarly conference several years ago she began to hear from other disabled people who revealed similar tales. Each had been berated by security personnel or casual onlookers, expelled from bathrooms, parking, and other accommodations because, as she put it, "they did not 'fit' the register of being disabled" (Fritsch, 2013: 136). At the small college where I teach, I've heard stories of colleagues with cerebral palsy, post-polio syndrome, and "invisible" neurological afflictions who have been hounded by passersby who insist they "don't look" disabled enough to use ADA-designated parking; I have also engaged in long, circular arguments with college facilities managers and ADA compliance officers, who remain convinced that the existing law extends only to individuals who use wheelchairs. Thus they plan campus accommodations around an idealized vision of wheelchair mobility.[2]

If the existing access symbol is ubiquitous, it is also deeply misleading. The result of a compromise, it remains imperfect at best. In the past 100 years, most disabled people realize that the conditions of their day-to-day lives have vastly improved. But the idea of access, and the laws meant to enforce it, have not solved the problem of lack of access. And, in some ways, the pervasive presence of the wheelchair symbol is misleading. It can suggest that access for disabled people is no longer a pressing issue. Ultimately, any solution to the lingering and very real problems of access that continue to exist must take the symbol—and all that it signifies—into account. Only then will the ISA live up to its original promise.

Notes

1   The committee members were: Glenn Barnes, David M. Capozzi, Arlene Dickinson, Frank Gehry Partners, Lizbeth Goodman, Paddy Harrington, Rabia Khedr, Robert Probst, Bill Shannon, Gary Taxali, and Mark Wafer.

2   The result of this misunderstanding is that issues like distance and terrain can be forgotten; after all, this erroneous logic follows, wheelchairs can travel easily over longer stretches of paths and sidewalks. And so accommodations like disabled parking lots can be moved away from the center of campus. If, as I've seen, all accommodations for the mobility impaired are measured according to an idealized understanding of wheeled access, parking for disabled people must always make way for bike racks and pedestrian malls or can be transformed overnight into loading docks.

BIBLIOGRAPHY

Primary Sources

Accessible Icon Project (2013), "The Accessible Icon." Accessed October 5. http://www. accessibleicon.org/

Ackermann, R. (1811), *The Repository of Arts, Literature, Commerce, Manufactures, Fashions, and Politics*, 1st series, vol. 6.

AIGA (American Institute of Graphic Arts) (1981), *Symbol Signs: The System of Passenger/Pedestrian Oriented Symbols Developed for the US Department of Transportation*, New York: United States Department of Transportation.

Ainsworth, G. (ed.) (1845), *Ainsworth's Magazine* 8: 115.

ANSI (American National Standards Institute). (1961), *ANSI 117.1: Accessible and Usable Building Facilities*, New York: ANSI.

Anon. (1825), *The Improved Bath Guide or Picture of Bath and Its Environs*, Bath: S. Simms.

Anon. (1857), "Mr Heath's Bath Chairs in the Art Treasures Exhibition." *The Manchester Guardian*, November 3: 3.

Anon. (1859), "Carroll's New York City Directory."

Anon. (1883), "The Turner Memorial. Liverpool." *Building News*, December 21: 999.

Anon. (1902), *Catalogue of J. & A. Carter, Manufacturers of Bath Chairs, Invalid Furniture & Appliances.*

Anon. (1916), "Inclined Sidewalk for a Wheeled Invalid Chair." *Popular Science* 88 (January): 473.

Anon. (1919), "Automobile Notes." *Granite Falls Record*, March 15: 6.

Anon. (1920), "Lively Cripples Who are Expert Drivers." *The Literary Digest* 45, May 22: 114.

Anon. (1944), "Disabled Vets Taught to Drive." *Los Angeles Times*, July 7: A1.

Anon. (1945), "Disabled War Veterans Taught to Drive Cars." *Los Angeles Times*, July 7, 1945: A1.

Anon. (1948), "UCLA Paraplegics." *Life Magazine*, April 5: 66, 69–70.

Anon. (1950a), "Preparing for Paraplegia." *Life Magazine*, June 12: 129–130, 132.

Anon. (1950b), "Scanning the News: Movie Filmed at Hospital." *Hospital Topics* 28(11): 5.

Anon. (1955a), "In Diversity Lies Industrial Success." *Los Angeles Times*, January 3: D70.

Anon. (1955b), "Profiles: Meet H.A. Everest." *Paraplegia News*, December 9(4).

Anon. (1956), "Our Members." *Sigma Signs*, 25.

Anon. (1957a), "President Asks Aid for Physically Handicapped." *Los Angeles Times*, May 24: 12.

Anon. (1957b), "Academics." *Sigma Signs*, 9–11.

Anon. (1966a), "Advanced Vehicle Concepts." *Sigma Signs*, 20.

Anon. (1977), "City to Enforce Special Parking for Handicapped." *Los Angeles Times*, June 12: GB6.

Arthur, P. (1967), "An Account of the Development and Execution of On-Site Graphics for Expo." *Print* 21 (March/April): 20–23, 50, 52, 55.

Arthur, P. (1993a), "A Cry for Help: Human Factors Research Needed." *Design Statements* 8(3) (Spring).

Arthur, P. (1993b), [Letter to Murphy], December 23. Collection of Brendan Murphy.

Arthur, P. (1994a), [Letter to Murphy], May 9. Collection of Brendan Murphy.

Arthur, P. (1994b), [Letter to Murphy], August 19. Collection of Brendan Murphy.

Arthur & Associates, Promotional Brochure (undated), (Self-Promotional Brochure, CCCA Concordia).

Associazione nazionale mutilati e invalidi del lavoro (1965), "Gli invalidi e le barriere architettoniche." [atti della Conferenza internazionale sulle barriere architettoniche: Stresa 17–20 giugno 1965] Roma: ANMIL.

Banta, K. V. (1957), "Handicapped Employment Takes Big Jump, Reports John Daly." *Radio, TV and Recording Technician-Engineer* 6(6): 9–10.

Belchick, Gerald (1998), Interview by Sharon Bonney. Disability Rights and Independent Living Movement Oral History Project. Regional Oral History Office. The Bancroft Library. University of California. Berkeley, CA.

Bond, A. R., (1914), "A Folding Wheel-Chair." *Scientific American*, 67.

Breslin, M. (1996–1998), Interview by Susan O'Hara. Disability Rights and Independent Living Movement Oral History Project. Regional Oral History Office. The Bancroft Library. University of California. Berkeley, CA.

Brewster, D. (1831), *The Life of Sir Isaac Newton*, London: J. Murray.

Brightwell, C. L. (1854), *Memorials of the Life of Amelia Opie: Selected and Arranged from Her Letters, Diaries, and Other Manuscripts*, Norwich: Fletcher and Alexander.

Buchanan, B. (1903), "The Bath Chair." *The Smart Set* 9(1): 155–160.

Canadian Corporation for the 1967 World Exhibition (1969), *General Report on the 1967 World Exhibition*, Ottawa: Queen's Printer.

Carroll, G. D. (1859), *Carroll's New York City Directory to the Hotels of Note, Places of Amusement, Public Buildings …. etc.: With a Description of and Directions When and How to Visit the Prominent Objects of Interest: Also to the Leading Mercantile Firms, in Every Commercial Pursuit*, New York: Carroll & Co.

Center for Universal Design at North Carolina State University (1997), "Seven Principles of Universal Design." Accessed September 12, 2016. http://universaldesign.ie/What-is-Universal-Design/The-7-Principles/

Chatelain, L. Jr. (Chair) (1961), *American Standard Specifications of Making Buildings and Facilities Accessible to and Usable by, the Physically Handicapped*, Washington: American Standards Association.

Chin, G. (1959), "Getting Acquainted." *Sigma Signs*, 6–8.

Cone, K. (1996–1998), Interview by David Landes. Disability Rights and Independent Living Movement Oral History Project. Regional Oral History Office. The Bancroft Library. Berkeley: University of California.

Dalland, Olav (2014), Email interchange with author. December 1.

Dickens, C. and Browne, H. K. (1848), *Dombey and Son*, London: Chapman and Hall.

"The Disability Challenge," Union of the Physically Impaired against Segregation, May, 1981 [Brochure].

Editorial (1955), "Steps, Stairs, and Stumbling Blocks." *Paraplegia News*, August: 2.

Eisenhower, D. D. (1960), *Public Papers of Presidents of the United States*, January 1–December 31.

Fay, F. A. (1965), "What You Can Do about Accessibility." *Sigma Signs*, 22–23.

Fay, F. A. (2001), Interview by Fred Pelka. Disability Rights and Independent Living Movement Oral History Project. Regional Oral History Office. The Bancroft Library. Berkley: University of California.

Friswell, J. H. (1864), *The Gentle Life: Essays in Aid of the Formation of Character*, London: S. Low, Son, and Marston.

General Accounting Office (GAO) (1975), *Further Action Needed to Make All Public Buildings Accessible to the Physically Handicapped, Department of Defense, Department of Health, Education, and Welfare, Department of Housing and Urban Development, General Services Administration: Report to the Congress*, Washington: U.S. General Accounting Office.

Haggard, H. R. (1895), *Joan Haste*, London: Longmans, Green.

Hasluck, P. N. (1900), *Cyclopaedia of Mechanics*, London: Cassell.

Hendren, S. (2013), "New Handicapped Sign Heads to NY." *Around the Nation*, NPR (Transcript). Washington, DC. Accessed September 30, 2015. http://www.npr.org/templates/transcript/transcript.php?storyId=189523504

Hendren, S. (2015), Interview with Author. June 24, 2015.

Hunt, P. (1972), "Letter to the Editor." *The Guardian*, September 2, 1972: 5.

Heumann, Judith. (1998-2001), Interview by Susan Brown, David Landes, and Jonathan Young.. Disability Rights and Independent Living Movement Oral History Project. Regional Oral History Office. The Bancroft Library. University of California. Berkeley, CA.

International Committee on Technical Aids (ICTA). (1969), *Symbol of Accessibility*, Stockholm: ISRDICTA.

International Society for Rehabilitation of the Disabled., Duncan, B., Hammerman, S., & United Nations Expert Group Meeting on Barrier Free Design (1975), *Barrier Free Design: Report of the United Nations Expert Group Meeting on Barrier Free Design Held June 3–8, 1974 at the United Nations Secretariat, New York*, New York: Rehabilitation International.

Jackson, J. S. (1973), *Proceedings of the 1973 Carnahan Conference on Electronic Prosthetics*, Lexington: University of Kentucky, Office of Research and Engineering Services.

Joyce, M., Nugent, T. J. and Lien, D. (1979), "Primer for Community Action." Minnesota State Council for the Handicapped.

Kamenetz, H. L. (1960), *The Wheelchair Book; Mobility for the Disabled*, Springfield, IL: C.C. Thomas.

Kliment, S. A. (1975), *Into the Mainstream: A Syllabus for a Barrier-Free Environment*, n.p.: American Institute of Architects.

La Rocca, J. and Turem, J. S. (1978), *The Application of Technological Developments to Physically Disabled People*, Washington, DC: Urban Institute.

Lindley, J. (2015), [Interpretation Letter], *Manual on Uniform Traffic Control Devices*, May 28. Accessed November 30, 2016. http://mutcd.fhwa.dot.gov/resources/interpretations/2_09_111.htm

Lockhart, F. B. (1971), *London for the Disabled*, London: Ward, Lock.

Marks, A. A. (1896), *A Treatise on Artificial Limbs with Rubber Hands and Feet*, New York City: A.A. Marks.

The Mental Health Law Project (1973), *Basic Rights of the Mentally Handicapped*, Washington, DC.

Merlin's "Invalid or Gouty Chair" and the Origin of the Self-propelled Wheelchair. Weiner MF1, Silver JR2.

Milner, J., Urquhart, D., and Cox, D. (1991), "Universal Design and Designer Awareness: The Constraints of Architectural Education." *The Report of the CIB Expert Seminar on Building Non-handicapping Environments*. Accessed October 12, 2016. www.independentliving.org/cib/cibbudapest19.html

Montan, K. (1974), *The Swedish Institute for the Handicapped – A Survey*, Bromma: Handikappinstitutet.

Mueller, J. (1996), *Case Studies on the Principles of Universal Design*, Raleigh: Center for Universal Design, North Carolina State.

Murphy, B. (1993), "Symbols of Access: Revision and Development of Symbols for the Sight-, Hearing-, Speech- and Mobility Impaired." Master of Fine Arts Thesis. University of Cincinnati.

Murphy, B. (2016), Interview with Author. August 20, 2016.

National Research Council Canada (1965), National Building Code of Canada.

National Society for Crippled Children and Adults (1965), *Proceedings of the National Institute on Making Buildings and Facilities Accessible to and Usable by the Physically Handicapped, November 21–24, 1965*, Chicago: National Society for Crippled Children and Adults.

New York State Council of Parks and Outdoor Recreation (1967), Outdoor Recreation for the Physically Handicapped. A Handbook of Design Standards. Albany [Brochure].

Nugent, T. J. (1950), *Paraplegic and Special Corrective Therapy: Rehabilitation Program-Annual Report*, 1–4.

Nugent, T. J. (1961), "Design of Buildings to Permit their Use by the Physically Handicapped." *New Building Research*. BRI Publication 910. Washington, DC: Building Research Institute.

Nugent, T. J. (c. 1963), Archival Interview. Accessed July 15, 2016. https://archives.library.illinois.edu/Electronic%20Records/video

Nugent, T. J. (2004–2005), Interview by Fred Pelka. Disability Rights and Independent Living Movement Oral History Project. Regional Oral History Office. The Bancroft Library. Berkeley: University of California.

Oldsmobile Division, General Motors Corporation (1946), "Oldsmobile's 'Valiant' Driving Controls: For Disabled Veterans and Other Handicapped Persons." Lansing, MI: Oldsmobile Service.

Ostroff, E., Limont, M., and Hunter, D. G. (2002), *Building a World Fit for People: Designers with Disabilities at Work*, Boston, MA: Adaptive Environments Center.

Peach, R. E. M. (1893), *Street-lore of Bath: A Record of Changes in the Highways and Byways of the City*, London, Simpkin, Marshall and Bath: E.R. Blackett.

President's Committee on Employment of the Handicapped (1957a). *Proceedings*.

President's Committee on Employment of the Handicapped (1957b), "Ten Years of Teamwork" [Pamphlet].

President's Committee on Employment of the Handicapped (1972), "Twenty-Five Years of Volunteers in Partnership" [Pamphlet].

President's Committee on Employment of the Handicapped (1977), "People Are Asking about Displaying the Symbol Access" [Pamphlet].

Rehabilitation International (1978), [Delegate Assembly Board Meeting], Baguio I, Philippines, January.

Rehabilitation International (2013), "Symbol of Access." *Rehabilitation International*. Accessed November 15, 2015. http://www.riglobal.org/symbol-of-access/

Rehabilitation International, Association for the Physically Disabled of Kenya (APDK) (1993), *17th World Congress of Rehabilitation International: September 7th–11th, 1992, Nairobi, Kenya. Accelerating Efforts to Equalization of Opportunities: Strategies for the 1990s*, Kenya: APDK.

Slavitt, E. B., and Pugh, D. J. (American Bar Association. Section of Real Property, Probate, and Trust Law) (2000), *Accessibility under the Americans with Disabilities Act and Other Laws: A Guide to Enforcement and Compliance*, Chicago, IL: Section of Real Property, Probate, and Trust Law, American Bar Association.

Society of Automotive Engineers (1945), "War Engineering Board, Vehicle Controls for Disabled Veterans" [Brochure].

Society for Environmental Graphic Design (1994), Memorandum on Brendan Murphy's Accessibility Symbols.

Specifications and Drawings of Patents Issued from the U.S. Patent Office P 649 150,022 Vehicle-Wheels. P. Gendron, Improvement in Children Carriages Toledo, Ohio (filed Aug 11, 1873).

Specifications and Drawings of Patents Issued from the U.S. Patent Office US 2095 411 A. H. A. Everest et al. Folding Wheel Chair, Los Angeles California (filed February 11, 1936).

Stanley, G. (1964), Memorandum to John Matheson. March 23, 1964.

Stein, K. (2016), Interview with Author. July 25, 2016.

Stein, R. and Linde, T. (1958), "The Greek Way." *Sigma Signs*, 12.

Stein, T. A. (1962), "A Program to Eliminate and Prevent Architectural Barriers to the Handicapped: Quarterly Progress Report." September.

Stein, T. A. (United States, President's Committee on Employment of the Handicapped) (1965), *Architectural Barriers: Progress Report, July 1962–July 1965*, Washington, DC.

Thompson, L. (1948–50), "From the Office of the President." *Sigma Signs* 1: 1.

U.S. National Commission on Architectural Barriers to Rehabilitation of the Handicapped (1968), *Design for All Americans: A Report*, Washington: U.S. Government Printing Office.

United Nations Convention on the Rights of Persons with Disabilities. Accessed February 10, 2011. http://www. un.org/disabilities/default.asp?id=260

Webster, J. and Dyce, A. (1859), *The Works of John Webster: With Some Account of the Author, and Notes*, London and New York: Routledge, Warne, and Routledge.

Whitehouse, R. (2016), Telephone Interview with Author. August 22, 2016.

Zukas, H. (1998), Interview by Sharon Bonney. Disability Rights and Independent Living Movement Oral History Project. Regional Oral History Office. The Bancroft Library. Berkeley: University of California.

Secondary Sources

Abley, M. (2007), "Expo's Language Legacy? Its Own Name." *Montreal Gazette*, April 28.

Acton, N. (1970), "The New Decade." *The Guardian*, April 23: 17.

Acton, N. (2000), [Letter], *WE Magazine*, April/March: 10.

Adrian, L. (1968), "Wheeler Deal." *Spectator*, April 4: 14.

Anderson, H. (1977), "Business Rolls along at Wheelchair Firm: Biggest Producer Began." *Los Angeles Times*, September 18: H3.

Anker, P. (2010), *From Bauhaus to Ecohouse: A History of Ecological Design*, Baton Rouge, LA: Louisiana State University.

Anon. (1966b), "Barrier Bits." *Rehabilitation Record* 7(6): 23–25.

Anon. (1967a), "Expositions: Snafus of Success." *Time Magazine*, May 12, 89(19): 70.

Anon. (1967b), "Design for the Disabled." *The Times* (New York), September 9.

Anon. (1967c), "Times Diary." *The Times* (London), September 9: 10.

Anon. (1967d), "Expo Says 16,000 Have Used Its Aids to the Handicapped." *New York Times*, September 9: 12.

Anon. (1967e), "Wheelchair Can Be an Asset to Fight Crowds." *Bridgeport Post*, October 8: 75.

Anon. (1968a), "Att Leva a med Handikapp [Living with a Disability]." *FORM* special issue 10.

Anon. (1968b), "Seminarium: manniska-miljo [Man and the Environment]." *FORM* 64(5): 323.

Anon. (1968c), "Miljö för alla?" *Dagens Nyheter*, July 28, 1968: 4.

Anon. (1969), "In World of Scandinavian Fashion, Function Is the Key." *New York Times*, September 20: 32.

Anon. (1970a), "Rehabilitation International Adopts International Symbol of Access for the Disabled." *Rehabilitation in Canada* (December): 6.

Anon. (1970b), "Rehabilitation International." *Nursing Times,* May 28, 1970: 674.

Anon. (1975), "Blue Curbs which Denote Parking for Handicapped." *Los Angeles Times*, December 7.

Anon. (1977), "The Old Order." *Paraplegia News*, March: 45.

Anon. (1981), "Editorial." *The Disability Challenge* 1: 2–8.

Anon. (1982), [Advertisement], *Rocky Mountain News*, June 7: 37.

Anon. (2011), "Selwyn Goldsmith." *Daily Telegraph*. Accessed October 2, 2015. http://www.telegraph.co.uk/news/obituaries/technology-obituaries/8435991/Selwyn-Goldsmith.html#disqus_thread

Anthony, K. (2001), *Designing for Diversity: Gender, Race, and Ethnicity in the Architectural Profession*, Champaign: University of Illinois Press.

Arthur, P. and Passini, R. (1992), *Wayfinding: People, Signs, and Architecture*, Ontario: McGraw-Hill Ryerson Ltd.

Attfield, J. (2000), *Wild Things: The Material Culture of Everyday Life*, Oxford: Berg.

Baker, B. (2011), "Enabling a New Icon." *Boston Globe*, February 21. Accessed February 13, 2015. http://www.boston.com/news/education/higher/articles/2011/02/21/cambridge_artist_sara_hendren_promotes_wheelchair_symbol_update/?fb_ref=art&fb_source=profile_oneline

Baker, B. (2013), "A Symbolic Salute to Progress." *Boston Globe*, December 14, 2013: A1

Bakker, W. (2013), "Icograda and the Development of Pictogram Standards: 1963– 1986." *Iridescent* 2(2): 38–48.

Bank-Mikkelsen, N. E. (1969), "A Metropolitan Area in Denmark: Copenhagen," in Kugel, R. (ed.), *Changing Patterns in Residential Services for the Mentally Retarded*, Washington: President's Committee on Mental Retardation.

Banks, S. (1997), "Vets Bring Old Hospital to Life for Students." *Los Angeles Times*, March 16: 1.

Barnartt, S. and Scotch, R. (2001), *Disability Protests: Contentious Politics 1970–1999*, Washington, DC: Gallaudet University Press.

Bartolucci, M. (1992), "Making a Chair Able by Design." *Metropolis* 12(4): 29–33.

Baskin, P. (2013), "A Team of Academics Redesigns an Icon." *The Chronicle of Higher Education*, May 20. Accessed November 27, 2016. http://www.chronicle.com/article/New-York-City-Embraces-a/139355/?key=TGxwJQUwYHNAMS1rY2tIZj4GanRsNhp0YXVMOCl7blpSEw%3D%3D

Ben-Moshe, L. and Powell, J. J. W. (2007), "Sign of our Times? Revis(it)ing the International Symbol of Access." *Disability and Society* 22(5): 489–505.

Bendixson, T. (1968), "Signs for Disabled." *Guardian*, November 20: 9.

Bergman, H. (1968), "Schools Are Not for Teaching." *FORM* 64(5): 319.

Bird, D. (1974), "Handicapped Drivers Win Exemption after 3½ Hour Midday Traffic Jam." *New York Times*, March 5, 1974: 19.

Bowe, F. (1978), *Handicapping America: Barriers to Disabled People*, New York: Harper & Row.

Boys, J. (2014), *Doing Disability Differently: An Alternative Handbook on Architecture*, New York: Routledge.

Brandt, E. N. and Pope, A. M. (eds.) (1997), *Enabling America: Assessing the Role of Rehabilitation Science and Engineering*, Washington, DC: National Academy Press.

Brattgard, S. (2002, 1972), "Sweden Fokus, A Way of Life for Living," in Lancaster-Gaye, D. (ed.), *Personal Relationships, the Handicapped and the Community*, London: Routledge.

Bresnahan, K. (2011), "'An Unused Esperanto': Internationalism and Pictographic Design, 1930–1970." *Design and Culture*, March, 3(11): 5–24.

Briggs, A. (1962), "The Welfare State in Historical Perspective." *European Journal of Sociology*, December, 2(2): 221–258. (Reprinted in BBC (2013), "Gone for a Decade." Accessed September 15, 2014. http://www.bbc.com/news/blogs-ouch-23061676)

Brodsly, D. (1981), *L.A. Freeway, an Appreciative Essay*, Berkeley: University of California Press.

Brown, S. E. (2008), "Breaking Barriers; The Pioneering Disability Students Services program at the University of, 1948–1960," in Tamura, E. (ed.), *The History of Discrimination in U.S. Education*, New York: Palgrave: 165–192.

Browning, N. L. (1947), "Paralyzed Veterans Go to College in Wheelchairs." *Chicago Tribune*, February 4: 6.

Brunnström, L. (1997), *Svensk industridesign: en 1900-talshistoria* [Swedish Industrial Design: A 20th-Century History], Stockholm: Norstedts.

Bull, N. (1963), "A Different Window." *Magic Carpet* 15(1): 12.

Burks, E. C. (1967), "Towaways Here Anger Physicians: Handicapped Also Object to Extension of Parking Ban but Mayor Stands Firm." *New York Times*, January 25: 1.

Busch, A. (1994), "Signs of the Times." *Metropolis Magazine* 13(12): 45.

Busch, A. (1995), "Designing for Disability." *Print* 49(2): 44–49.

Byrom, B. (2001), "A Pupil and a Patient: Hospital-Schools in Progressive America," in Longmore, P. and Umansky, L. (eds.), *The New Disability History: American Perspectives*, New York: New York University Press: 133–156.

Caniff, C. E. (1962), "Architectural Barriers—A Personal Problem." *Rehabilitation Literature* 23(January): 13–14.

Cartwright, N., Cat, J., Fleck, L., and Uebel, T. E. (1996), *Otto Neurath: Philosophy Between Science and Politics*, Cambridge, MA: Cambridge University Press.

Catanese, L. (2012), "Thomas Lamb, Marc Harrison, Richard Hollerith and the Origins of Universal Design." *Journal of Design History* 25(2): 206–217.

Chamberlain, G. (2014), "Living Potential, Not Limitation, Has Always Been Nugent's Goal." News Bureau, University of Illinois. Accessed December 1, 2016. https://news.illinois.edu/ii/14/0918/timothy_nugent_pioneering_disability_services.html

Choksi, N. (2014), "The Handicap Symbol Gets an Update—At Least in New York State." *Washington Post*, July 20. Accessed November 30, 2016. https://www.washingtonpost.com/blogs/govbeat/wp/2014/07/29/the-handicap-symbol-gets-an-update-at-least-in-new-york-state/?utm_term=.c3ce5d28f76a

Chouinard, V., Hall, E., and Wilton, R. (eds.) (2010), *Toward Enabling Geographies: 'Disabled' Bodies and Minds in Society and Space*, Burlington: Ashgate.

Cimons, M. (1979), "Activist Leads Fight for Rights of Disabled." *Los Angeles Times*, May 31: B8.

Clarke, A. J. (2013), "'Actions Speak Louder': Victor Papanek and the Legacy of Design Activism." *Design and Culture* 5(2): 151–168.

Clarke, A. J. (2014), "Designer for the Real World." Public lecture, Maryland Institute College of Art, April 8.

Clarkson, J., Keates, S., Coleman, R., and Lebbon, C. (eds.) (2003), *Inclusive Design: Design for the Whole Population*, London: Springer London.

Coleman, R., Clarkson, J., Dong, H., and Cassim, J. (2007), *Design for Inclusivity: A Practical Guide to Accessible, Innovative and User-Centred Design*, Aldershot: Gower.

Compton, N. (1967), "Expo 67." *Commentary*, July 1: 32–39.

Cooper, R. A. et al. (2003), "Wheelchair Ergonomics," in Kumar, S. (ed.), *Perspectives in Rehabilitation Ergonomics*, London, and Bristol, PA: Taylor & Francis: 281–312.

Corker, M. and Shakespeare, T. (2002), *Disability/Postmodernity: Embodying Disability Theory*, London and New York: Continuum.

Cosgrove, B. (2014), "LIFE With Brando: Early Photos of a Legend in the Making." *Life Magazine*, November 5. Accessed December 20, 2014. http://time.com/3579204/life-with-brando-early-photos-of-an-icon-in-the-making/

Council for Exceptional Children (1976), *Exceptional Child Education Abstracts* 8.2, Volume 8, Summer 1976.

Covey, H. C. (1998), *Social Perceptions of People with Disabilities in History*, Springfield, IL: Charles C. Thomas.

Creagh, L., Kåberg, H., and Lane, B. M. (eds.) (2008), *Modern Swedish Design: Three Founding Texts*, New York: Museum of Modern Art.

Crowther, B. (1950), "What Price Glory." *New York Times*, July 30: xi.

DeJong, G. (1984), *Independent Living and Disability Policy in the Netherlands: Three Models of Residential Care and Independent Living*, International Exchange of Experts and Information in Rehabilitation, World Rehabilitation Fund, Inc.

Delaney, M. (1967), "STOP: Expo Designers at Work." *Saturday Night*, May: 23–25.

DeLoach, C. (1992), "The Independent Living Movement." Region V Rehabilitation Continuing Education Program ADA Train the Trainer Program. Carbondale, Southern Illinois University at Carbondale Rehabilitation Institute.

Denly, O. A. (1964), "The User's Viewpoint." *Paraplegia* 2: 42–48.

Depoy, E. and Gilson, S. (2010), "Disability Design and Branding: Rethinking Disability within the 21st Century." *Disability Studies Quarterly* 30(2). Accessed August 3, 2015. http://dsq-sds.org/article/view/1247/1274

Deque Systems (2013), "Accessibility Logo Receives a 21st Century Makeover." *Deque*. September 6. Accessed November 27, 2016. http://www.deque.com/blog/accessibility-logo-receives-21st-century-makeover/

Doherty, B. (1995), "Unreasonable Accommodation." *Reason* 72(4): 18.

Dolmage, J. (2005), "Disability Studies Pedagogy, Usability and Universal Design." *Disability Studies Quarterly* 25(4).

Dunne, A. (1999), *Hertzian Tales*, Cambridge, MA: MIT Press.

Ebert, R. (2011), *Life Itself: A Memoir*, New York: Grand Central Publishing.

Eddy, W. A. (1954), *F.D.R. Meets Ibn Saud*, New York: American Friends of the Middle East.

Ede, M. (1990), "Bath and the Great Exhibition of 1851." *Bath History* 3: 138–158.

Eisland, N. L. (1994), *The Disabled God: Toward a Liberatory Theology of Disability*, Nashville, TN: Abingdon Press.

Elder, Alan (2005), *Made in Canada: Craft and Design in the Sixties*, Montreal: McGill-Queen's University Press.

Ellseby, R. (1995), "Signs of the Times." *Office Systems* 64(12): 6

El Osman, M. (1975), "Barrier-Free Architecture: Yesterday's Special Design Becomes Tomorrow's Standard." *AIA*, March, 63(3): 40–44.

Epstein, S. (1937), "The Classic. Art, History and the Crutch." *Annals of Medical History* 9: 304.

Evans, B. (1997), "Author of Seminal Book on Disabled Design Reacts." *Architect's Journal* November 20, 206(26).

Fallan, K. (2007), "How an Excavator Got Aesthetic Pretensions—Negotiating Design in 1960s' Norway." *Journal of Design History* 20(1): 43–59.

Fallan, K. (2011), "The 'Designer'—The 11th Plague": Design Discourse from Consumer Activism to Environmentalism in 1960s Norway." *Design Issues* 27(4): 30–42.

Fallan, K. (ed.) (2012), *Scandinavian Design: Alternative Histories*, Oxford: Berg.

Fineder, M. and Geisler, T. (2010), "Design Criticism and Critical Design in the Writings of Victor Papanek (1923–1998)." *Journal of Design History* 23(1): 99–106.

Finkelstein, V. (1975), "Discovering the Person in Disability." *Magic Carpet* 26: 31–38.

Fischer, A. M. E. (2008), "We're Not That Far from Famous After All." *The Daily News*. Accessed November 1, 2016. http://tdn.com/news/we-re-not-that-far-from-famous-after-all/article_1591b64d-f8ba-58e8-b7f6-fd7bdd69c995.html

Fleischer, D. and Zames, F. (2011), *The Disability Rights Movement: From Charity to Confrontation*, Philadelphia, PA: Temple University Press.

Flinchum, R. (1997), *Henry Dreyfuss, The Industrial Designer and His Work*, New York: Cooper-Hewitt, National Design Museum.

Francke, L. and Francke, L. (1967), "The Handicapped at Expo: Special Facilities Aid Wheelchair Tourists and Aged Visitors." *New York Times*, May 28: xxii.

Fritsch, Kelly (2013), "Neoliberal Circulation of Affects: Happiness, Accessibility and the Capacitation of Disability as Wheelchair." *Health, Culture and Society* 5(1): 135–149.

Fulford, R. (1968), *This Was Expo*, Toronto: McClelland and Stewart.

Gallagher, H. (1974), "Barriers to the Handicapped." *Washington Post*, December 13: A31.

Gallagher, H. (1985), *FDR's Splendid Deception: The Moving Story of Roosevelt's Massive Disability—and the Intense Efforts to Conceal It from the Public*, New York: Dodd, Mead.

Garland-Thomson, R. (ed.) (1996), *Freakery: Cultural Spectacles of the Extraordinary Body*, New York: New York University Press.

Garland-Thomson, R. (1997), *Extraordinary Bodies: Figuring Physical Disability in American Culture and Literature*, New York: Columbia University Press.

Garland-Thomson, R. (2005), "Feminist Disability Studies: A Review Essay." *Signs: A Journal of Women and Culture* 2: 1557–1587.

Garland-Thomson, R. ([2002] 2011a), "Integrating Disability, Transforming Feminist Theory," in Hall, K. Q. (ed.), *Feminist Disability Studies*, Bloomington: Indiana University Press: 13–47.

Garland-Thomson, R. (2011b), "Misfits: A Feminist Materialist Disability Concept." *Hypatia: A Journal of Feminist Philosophy* 26(3): 591–609.

Garland-Thomson, R. (2013), "Disability Studies: A Field Emerged." *American Quarterly* 65(4): 915–926.

Geist, F. et al. (2003), "Disability Law in Germany." *Journal of Comparative Labour Law and Policy* 24: 563–576.

Gelfer-Jørgensen, M. (2003), "Scandinavianism—A Cultural Brand," in Halén, W. and Wickman, K. (eds.), *Scandinavian Design beyond the Myth: Fifty Years of Design from the Nordic Countries*, Stockholm: Arvinius: 17–26.

Gerber, D. (2000), *Disabled Veterans in History*, Ann Arbor: University of Michigan Press.

Gerrard, M. (1981), "Excluded from Vehicles Because of Faulty Lifts: 20 in Wheelchairs Protest at Bus Stop." *Los Angeles Times*, March 12: D3.

Gleeson, B. (1998), *Geographies of Disability*, London: Routledge.

Gloag, J. (1964), *The Englishman's Chair: Origins, Design, and Social History of Seat Furniture*, London: Allen and Unwin.

Goffman, E. (1980), *Behavior in Public Places: Notes on the Social Organization of Gatherings*, Westport, CO: Greenwood Press.

Goldberg, R. T. (1981), *The Making of Franklin D. Roosevelt: Triumph over Disability*, Cambridge, MA: Abt Books.

Goldsmith, S. (1963), *Designing for the Disabled*, London: RIBA Publications Ltd.

Goldsmith, S. (1965), "Further Thoughts on Design for the Disabled." *The Architect's Journal*, 142: 971–979.

Goldsmith, S. (1967), "The Disabled: A Mistaken Policy." *RIBA Journal*, 7: 387–389.

Goldsmith, S. (1967), *Designing for the Disabled*, 2nd edition, London: RIBA Publications Ltd.

Goldsmith, S. (1968a), "The Signposting of Arrangements for Disabled People in Buildings." *Rehabilitation*, January–March, 64:11–18.

Goldsmith, S. (1969a), "The Long Search for a Symbol." *Design Journal* 251: 45.

Goldsmith, S. (1969b), *A Symbol for Disabled People*, London: RIBA.

Goldsmith, S. (1976), Designing for the Disabled, 3rd edition, London: RIBA Publications Ltd.

Goldsmith, S. (1983), "The Ideology of Designing for the Disabled," in *Proceedings of the Fourteenth International Conference of the Environmental Design Research Association* (EDRA 14), Lincoln, Nebraska: 198–214.

Goldsmith, S. (1997), *Designing for the Disabled: The New Paradigm*, London: Taylor & Francis.

Goldsmith, Selwyn (2000), *Universal Design: A Manual of Practical Guidance for Architects*, Architectural Press.

Golledge, R. G. (ed.) (1999), *Wayfinding Behavior: Cognitive Mapping and Other Spatial Processes*, Baltimore, MD: Johns Hopkins University Press.

Gordon College (2014), "Powerful Advocacy in Practice: Gordon's Impact in New York State Assembly." June 26. Accessed November 29, 2016. http://www.gordon.edu/article.cfm?iArticleID=1624

Green, T. (1977), "Effort Grows to Provide Access for Handicapped." *Los Angeles Times*, May 22: 14.

Gritzer, G. and Arluke, A. (1985), *The Making of Rehabilitation Medicine: A Political Economy of Medical Specialization, 1890–1980*, Berkeley and Los Angeles: University of California Press.

Groce, N. (1985), *Everyone Here Spoke Sign Language: Hereditary Deafness on Martha's Vineyard*, Cambridge, MA: Harvard University Press.

Groce, N. (2002), *From Charity to Disability Rights: Global Initiatives of Rehabilitation International, 1922–2002*, New York: Rehabilitation International.

Grosz, E. (1994), *Volatile Bodies: Toward a Corporeal Feminism*, Bloomington: Indiana University Press.

Gudis, C. (2004), *Buyways: Billboards, Automobiles, and the American Landscape*, London: Psychology Press.

Guffey, E. (2015a), "The Disabling Art Museum." *The Journal of Visual Culture* 14(1): 61–73.

Guffey, E. (2015b), "The Scandinavian Roots of the International Symbol of Access." *Design and Culture* 7(3): 357–376.

Haigh, S. (2015), "Peppier Handicapped Symbol Meets Resistance." *San Jose Mercury News*, Accessed October 16, 2015. http://www.mercurynews.com/2015/10/16/peppier-handicapped-symbol-meets-resistance/

Halén, W. (2003), "Fifty Years of Scandinavian Design—and After." in Halén, W. and Wickman, K. (eds), *Scandinavian Design Beyond the Myth: Fifty Years of Design from the Nordic Countries*, Stockholm: Arvinius: 7–16.

Hamraie, A. (2012), "Universal Design Research as a New Materialist Practice." *Disability Studies Quarterly* 32(4): Accessed August 21, 2015. http://dsq-sds.org/article/view/3246

Hamraie, A. (2013), "Designing Collective Access: A Feminist Disability Theory of Universal Design." *Disability Studies Quarterly* 33(4). Accessed June 3, 2015. http://dsq-sds.org/article/view/3871

Hamraie, A. (2017), *Building Access*, New York: New York University Press.

Hannson, L. (2007), "The Power of Design—Allies Fighting Design Exclusion," in Brembeck, H., Ekstrom, K., and Morck, M. (eds.), *Little Monsters: (De) Coupling Assemblages of Consumption*, Berlin: Lit Verlag: 15–28.

Herwig, O. (2008), *Universal Design: Solutions for Barrier-free Living*, Berlin: de Gruyter.

Hicks, J. (2013), "A New Bern Resident Is Trying to Change the Way People View the Handicap Symbol." ABC News Channel 12. February 13. Accessed November 29, 2016. http://www.wcti12.com/news/a-new-bern-resident-is-trying-to-change-the-way-people-view-the-handicap-symbol-/15318844

Hodgson, P. (1972), "Sidelines Disablement." *Times*, London, October 2: 9.

Hosey, L. (2001), "Hidden Lines: Gender, Race, and the Body in *Graphic Standards*." *Journal of Architectural Education* 55(2): 101–112.

Hughes, F. (1963), "Lessons in Courage Aid Students at U.I." *Chicago Daily Tribune*, January 26: W17.

Husz, O. (2011), "Passionate about Things: The Swedish Debate on Throwawayism (1969–61)." *Revue d'Histoire Nordique* 7(2): 135–160.

Huxtable, A. L. (1980), "Danish Design: From Its Famous Past to the Present." *New York Times*, August 21.

Imrie, R. (1996), *Disability and the City: International Perspectives*, New York: St. Martin's Press.

Imrie, R. (2002), "Architects' Conceptions of the Human Body." *Environment and Planning D: Society and Space* 21(1): 47–65.

Imrie, R. (2012), "Universalism, Universal Design, and Equitable Access to the Built Environment." *Disability and Rehabilitation* 34(10): 873–882.

Imrie, R. and Hall, P. (2001), *Inclusive Design: Designing and Developing Accessible Environments*, New York: Spon Press.

Inclusive Design Research Centre (2013), "Lieutenant Governor to Launch Student Challenge to Redesign Traditional Wheelchair Symbol." Accessed November 30, 2016. http://idrc.ocadu.ca/about-the-idrc/idrc-news/474-reimagine

Jacob, J. (1985), *John Joseph Merlin: The Ingenious Mechanick*, London: Greater London Council.

Jasmin, Y. (1997), *Le Petite Historie d'Expo 67*, Montreal: Québec/Amérique.

jgeboers. (2013), "Reimagining and Redesigning Accessibility." *Up-and-Coming*, December 4. Accessed November 30, 2016. http://jpress.journalism.ryerson.ca/perceptionmag/2013/12/04/reimagining-and-redesigning-accessibility/

Johnson, J. (1995), "Designer Revamps Wheelchair-Access Symbol." *Cincinnati Enquirer* February 22, 1995: 37.

Johnson, M. (1992), "Jerry's Kids (Ethics of the Jerry Lewis Labor Day Telethon)" (Editorial), *The Nation*, September 14, 255(7): 232.

Johnson, R. (ed.) (1897), *A History of The World's Columbian Exposition, Chicago*, New York: D. Appleton.

Jones, G. (1836), "A Defence of Dr. Golding." *The Lancet*, Volume 2. "Abstract of Mr Pettigrew': 835–837.

Kamenetz, H. L. (1969), "A Brief History of the Wheelchair." *Journal of the History of Medicine and Allied Sciences* 24(2): 205–210.

Kirkwood, S. (n.d.), "Can We Design a Truly Inclusive Accessibility Icon?" *AIGA Magazine*. Accessed November 29, 2016. http://www.aiga.org/inclusive-accessible-icon-project-icon-wheelchair

Kneebone, P. (1969), "Letter to the Editor." *Design Journal* 252: 73.

Knittel, S. (2015), *The Historical Uncanny: Disability, Ethnicity, and the Politics of Holocaust Memory*, New York: Fordham University Press.

Koefoed, J. (2012), "Skarberen af Verdens Mest Udbredte Symbol Besøgte Gudhjem [Author of the World's Most Widely Known Symbol Visits Gudhjem]" July 15. Accessed November 5, 2016. http://www.lisahoyrup.dk/jk/skaberen-af-verdens-mest-udbredte-symbol-besøgte-gudhjem/

Korvenmaa, P. (2009), *Finnish Design: A Concise History*, Helsinki: University of Art and Design.

Large, M. (2001), "Communication among All People, Everywhere: Paul Arthur and the Maturing of Design." *Design Issues*, Spring, 17(2): 81–90.

Leibrock, C. (1994), "Dignified Options to ADA Compliance." *Facilities Design and Management*, June: 56.

Lembke, D. (1975), "Handicapped: 'Pushy' New Political Force." *Los Angeles Times*, July 16: B1.

Lewis, C. S. (1994), "International Aspects of the Duality Issue," in Nelson, J. A. (ed.), *The Disabled, The Media and the Information Age*, Westport, CT: Greenwood Press.

Lie, I. K. (2014), "'Vardagsvaror' for den virkelige verden: Victor Papaneks relasjon til det nordiske designmiljøet på 1960- og 70-tallet ['Vardagsvaror' for the Real World: Victor Papanek's Relation to the Nordic Design Environment in the 1960s and 70s]." Masters thesis, University of Oslo.

Lifchez, R. (1987), *Rethinking Architecture: Design Students and Physically Disabled People*, Berkeley: University of California Press.

Lindkvist, L. (2003), "Ergonomic Design for All," in Halén, W. and Wickman, K. (eds.), *Scandinavian Design beyond the Myth: Fifty Years of Design from the Nordic Countries*, Stockholm: Arvinius: 115–122.

Linker, B. (2011), *War's Waste: Rehabilitation in World War I America*, Chicago: University of Chicago Press.

Linton, S. (1998), *Claiming Disability: Knowledge and Identity*, New York: New York University Press.

Little, E. D. (1977), "A Plea for Unhobbling the Disabled." *New York Times*, March 27: 486.

Loebl, W. Y. and Nunn, J. F. (1997), "Staffs as Walking Aids in Ancient Egypt and Palestine." *Journal of the Royal Society of Medicine* 90: 450–454.

Lomazow, S. and Fetmann, E. (2009), *FDR's Deadly Secret*, New York, NY: Public Affairs.

Longmore, P. (2003), *Why I Burned My Book and Other Essays on Disability*, Philadelphia, PA: Temple University Press.

Longmore, P. K. and Goldberger, D. (2000), "The League of the Physically Handicapped and the Great Depression: A Case Study in the New Disability History." *The Journal of American History*, December, 87(3): 888–922.

Lundahl, G. (1969), "SDO i kris" *Form* 65(8): 372.

Lynch, K. (1960), *The Image of the City*, Cambridge, MA: MIT Press.

Mace, R. (1998), "A Perspective on Universal Design." Presentation made at "Designing for the 21st Century: An International Conference on Universal Design." Accessed June 19, 1998. https://www.ncsu.edu/ncsu/design/cud/about_us/usronmacespeech.htm

Mace, R. (1985), "Universal Design: Barrier-Free Environments for Everyone." *Designer's West* 33(1): 147–152.

Madge, P. (1993), "Design, Ecology, Technology: A Historiographical Review." *Journal of Design History* 6(3): 149–166.

Madsen, J. (2004), "Compliance or Defiance?" *Buildings* 98(6): 94–96.

McDonald, I. (1967), "Expo Thousands Say Au Revoir: Canada's Camelot Slips Away." *Vancouver Sun*, October 28: 1.

McIntyre, L. (2015), *RIBA Trust: Selwyn Goldsmith (1932–2011) and the Architectural Model of Disability: A Retrospective of the Man and the Model*, London: RIBA.

Meister, D. (1999), *The History of Human Factors and Ergonomics*, London: Erlbaum.

Middleton, M. (1963), "Icograda. London, 1963." *Society of Industrial Artists Journal* 15: 9–12.

Miedema, G. (2005), *For Canada's Sake: Public Religion, Centennial Celebrations, and the Remaking of Canada in the 1960s*, Montreal: McGill-Queen's University Press.

Mitchell, D. and Snyder, S. (2006), *Cultural Locations of Disability*, Chicago: University of Chicago Press.

Mollerup, P. (2006), *Wayshowing: A Guide to Environmental Signage Principles and Practices*, Baden, Switzerland: Lars Müller Publishers.

Montan, K. (2000), "Letter to the Editor." *Journal of Prosthetics and Orthotics International* 24(1): 85.

Moore, C. and Bloomer, K. (1977), *Body, Memory and Architecture*, New Haven, CT: Yale University Press.

Morgan, M. (1976), "Beyond Disability: A Broader Definition of Architectural Barriers." *AIA Journal*, May 65(5): 50–53.

Murphy, B. (1994), "More Accessible Symbols." *Step-By-Step Graphics* 10(6): 15.

Nelson, M. (1986), "Church Builder Led Revolution." *NewsOK*, July 22.

Neurath, M and Kinross, R. (2009), *The Transformer: Principles of Making Isotype Charts*. London: Hyphen Press.

Nightingale, F. (1858), *Subsidiary Notes as to the Introduction of Female Nursing into Military*, London: Harrison & Sons.

Nugent, T. J. (1961), "A National Attack on Architectural Barriers." *New Building Research*, Fall: 51–66.

Nunn, J. F. (2002), *Ancient Egyptian Medicine*, Norman: University of Oklahoma Press.

Ogden, C. K. (1931), *Debabelization*, London: Kegan Paul.

Oliver, M. (1983), *Social Work with Disabled People*, London: Macmillan, for the British Association of Social Workers.

Oliver, M. (1990), *The Politics of Disablement: A Sociological Approach*, New York: St. Martin's Press.

Oppenheim, C. (1975), "Handicapped ask City for Access to Buildings." *Chicago Tribune*, February 23: 35.

Oppert, F. (1867), *Hospitals, Infirmaries and Dispensaries: Their Construction, Interior Arrangements and Management, etc.*, London: John Churchill and Sons.

Papadosifos, N. (2014), "The Complications of Crutches—A Summary of a Systematic Review of the Literature." *AGR Note* 1(4): 1–2.

Papanek, V. (1971), *Design for the Real World*, New York: Pantheon Books.

Papanek, V. (1976), "Twelve Methodologies for Design." Proceedings of the ISCIO "Design for Need" Symposium.

Parker, G. (2014), *Imprudent King: A New Life of Philip II*, New Haven and London: Yale University Press.

Parry, C. H. (1825), *Collections from the Unpublished Medical Writings of the Late Caleb Hillier*, London: Underwoods.

Percy, S. L. (1989), *Disability, Civil Rights, and Public Policy: The Politics of Implementation*, Tuscaloosa: University of Alabama Press.

Perez, S. (2007), *La santé de Louis XIV: une biohistoire du Roi-Soleil*, Seyssel: Champ Vallon.

Perkins, F. (1946), *The Roosevelt I Knew*, New York: The Viking Press.

Phelps, J. (2012), "Gordon College Adds New 'Accessiblity Icon' to Parking Lots." *Salem News*. Accessed December 1, 2016. http://www.salemnews.com/news/local_news/gordon-college-adds-new-accessiblity-icon-to-parking-lots/article_a8590fe4-61bb-545e-8662-6b9b3e4622b4.html

Pierson, J. (1995), "Form and Function: A Symbol Is Worth a Thousand Words about Acceptance." *Wall Street Journal*, February 17: B1.

Plumptre, T. (1967), "At Expo, A Low Neck Can Avert Blushes." *Globe and Mail Reporter*, May 30.

Poore, C. (2007), *Disability in Twentieth-Century German Culture*, Ann Arbor: University of Michigan Press.

Powell, J. J. W. and Solga, H. (2009), "The Icons of Access: From Exclusion to Inclusion." *Stimulus Respond* 'icon' issue: 90–95.

Powell, R. D. (1886), *On Diseases of the Lungs and Pleuræ Including Consumption*, New York: W. Wood.

Preiser, W. F. E. and Ostroff, E. (2001), *Universal Design Handbook*, New York: McGraw-Hill.

Prosen, H. (1965), "Physical Disability and Motivation." *Canadian Medical Association Journal*, June 12, 92(24): 1261–1265.

Pullin, G. (2009), *Design Meets Disability*, Cambridge, MA: MIT Press.

Pynt, J. and Griggs, J. (2008), "Nineteenth-Century Patent Seating: Too Comfortable to Be Moral?" *Journal of Design History*, September 1, 21(3): 2.

Racine, M. (2010), "The Ambiguous Modernity of Designer Julien Hebert," in Kenneally, R. R. and Sloan, J. (eds.), *Expo 67: Not Just a Souvenir*, Toronto: University of Toronto Press: 93–108.

Ranzal, E. (1973), "Mayor to Review Parking Permits." *New York Times*, August 2, 1973: 39.

Rehabilitation International (RI) (2017), Fact Sheet. http://www.riglobal.org/wp-content/uploads/2016/03/RI-Fact-Sheet-Symbol-of-Accessibility.pdf

Reiti, J. (2013), "Ontario Contest to Alter Wheelchair Logo Finds No Winner." CBC News, November 2. Accessed November 30, 2016. http://www.cbc.ca/amp/1.2326012

Rhodes, H. (1915), 'Atlantic City: Seeing America at Last." *Colliers* 54(1): 11–12.

Rider, J. H. (1895), *Joan Haste*, London: F.S. Wilson.

Ripley, W. J. (1977), "Book Review: Selwyn Goldsmith's *Designing for the Disabled.*" *Rehabilitation World* 3(2): 25–27.

Robach, C. (2004), *Poppigt sakligt politiskt 1960-talets konsthant- verk och design på Nationalmuseum* [Pop's Political Objectives: Art from the 1960s in the National Museum], Stockholm: Nationalmuseum.

Roberts, L. (2007), "Brand Scandinavia." *Campaign* 20: 33.

Roberts and Crigger. (1949), "Wheelchair Vets Trek to Springfield in Vain Effort to Keep Division Open." Galesburg *Illini* 25: 1.

Roosevelt, J. (1959), *The Saturday Evening Post* 232: 136.

Rose, D. W. (2003), *March of Dimes*, Charleston, SC: Arcadia Publishing.

Rose, S. (2012), "The Right to a College Education? The G.I. Bill, Public Law 16, and Disabled Veterans." *Journal of Policy History* 24(1): 26–52.

Rose, S. (2017), *No Right to Be Idle: The Invention of Disability, 1850–1930*, Chapel Hill: University of North Carolina Press.

Rubin, G. (1975), "The Traffic in Women: Notes on the Political Economy of Sex" in Reiter, Rayna R. (ed.), *Toward an Anthropology of Women*, New York: Monthly Review Press: 157–210.

Rusk, H. (1946), "Bill to Provide Automobiles for Amputees..." *The Times*, July 28: 34.

Rusk, H. (1966), "Handicap for Disabled: Lack of Access to Buildings Thwarts a Cripple's Effort to Lead Normal Life." *New York Times*, June 19: 87.

Rusk, H. (1967), "Handicapped Drivers: Car and a Place to Park Are Essential for Many with No Other Way to Travel." *The Times*, January 29: 79.

Sandell, R. and Dodd, J. (2010), "Activist Practice," in Sandell, R., Dodd, J., and Garland-Thomson, R. (eds.), *Re-Presenting Disability: Activism and Agency in the Museum*, London and New York: Routledge: 3–22.

Sanford, J. (2012), *Universal Design as a Rehabilitation Strategy*, New York: Springer.

Saxton, G. (1967), "Expo 67 Rolls Out Red Carpet for Handicapped Visitors." *Journal of Rehabilitation*, May–June, 33(3): 13.

Schipper, F. (2009), "Unravelling Hieroglyphs: Urban Traffic Signs and the League of Nations." *Metropoles* 6: 65–100. Accessed July 1, 2015. https://metropoles. revues.org/4062

Schweik, S. (2009), *The Ugly Laws*, New York: New York University Press.

Scotch, R. K. (2001), *From Good Will to Civil Rights: Transforming Federal Disability Policy*, 2nd edition, Philadelphia, PA: Temple University Press.

Serlin, D. (2004), *Replaceable You: Engineering the Body in Postwar America*, Chicago: University of Chicago Press.

Serlin, D. (2012), "Architecture and Social Justice." *Boom*, Spring, 2(1).

Shakespeare, T. (2006), *Disability Rights and Wrongs*, Abingdon: Routledge.

Shapiro, J. (1993), *No Pity: People with Disabilities Forging a New Civil Rights Movement*, New York: Times Books/Random House.

Shea, T. (2014), "A Valiant Effort! 1947 Oldsmobile 66." *Hemmings Classic Car*, July: 118.

Simonsen, E. (2005), "Disability History in Scandinavia: Part of an International Research Field." *Scandinavian Journal of Disability Research* 7(3–4): 137–154.

Smith, M. A. P. (1859), *Six Years' Travels in Russia. By an English Lady*, London: Hurst and Blackett.

Smith, S. (1969), "A Chair's-Eye View of the Loop." *Chicago Tribune*, May 31: 9.

Smolowe, J. (1979), "To the Wheelchair Shopper, City Is Obstacle Course.." *New York Times*, December 25: 26.

Sparrow, C. (2014), *Greeves: The Complete Story*, Marlborough: The Crowood Press.

Steinfeld, E. (1979), *Access to the Built Environment: A Review of the Literature*, Washington: U.S. Department of Housing and Urban Development Office of Policy and Development Research.

Steinfeld, E. and Maisel, J. (2012), *Universal Design: Creating Inclusive Environments*, Hoboken, NJ: John Wiley and Sons.

Sterry, J. (1883), "Lays of a Lazy Minstrel." *Punch* November 10, 84/85: 227.

Stick, R. (1976), "The Handicapped Child Has a Right to an Appropriate Education." *Nebraska Law Review* 55(4): 637–682.

Stiker, H. (1999), *A History of Disability*, W. Sayers (trans.), Ann Arbor: University of Michigan Press.

Stockton, F. R. (1900), *Pomona's Travels*, Vol III. New York: Scribers & Sons.

Stone, K. (1997), *Awakening to Disability: Nothing about Us without Us*, Volcano, CA: Volcano Press.

Story, M., Mueller, J., and Mace, R. (1998), *The Universal Design File: Designing for People of All Ages and Abilities*, Raleigh: Center for Universal Design: 6.

Swain, J, Finkelstein, V., French, S., and Oliver, M. (eds) (1993), *Disabling Barriers, Enabling Environments*, London: Sage Publications.

Swete, H. (1870), *Handy Book of Cottage Hospitals*, London: Hamilton, Adams.

Tarschys, R. (1968), "Designideolog från USA maratonföreläser." *Dagens Nyheter*, July 23.

Theall, D. (2001), *Virtual Marshall McLuhan*, Montreal: McGill-Queen's University Press.

Thomas, C. (1999), *Female Forms: Experiencing and Understanding Disability*, Buckingham and Philadelphia, PA: Open University Press.

Thorpe, A. (2012), *Architecture & Design versus Consumerism: How Design Activism Confronts Growth*, New York: Routledge.

Tilt, E. J. and Etter, H. (1881), *A Handbook of Uterine Therapeutics and of Diseases of Women*, New York: Wood.

Tim, M. (1982), "The Selma of Handicapped Rights." *Denver Post*, April 14: 54.

Titchkosky, T. (2011), *The Question of Access: Disability, Space, and Meaning*, Toronto: University of Toronto Press.

Tobin, J. (2013), *The Man He Became: How FDR Defied Polio to Win the Presidency*, New York: Simon & Schuster.

Tomlinson, N. and Stevens, J. (1972), "Reflections on the Process of Visual Design." *Instructional Science*, March, 1(1): 89–119.

Toombs, H. J. (1931a), "Architectural Suggestions—Ramps and Steps." *The Polio Chronicle*, August: 1.

Toombs, H. J. (1931b), "Architectural Suggestions—Bathrooms." *The Polio Chronicle*, September: 4.

Toombs, H. J. (1938), Letter to M Le Hand, Franklin D. Roosevelt Library.

Toombs, H. J. (2016), *Designing the Olympics: Representation, Participation, Contestation*, London: Routledge.

Tremblay, M. (1996), "Going Back to Civvy Street: A Historical Account of the Impact of the Everest and Jennings Wheelchair for Canadian World War II Veterans with Spinal Cord Injury." *Disability & Society* 11(2): 149–170.

Tunstall, J. (1860), *The Bath Waters: Their Uses and Effects in the Cure and Relief of Various Chronic Diseases*, 2nd edition, London: John Churchill.

Turner, B. S. (2006), *Vulnerability and Human Rights*, University Park: Pennsylvania State University Press.

Vanderheiden, G. (1996), *Universal Design: What It Is and What It Isn't*, Madison, WI: Trace R&D Center.

Van Hampton, T. (2009), "Britain's 3-Wheel Solution to Mobility for the Disabled." *New York Times*, December 3.

Vanhemert, K. (2013), "How a Guerrilla Art Project Gave Birth to NYC's New Wheelchair Symbol." *Co.Design.* June 6. Accessed November 27, 2016. https://www.fastcodesign.com/1672754/how-a-guerrilla-art-project-gave-birth-to-nycs-new-wheelchair-symbol

Verville, R. (2009), *War, Politics, and Philanthropy: The History of Rehabilitation Medicine*, Lanham, MD: University Press of America.

von Eckart, W. (1976), "Obstacles to Access." *Washington Post*, January 10: B1.

Wainwright, D. (1967), "The Design Intent for Expo 67." *Design*, January: 31.

Walker, S. (2006), *Sustainable by Design: Explorations in Theory and Practice*, London; Sterling, VA: Earthscan.

Wall, M. (2007), *From Where I Sit, From Where You Stand: A Roll through Life.* Amazon Author House ebook. Accessed February 11, 2014. https://www. amazon.com/Where-Sit-You-Stand-ebook/dp/B003TFELPI/ref=sr_1_1?s=books &ie=UTF8&qid=1486476903&sr=1-1&keywords=9781452034300

Ward, M. (1975), "Fighting for Change from a Wheelchair: World Not Built for the Handicapped." *Los Angeles Times*, March 2: SG1.

Warner, R. (1801), *The History of Bath*, Bath: Printed by R. Cruttwell and sold by G. G. and J. Robinson, London.

Wendell, S. (1996), *The Rejected Body: Feminist Philosophical Reflections on Disability*, New York: Routledge.

Whiteley, N. (1993), *Design for Society*, London: Reaktion Books.

Widengren, G. (ed.) (1994), *Tanken och handen: Konstfack 150 år*, Stokholm: Page One.

Williamson, B. (2012a), "Getting a Grip; Disability in American Industrial Design of the Late Twentieth Century." *Winterthur Portfolio* (Winter) 46(1): 213–236.

Williamson, B. (2012b), "The People's Sidewalks." *Boom* (Spring) 2: 1.

Wolfe, S. (1961), "Education—in Wheel Chairs!: Disabled Students Are Learning at U. of I." *Chicago Daily Tribune*, October 16: B17.

Wolfson, P. L. (2015), "Enwheeled: Two Centuries of Wheelchair Design, from Furniture to Film." Masters thesis, Parsons/Cooper-Hewitt National Design Museum, Smithsonian Institution and Parsons The New School for Design.

Woods, B. and Watson, N. (2004a), "In Pursuit of Standardization: The British Ministry of Health's Model 8F Wheelchair, 1948–1962." *Technology and Culture* 45(3): 540–551.

Woods, B. and Watson, N. (2004b), "The Social and Technological History of Wheelchairs." *The International Journal of Therapy and Rehabilitation* 11(9): 407–410.

Woods, B. and Watson, N. (2005b), "No Wheelchairs Beyond This Point: A Historical Examination of Wheelchair Access in the Twentieth Century in Britain and America." *Social Policy and Society* 4(1): 97–105.

Woods, B., Watson, N., and MacKenzie, D. (2004), A Historical Sociology of the Wheelchair. Full Report of Research Activities and Results, Economic and Social Research Council, 2004. Accessed May 14, 2015. http://www.esrc.ac.uk

Wright, B. A. (1993), "Division of Rehabilitation Psychology: Roots, Guiding Principle, and a Persistent Concern." *Rehabilitation Education* 38: 63–65.

Wright, G. N. (1989), "Rehabilitation Counseling: International Professional Preparation and Practice." *Rehabilitation Education* 3: 233–237.

Yergin, D. (1991), *The Prize: The Epic Quest for Oil, Money and Power*, New York: Simon & Schuster.

INDEX